40.00

£25

D1356038

uu

This is the first comprehensive study in English of Heiner Müller, considered one of the most important German playwrights of the twentieth century. Often regarded as Brecht's most significant spiritual heir, Müller wrote almost all his texts in direct response to other literary works and posed even more radical challenges to received notions of originality than Brecht. In his study Jonathan Kalb analyzes Müller's artistic method, which was to take on the mantle of other writers, occupying the "bodies" of their works like a historically subversive vampire or virus. Among these artists Kalb looks at Müller's relationships with Brecht, Shakespeare, Beckett, and Wagner. This book attempts not to unmask Müller but rather to illuminate his work and thought by way of his carefully chosen alter egos.

Müller's death in 1995 also marked a turning-point in German social history as the country began to feel the effects of the end of the Cold War. Müller's career spanned both sides of this divide and this book offers a view not only of an influential dramatist but also of twentieth-century politics and culture.

The book contains valuable illustrations from key productions and will be of interest to scholars and students of theater history and twentieth-century culture.

The Theater of Heiner Müller

CAMBRIDGE STUDIES IN MODERN THEATRE

Series editor
Professor David Bradby, *Royal Holloway, University of London*

Advisory board
Martin Banham, *University of Leeds*
Jacky Bratton, *Royal Holloway, University of London*
Tracy Davis, *Northwestern University*
Richard Eyre
Michael Robinson, *University of East Anglia*
Sheila Stowell, *University of Birmingham*

Volumes for Cambridge Studies in Modern Theatre explore the political, social and cultural functions of theater while also paying careful attention to detailed performance analysis. The focus of the series is on political approaches to the modern theater with attention also being paid to theaters of earlier periods and their influence on contemporary drama. Topics in the series are chosen to investigate this relationship and include both playwrights (their aims and intentions set against the effects of their work) and process (with emphasis on rehearsal and production methods, the political structure within theater companies, and their choice of audiences or performance venues). Further topics will include devised theater, agitprop, community theatre, para-theater and performance art. In all cases the series will be alive to the special cultural and political factors operating in the theaters they examine.

Books published
Brian Crow with Chris Banfield, *An introduction to post-colonial theatre*
Maria DiCenzo, *The politics of alternative theatre in Britain, 1968–1990: 7:84 (Scotland)*
Jo Riley, *Chinese theatre and the actor in performance*
Jonathan Kalb, *The Theater of Heiner Müller*

The Theater of Heiner Müller

Jonathan Kalb

CAMBRIDGE
UNIVERSITY PRESS

PUBLISHED BY THE PRESS SYNDICATE OF THE UNIVERSITY OF CAMBRIDGE
The Pitt Building, Trumpington Street, Cambridge CB2 1RP, United Kingdom

CAMBRIDGE UNIVERSITY PRESS
The Edinburgh Building, Cambridge CB2 2RU, United Kingdom
40 West 20th Street, New York, NY 10011–4211, USA
10 Stamford Road, Oakleigh, Melbourne 3166, Australia

First published 1998

Printed in the United Kingdom at the University Press, Cambridge

Typeset in Trump [CE]

A catalogue record for this book is available from the British Library

Library of Congress cataloguing in publication data

Kalb, Jonathan
The Theater of Heiner Müller / by Jonathan Kalb.
    p. cm. – (Cambridge studies in modern theatre)
Includes bibliographical references and index.
ISBN 0 521 55004 1 (hardback)
1. Müller, Heiner, 1929– – Criticism and interpretation.
2. Theater – Germany (East) – History. 1. Title. II. Series.
PT2673.U29Z725   1998
832′.914 – dc21   97–23861   CIP

ISBN 0 521 55004 1 hardback

for Stanley Kauffmann

What I claim is to live to the full the contradiction of my time, which may well make sarcasm the condition of truth.

Roland Barthes, *Mythologies* (1957)

Contents

Contents

Illustrations

Acknowledgements

This project benefited from the generous help of numerous friends, colleagues, and acquaintances. Elmar Engels, whose indefatigable clipping fingers have kept me informed about German theater for a decade, was unstinting with hospitality and advice. Also in Germany, Gisela Engels, Hans-Thies Lehmann, Genia Schulz, Alexander Weigel, Maik Hamburger, Holger Teschke, Stefan Suschke, Renate Ziemer, and Andrzej Wirth offered multifarious forms of support and assistance. Thanks as well to Mona Heinze, Helen Fehervary, Marc Silberman, Patricia Simpson, Katherine Lahti, and Paul Schmidt in the United States, to Victoria Cooper and Chris Lyall Grant at Cambridge University Press, and to series editor David Bradby.

Stanley Kauffmann and Marvin Carlson were extraordinarily generous with time taken to read the manuscript critically, and the book is better for their comments and suggestions. I am grateful as well to John Rouse and the Byrd Hoffman foundation for lending important video material.

The help of Carlos Hortas, Dean of Humanities and Arts at Hunter College, was crucial in arranging the leave of absence from teaching that I needed to finish writing. He and Hunter Provost Laura Schor also offered support in the form of money for international travel. Beyond that, travel and research for the book were supported by a grant from the International Research & Exchanges Board, with funds provided by the US Department of State (Title VIII program) and the National Endowment for the Humanities. None of these organizations is responsible for the views expressed.

The editors of *New German Critique*, *Theater*, and *Heiner Müller: ConTEXTS and HISTORY* have my thanks for permission to reprint previously published material. Grateful acknowledgement is made to Suhrkamp Verlag for permission to quote from Heiner Müller's works in my own English translations, and to Verlag der Autoren for permission to quote in English from his *Gesammelte Irrtümer* volumes. The copyright notices below pertain to the permissions to quote in English from the works of Bertolt Brecht kindly granted by Methuen, London, and by Arcade Publishing, New York.

I am grateful to Heiner Müller for taking the time to meet and answer questions.

Most of all, I am grateful to my wife, Julie Heffernan, for patient and insightful reading of drafts, for caring for our children while I traveled, and for the love and faith that made this long project endurable.

Chronology

1929	Heiner Müller is born on January 9 in the Saxon village of Eppendorf.
1933	His father, a Social Democrat, is beaten and arrested by the SS, sent to a concentration camp, released a year later, thereafter unemployed.
1938	The family moves to the Mecklenburg town of Waren where Heiner Müller attends elementary and secondary school.
1939–45	Compulsory membership in the Hitler Youth. Brief incarceration in an American prison camp at war's end.
1947	Müller's father becomes Bürgermeister of the Saxon town of Frankenberg in the Soviet Occupation Zone, soon to become the German Democratic Republic.
1951	Müller remains in the GDR when his family flees to the West in a political scandal; he moves to Berlin. First marriage: to a pregnant girlfriend from Frankenberg, ends quickly in divorce.
1953–55	Employee of the East German Writers' Union.
1954	Second marriage: to Inge Schwenker, a poet and author of children's books, later a collaborator on his plays.
1956	*Der Lohndrücker* (*The Scab*) – premiere 1958 in Leipzig.
1957	*Die Korrektur* (*The Correction*) – revised to satisfy Party criticism – premiere 1958 in East Berlin.
1959	Heinrich Mann Prize (with Inge Müller).
1961	*Die Umsiedlerin* (*The Resettler*) is closed by GDR authorities after the dress rehearsal. Müller is expelled from the Writers' Union.

1964   *Philoktet (Philoctetes)* – premiere 1968 in Munich – GDR premiere 1977 in Berlin.

1965   The premiere production of *Der Bau (The Construction Site)* is cancelled in Berlin after the text is severely attacked in the Communist Party's Central Committee – premiere 1980 in East Berlin.

1966   Suicide of Inge Müller.

1967   First production of a Müller play in the West – *Ödipus Tyrann (Oedipus Rex)* in Bochum.

1968   *Der Horatier (The Horatian)* – premiere in West Berlin 1973. Third marriage: to Ginka Tscholakowa, a Bulgarian Germanist, ends in divorce in the early 1980s.

1969   Collaboration with Party functionaries on the adaptation *Waldstück (Forestplay)*.

1970   *Mauser* – premiere 1975 in Austin, Texas – never performed in the GDR.

1971   *Germania Tod in Berlin (Germania Death in Berlin)* – premiere 1978 in Munich – GDR premiere 1989 in Berlin. *Macbeth* – premiere 1972 in Brandenburg – elicits a lengthy critical attack by the philosopher Wolfgang Harich.

1972   *Zement (Cement)* – premiere 1973 in Berlin.

1974   *Die Schlacht (The Battle)* – premiere 1975 in Berlin. First volume of Müller texts appears in the West.

1975   Lessing Prize. First trip to the United States, for a teaching residency in Austin, Texas.

1976   *Leben Gundlings Friedrich von Preussen Lessings Schlaf Traum Schrei (Gundling's Life Frederick of Prussia Lessing's Sleep Dream Scream)* – premiere 1979 in Frankfurt-on-Main.

1977   *Hamletmaschine (Hamletmachine)* – premiere 1979 in Paris.

1978   *Untergang des Egoisten Fatzer (Downfall of the Egoist Fatzer)* – premiere in Hamburg. Second trip to the United States.

1979   *Der Auftrag (The Mission)* – premiere 1980 in East Berlin, directed by Müller and Tscholakowa.

1980   *Quartett (Quartet)* – premiere 1982 in Bochum.

1982   *Verkommenes Ufer Medeamaterial Landschaft mit Argonauten (Despoiled Shore Medeamaterial Landscape with Argonauts)* – premiere 1983 in Bochum. Co-directs *Macbeth* in East Berlin.

1984   *Bildbeschreibung (Description of a Picture)* – premiere 1985 in Graz.

1985   *Anatomie Titus Fall of Rome (Anatomy of Titus Fall of Rome)* – premiere in Bochum.

1986   GDR National Prize, First Class.

1987   Completion of the five-part *Wolokolamsker Chaussee (Volokolamsk Highway)*.

1988   Directs a revival of *The Scab* in East Berlin.

1989–90 Directs the eight-hour *Hamlet/Machine* in East Berlin during public unrest around the fall of the Berlin Wall.

1990   Becomes President of the Akademie der Künste (East). Kleist Prize. Experimenta 6 festival in Frankfurt-on-Main dedicated exclusively to his work.

1991   Becomes part of new group leadership of the Berliner Ensemble. European Theater Prize. Directs *Mauser* in Berlin.

1992   *Mommsen's Block*. Fourth marriage: to Brigitte Maria Mayer, a photographer thirty-seven years his junior. Publication of the autobiography *Krieg ohne Schlacht (War without Battle)*.

1993   Revelations of contacts with the Stasi dating back to 1978. Directs Wagner's *Tristan and Isolde* at the Bayreuther Festspielhaus.

1994   Directs *Quartet* in Berlin. Operation for cancer in Munich, convalescence in California.

1995   Becomes sole artistic leader of the Berliner Ensemble and directs Brecht's *The Resistible Rise of Arturo Ui* there. Death in Berlin on December 30.

Note on the text

To economize on footnotes, quotations from Heiner Müller's works are cited in bracketed numerical references within the text from the following sources. Volume number (as listed here) precedes page number, separated by a slash mark. The volume number is omitted where the volume is apparent from the context, and in extended discussion of a particular text it is given in the first quotation only. All translations are mine unless otherwise mentioned, notably in volume 19 of this list. Foreign titles are given the first time in the original language and English, thereafter only in English.

  0 Heiner Müller, *Krieg ohne Schlacht: Leben in zwei Diktaturen* (Cologne: Kiepenheuer & Witsch, expanded edition 1994).

  1 Heiner Müller, *Geschichten aus der Produktion 1* (Berlin: Rotbuch Verlag, 1974).

  2 Heiner Müller, *Geschichten aus der Produktion 2* (Berlin: Rotbuch Verlag, 1974).

  3 Heiner Müller, *Die Umsiedlerin oder Das Leben auf dem Lande* (Berlin: Rotbuch Verlag, 1975).

  4 Heiner Müller, *Theater-Arbeit* (Berlin: Rotbuch Verlag, 1975).

  5 Heiner Müller, *Germania Tod in Berlin* (Berlin: Rotbuch Verlag, 1977).

  6 Heiner Müller, *Mauser* (Berlin: Rotbuch Verlag, 1978).

  7 Heiner Müller, *Herzstück* (Berlin: Rotbuch Verlag, 1983).

  8 Heiner Müller, *Shakespeare Factory 1* (Berlin: Rotbuch Verlag, 1985).

  9 Heiner Müller, *Shakespeare Factory 2* (Berlin: Rotbuch Verlag, 1989).

10 Heiner Müller, *Kopien 1* (Berlin: Rotbuch Verlag, 1989).

11 Heiner Müller, *Kopien 2* (Berlin: Rotbuch Verlag, 1989).

12 Heiner Müller, *Germania 3: Gespenster am Toten Mann* (Cologne: Kiepenheuer & Witsch, 1996).

13 Heiner Müller, *Rotwelsch* (Berlin: Merve, 1982).

14 Heiner Müller, *Gesammelte Irrtümer* (Frankfurt-on-Main: Verlag der Autoren, 1986).

15 Heiner Müller, *Gesammelte Irrtümer 2* (Frankfurt-on-Main: Verlag der Autoren, 1990).

16 Heiner Müller, *Gesammelte Irrtümer 3* (Frankfurt-on-Main: Verlag der Autoren, 1994).

17 Heiner Müller, *Zur Lage der Nation* (Berlin: Rotbuch Verlag, 1990).

18 Heiner Müller, *Jenseits der Nation* (Berlin: Rotbuch Verlag, 1991).

19 Heiner Müller, *Germania*, ed. Sylvère Lotringer, trans. Bernard and Caroline Schütze (New York: Semiotext(e), 1990).

20 Heiner Müller, *Gedichte* (Berlin: Alexander Verlag, 1992).

1 Müller as Müller: Introduction

The history of culture is replete with profound examples of self-contradiction. From Plato to Rousseau to Artaud to Heiner Müller, every era has produced virtuosic wrigglers, artists who, through whimsy, frenzy, illness, extravagance of imagination, deep attachment to the theater, or some other cause that tends to be suspicious to others, have identified themselves as chameleons and flourished in the course of rejecting singular identity more resolutely than most of their peers. In all of this dauntingly various company, however, there is no major artist whose basic character is likely to remain as provisional, as much a matter of lasting fundamental debate, as this East German born in Saxony in 1929. The elementary question of identity – who is he? – is, even after decades of close attention by German journalists and scholars, still the most interesting one to ask about Heiner Müller.

It may be that the question is easier to isolate outside of the lands that lavished so much attention on him. Consider his death on December 30, 1995, for example. Nothing in Müller's life became him like the leaving of it. During the week before his sixty-seventh birthday on January 9, dangerously packed crowds attended a marathon reading of his works at the Berliner Ensemble, the theater he led, which had been seldom known for full houses since reunification. After a similarly teeming all-night vigil at the Volksbühne, billed as "Whisky and Cigars" and replete with both in homage to his preferred instruments of pleasure and self-destruction, an impromptu procession numbering in the thousands made its way up Friedrichstrasse and, stopping for red lights, attended the burial of this occasionally condemned figure in the hallowed ground of the Dorotheenstädtischen Friedhof. There, in the presence of political dignitaries like former West German President Richard von Weizsäcker, Berlin Mayor Eberhard Diepgen, Cultural Minister Steffen Reiche and theatrical dignitaries such as Robert Wilson, Bernhard Minetti, Claus Peymann and Thomas Langhoff, Müller was buried in the company of Brecht, Fichte, Hegel, Eisler, Becher, Schinkel, Seghers, and Heinrich Mann. New German Cinema star Volker Schlöndorff filmed it all from a scaffold erected over a gravestone.

Meanwhile in America, on the day after Müller's death the *New York Times* printed a tiny Reuters obituary, tucked into a three-inch box beside another for Arnold Schwarzenegger's bodybuilding trainer, followed up four days later by a 750-word piece by Eric Pace, perceptive but littered with factual errors.[1] That week the *Village Voice* offered me 300 words to do better, over which I stewed as a friend in Berlin faxed some 35,000 words worth of German journalism about the death, its meaning for the German theater, and for world culture. Another 40,000 words arrived the following week, and special issues of *Theater Heute* and *Theater der Zeit* dedicated to Müller were still to come. In late March, as if to apologize for previous neglect, a Sunday feature by Stephen Kinzer appeared in the *New York Times*, concerned a bit with Müller but primarily with the endangered tourist value of the Berliner Ensemble; it was entitled "Germany Can't Forget a Legendary *Director*" (my italics).[2]

In a way, the chasm between these German and American perspectives is at the heart of this study, which is colored on every page by an awareness of the utter marginality of its subject – a household name in and beyond his own country – in the United States. The book, the first general study of Müller to appear in English,[3] is the product of a continuing search on my part for a theater rarely found in the United States: an intellectually ambitious theater that undermines the insidious contract between complacent audiences and the dominant bourgeois dramatic tradition, engages with world history and the history of theater and drama, and brings all its abundant resources to bear shrewdly and innovatively on meaning, rather than redundantly illustrating and decorating texts with settings, costumes, light, gesture, and sound. For many years – rightly and wrongly, as I will explain – Müller seemed to me the most important representative of this theater. Beyond this, the rebarbative quality in his texts, their manifold and deliberate abrasiveness, always seemed grounded in an acknowledgement of the need, finally, for some sustenance in anarchy and nihilism, which have grown so common and cheaply self-congratulatory as the century draws to a close. (Every other pop music star and trendy art magazine hero today is a celebrated nihilist.)

Not just for Americans but for anyone who had followed Müller and his public reception, there was something absurdly excessive, something compensatory, about the remarkable outpouring of German ink and emotion at the dawn of 1996. Prominent and infamous as he was, he was the very opposite of a darling, beloved countryman in the eyes of either *Ossies* (Easterners) or *Wessies* (Westerners). Expelled from the East German Writers' Union in 1961 for a realistic play that spoke too frankly about the land reforms of the previous decade, he was banned from production and publication for years. Reborn later as an avant-gardist, he was "discovered" in the 1970s by Westerners eager to depict him as a prisoner of conscience, and was consequently privileged at home – the privileges and the avant-gardist forms both generating distrust there. By the 1980s the GDR (German Democratic Republic – East Germany) regime was hailing him as its preeminent dramatist, and in 1993 came revelations that, at least since 1978, he had been meeting with agents of the Stasi (*Staatssicherheit* – the secret police) to discuss fellow artists. His defense: "We talked about cultural politics. You can hold that against me. But why shouldn't I try to exercise influence when I had the possibility. I never saw a moral problem in that." [16/184–5]. Why, after all this, such sudden and universal zeal to enshrine and institutionalize him with monumental eulogies?

One answer is that many of those who wrote and spoke about Müller in the winter of 1996 were uttering feelings that they had not felt free to express, or perhaps acknowledge, before; for his culture's respect for him was often blended with unconscious fear of his reaction. He made everyone who observed him self-conscious about all their habits of constructing and monumentalizing heroes. Like Bernard Shaw in a different culture, Müller was one of the most frequently interviewed figures of his age, his opinion solicited on every event of moment in German letters, history and politics over several decades, the resulting bon mots appearing prominently in

mainstream publications throughout the four German-speaking countries. Whenever the subject turned to him, however, he proved
himself a master of deflection and evasion, typically denying that
questions had been formulated properly, turning attention back to the
questioner's motives, and sneering at the very idea of consistency.
Interviews are "performances," he said in one of his three volumes of
them entitled *Gesammelte Irrtümer* (*Collected Errors*): "The next day
you can say the opposite" [14/155]. He would not tolerate attempts to
define him, pin him down to any theses or ideologies, even complex
ones, and eventually even his admirers became sheepish about
whether the terms of their would-be praise could ever be acceptable.

Far from excluding myself, I admit to writing this book with
the following snap at a 1987 interviewer steadfastly in mind:

> You're trying constantly to unmask me. That's why you are
> doing this interview. You shine this flashlight on someone from
> your own abyss, and when there is nothing there you think he is
> unserious. In the end, your line of thought will lead you to
> Plato's exile of the poet.   [19/218]

So who was Heiner Müller? Let us see how far biography takes us.
Most of what is known about his personal life comes from his 1992
autobiography *Krieg ohne Schlacht* (*War without Battle*), which is
structured as a long interview and which he would never have
produced without the urging of the interviewers. *War without Battle*
skips over broad and significant territory, such as his children (four
from four marriages – "I have children but they don't interest me," he
said to the author Erich Fried in 1987[4]), his relationship to the other
young and officially undesirable writers who gathered at his apart-
ment during the 1960s and 1970s (Thomas Brasch's post-mortem
reflections on his "lauding to death [*Kaputtloberei*] of possible young
competitors" are especially interesting in this regard[5]), and his meetings with the Stasi.[6] It also contains the following disclaimer near the
end: "My interest in my person does not suffice to write an autobiography . . . Among the problematic parts of the text is its injustice to
people, also to my person" [366]. It is, to be sure, one of the most
unflattering autobiographies ever published, a problem Müller would

no doubt have cast as a virtue, if challenged, in the spirit of Walter Benjamin's remark that "[living] in a glass house is a revolutionary virtue par excellence. It is also an intoxication, a moral exhibitionism, that we badly need."[7]

He was born in Eppendorf, Saxony, an industrial village in one of Germany's most industrialized (and hence heavily polluted) regions, with brown coal and uranium reserves that were crucial to the Nazi and GDR economies as well as the Soviet nuclear program. Both Müller and his father would certainly have ended up as mine- or factory-workers had they not shown intelligence in school, and much detail from this industrial milieu finds its way into Müller's early plays. In January, 1933, his father, a minor official in the Social Democratic Party, was beaten and arrested by the SS (*Schutzstaffel* – Nazi guard troops employed as thugs) as his 4-year-old son looked on through a door-crack. A short 1958 prose text called "The Father" [5/ 20–6] traces the centrality of betrayal in Müller's consciousness and writing to that night, when his father knocked to say goodbye and he feigned sleep rather than answering. Sent to a concentration camp, the unrepentant socialist was released about a year later on condition that he not return to Eppendorf.

The family then lived with the paternal grandparents in another Saxon village for four years before relocating to Waren in the northern German state of Mecklenburg, where the father found work as an auditor. In an episode that foreshadows the son's famous sardonicism, the elder Müller was arrested again in 1940 after reading aloud to co-workers from *Mein Kampf* – Hitler's scathing comments about Bolsheviks – on the day of the non-aggression pact with the USSR. The entire Nazi period entailed severe financial hardship and humiliation for the family. During the long years of the father's unemployment, Müller was his only conversation partner, and he acquired his basic socialist orientation from those talks. *War without Battle* also describes the shame of being sent to eat nourishing meals at a sympathetic neighbor's house when the father was imprisoned, and the general isolation of being known as the child of a "criminal" (and a Saxon outsider in Mecklenburg besides) with whom other children weren't allowed to play.

According to Müller – and this is the most telling remark in an extraordinarily revealing book – the main result of these painful experiences was the development of "a hate potential, a need for revenge" [25], a comment he repeats and applies not merely to his personality but also his motivation as an author. He says his rage at capitalism, linked at all times in his mind with fascism, originates in "envy," the "childhood trauma" of "standing before shop windows and not being able to buy" [321]. The repeated confiscation of his father's library seems to have justified his stealing books from a house where his Hitler Youth group had stopped for canteen-water and from libraries around Waren he was employed to "de-Nazify" [35, 46]. The very establishment of the GDR was justified, to him, both as a dictatorship "to establish a new order" and as "a dictatorship against the people who had damaged my childhood" [181].

The key to fitting this unabashed vindictiveness into a larger picture is, I think, the accompanying recurrent references to isolation. Even after the war, when his father became mayor of the Saxon town of Frankenburg, Müller was ostracized, this time for being the beneficiary of Soviet-backed privilege, and every phase of his writing features figures such as Prometheus, Philoctetes, and Niet (the displaced ethnic German in *Die Umsiedlerin* [*The Resettled Woman* – hereafter *The Resettler*]) who feel, as he says of himself, that they don't "belong" anywhere [308]. This theme appears in his writing entirely without sentimentality until his final few years. The point is, his early island- or siege-mentality developed into significant adult attributes. First, it fed his political self-image as an outcast, or member of an underclass: "I really am a negro [*Neger*]" (1985);[8] "I'm certain that I could come to an understanding sooner with a Puerto Rican in New York, even if he takes my wallet away, than with a building-and-loan worker in Bochum" (1983) [14/140] – the implicit racism of such remarks, as well as the general presumptuousness behind the attitude, coming across better in English translation than in German. Second and probably more important, his siege-mentality ripened into a deeply personal Machiavellianism – an essentially apolitical drive – that could justify almost any behavior in the name of the private end of revenge dressed up as sundry national and international socialist ends: "It was always an error to believe that I'm a political poet," he said, adding that he regarded nearly everything –

communism, socialism, the GDR, friends, even the suicide of his second wife in 1966 – as "dramatic material" [183].

It is unclear to what extent the latter drive was already a factor in his crucial decision to remain in the GDR when his parents fled to the West in a 1951 political scandal (a building collapse for which his father bore administrative responsibility). He gave so many different explanations for staying – belief in the eventual triumph of Communism, a pregnant girlfriend, emulation of Brecht – that the truth may well lie more in confusion than conviction. In any case, having grown up in one dictatorship, he chose to spend most of the rest of his life in another, preferring the greater "pressure of experience" in a totalitarian environment. According to George Steiner, Jorge Luis Borges, who detested Juan Perón as a "Nazi," once answered as follows when asked whether he wished to escape the Peronist dictatorship in Argentina: "Don't be silly. Torture is the mother of metaphor."[9] Müller stated in 1990: "I know democracy only as a tourist; dictatorship is my corporeal experience" [17/94]. Besides, he added in his autobiography, dramatists thrive on "a certain relationship to power, also a fascination through power, a rubbing of oneself against power and a partaking in power, also perhaps a submission to power so that one takes part" [113]. In the poem "Vampire," written after the fall of the Berlin Wall, he writes nostalgically: "Vanished is the power against which my verse / Broke like surf, rainbow-colored."[10]

Remaining in the GDR, then, meant the chance to apply in a somewhat less dangerous context the many slippery strategies he had developed for maneuvering and surviving within the Third Reich. At one point, he mocks the "Western Germanists" who took seriously a 1966 discussion with him published in the journal *Sinn und Form* and reprinted in the first volume of his works to appear in the West in 1974: "For GDR readers it was clear that I was lying, that it had only to do with the possibility of producing *Der Bau*" (*The Construction Site*, a play he wrote in 1963-4) [197–8]. For him – a man whom the author Horst Drescher once dubbed the GDR's "most sincere and faithful son"[11] – "the 'Workers' and Farmers' State' was merely a pronouncement, like socialism, a phantom" [230], whose corruption he presumed. "For me it was never a problem to be treated unjustly. I knew there was no justice, neither from the one nor the other side, so I could never get really indignant about it" [75–6]. The main problem with this imperturbability, this penchant for strategic thinking, is that it invariably appears to others as untrustworthiness.

To follow the implications of the statements and anecdotes in *War without Battle* closely is to be filled often with repugnance for a man who describes himself as "cold" and "untouched" and whose irrational guilt from childhood – from the Nazi point of view, of course, he *was* always guilty, always did have something to hide – was channeled into a radical moral leveling that could rationalize all duplicity, guile, and ingratitude. For example, having studied English at the secondary school to which he won a scholarship, he was able to sweet-talk his way past an American prison-camp guard in 1945, but he has nothing but contempt for that guard and all the other American soldiers who believed the "propaganda" about German bestiality [39]. Having written harsh book reviews for the weekly *Sonntag* during his first years in Berlin – he supported himself then with journalism and an administrative job at the Writers' Union that made him suspicious to some theater people – he blames his harshness on those who assigned him bad books and maintains that the reviews "meant nothing to me" even though he felt like a "teacher" while writing them [80].

All his descriptions of dealing with GDR authorities tell of paranoia, hypocrisy, and bravado born of nervousness, yet, bizarrely, he expects the reader to regard the theoretical superiority of the GDR system as self-evident even when he is busy narrating its attempt to rid itself of him like a foreign body. His second and third produced plays, *Der Lohndrücker* (*The Scab*, 1956) and *Die Korrektur* (*The Correction*, 1958) – only a collaboration on an adaptation of John Reed's *Ten Days that Shook the World* (1956) preceded them – earned him notoriety and respect in theater circles but were regarded coolly by the Walter Ulbricht regime. The amateur production of his next work, *The Resettler*, was closed down after the dress rehearsal in 1961, its actors subjected to police interrogation and forced to practice "self-critique," the director sentenced to hard labor and expelled from the Communist Party. Müller, on Helene Weigel's advice, composed his own self-deprecatory self-critique to try to save himself but was expelled from the Writers' Union anyway, effectively closing off all avenues of publication and production to him. His reminiscence:

I can't remember that great shame came over me while putting together the self-critique. It had to do with my existence as an author . . . I also knew that, for example, Eisenstein had always practiced self-critique. He survived that way as an artist. Then, certainly, fear of prison came into play. Writing was more important to me than my morals. [179–80]

The closest I ever saw Müller come to facing squarely his essential uninterest in the moral issues raised by the events of his life was this reluctant, halting answer he gave to the interviewer Klaus Bednarz in a 1992 public encounter in Frankfurt-on-Main, caught on film in Michael Kluth's 1995 *Apokalypse mit Zigarre* (*Apocalypse with Cigar*):

> BEDNARZ: Are you really the sort of guy who's left cold by everything, or who hides behind what many think of as armor made of cynicism, irony and aestheticism?
> MÜLLER: That could all be the case. I don't know.
> [Catcalls and protests from the audience that he's avoiding the question.]
> MÜLLER: Excuse me. All questions are allowed. The main point is that I'm a writer. And that is perhaps, if you will, my actual existence. The other existence, the longer one writes, unfortunately becomes – and that is a point of alienation, I'd admit that – becomes more and more material for the literature one makes . . . And that is a problem. That is on the other hand, was, a thing that has made me mistrustful of myself, and also a thing that has given me a bad conscience in certain situations, a feeling of guilt. You also make yourself guilty when you describe a thing.[12]

Whatever the private effect of this guilt and mistrust of self, his public persona and the superficies of nearly all his texts stand out for their bone-coldness and lack of shame about self-contradiction. The very titles of *War without Battle* and *Collected Errors* describe the frames of belligerent subterfuge and protean elusiveness in which he preferred to see his life. The utterly idiosyncratic attitude of Genet's Leila in *Les Paravents* (*The Screens*) comes quickly to mind – a character who inexplicably "sets up house" with stolen items beside an outdoor rampart, indifferent to reality per se, hostile to all attempts to classify her morally, her happiness dependent on maintaining a deliberately mystifying public image and a perpetual state of mental embattlement.

It is difficult to say precisely when this embattled attitude congealed (see chapter 4), but it is recognizable in all the post-*Resettler* phases of Müller's career. Prevented from communicating with the GDR public openly and immediately in realistic plays about the problems of reconstruction, he turned to metaphorical critique in verse plays with classical subject matter (e.g. *Philoktet* [*Philoctetes*, 1958–64]; *Prometheus*, 1967–8), and continued his earlier experimentation with collage constructions that disrupted realistic narrative with mythical interludes (e.g. *Traktor* [*Tractor*, 1955/61]; *Zement* [*Cement*, 1972]). Then he dispensed with singular, dominant narratives entirely in favor of pastiches of thematically linked fragments and dense webs of quotations dealing with Germanic history and myth, the so-called "synthetic fragments": *Die Schlacht* (*The Battle*, 1951 and 1974); *Germania Tod in Berlin* (*Germania Death in Berlin*, 1956/71); *Leben Gundlings Friedrich von Preussen Lessings Schlaf Traum Schrei* (*Gundling's Life Frederick of Prussia Lessing's Sleep Dream Scream*, 1976); *Germania 3: Gespenster am Toten Mann* (*Germania 3: Ghosts at the Dead Man*, 1995).

Most of these works languished unproduced for years in the GDR, as Müller lived on, in his words, "money [given by] various friends. Well, not really friends, people with money."[13] In an interview with me in early 1989, he said that being banned was a matter of indifference for him: "It's all the same whether [a text] is read now or later. It doesn't matter one bit. Literature is always right in the face of politics."[14] Explaining in *War without Battle* why he accepted the GDR National Prize, First Class, in 1986 after years of official repression, he said:

> It didn't have to do with privileges but rather with work. One year later I was the most frequently performed author in the GDR . . . I wouldn't conduct myself any differently today. It's

important that my things come to have an effect, not
that I play the noble knight.   [356]

The fact of the contradiction aside – different roles were played for
different interviewers – which statement is true?

Undoubtedly the second. The way Müller handled his career in
the late 1970s and 1980s, cultivating an audience and reputation in
the West that he knew would make it difficult to ignore him at home,
is clear evidence of healthy ambition. What is interesting is his refusal
to regard his increasingly privileged position – he was allowed to
travel to the West after the mid 1970s, for instance – as an obligation
to support those less privileged, or to take other unambiguous moral
stands he wouldn't have taken before. "I had the luck to be in
Bulgaria" during the 1968 Soviet invasion of Czechoslovakia, he says,
referring to a time when he was still unknown outside the Berlin
theater and literary worlds, "so I wasn't embarrassed into signing or
not signing a paper for or against Prague" [212]. Twenty years later,
the world-famous author and nominee for the Nobel Prize was
surprised by a GDR television interviewer's question about the recent
arrest of dissident artists, and he gave an answer deflected to Northern
Ireland, which was subsequently broadcast in apparent support of the
GDR government [350]. Later he felt ashamed of this, but his impulse
not to speak for the dissidents is telling.

Moreover, with shame or not in that instance, Müller often did
express sympathy, in *War without Battle* and elsewhere, with the
GDR's authoritarian leaders, whom he described as victims: "The
first prisoners of the system are the leaders, the ruling tier is the
oppressed" [97]; "The Central Committee building was a high-
security area for the prisoners of power" [298]. And when he made
similar comments about Hitler and Stalin, or criticized the West
German left for remembering Auschwitz at the expense of Stalingrad
[346], or said he didn't care whether Carl Schmitt, a Nazi ideologue,
was right or wrong because his texts are good theater [272], one
suspected he was speaking more from a will to provoke than from
belief. The fact that one really could not be certain points to the chief
difficulty in formulating a critical response to him. Very distant from

any orthodox communist ideology by the end of his life, Müller viewed art as "a space of irresponsibility . . . [and] freedom – a dangerous and libidinously occupied field" [18/20] in which ideas were simply "material" to be played with. But unlike Duchamp and most other precursors to what became winsomely nihilistic post-modern thinking, he nevertheless confined himself most of the time to the serious, grounded, and ostensibly responsible subject-matter of history and politics. Half of his prodigious artistic effort went into formulating sensible-sounding social and political ideas while the other half went into throwing up smokescreens to prevent close rational scrutiny and extended argument of them. His famous hit-and-run aphorisms, a sort of conversational terrorism, were, in this sense, his compromises with himself.

Müller was not merely a provocateur; he was a clownish provocateur ("Second clown in the communist springtime," is a self-designation of two of his characters [1/92, 6/89]). The way he played fast and loose with facts from history and politics was, among other things, a clownish provocation geared specifically to his German context. Deferring to apparent erudition, his primary public could be counted on *not* to challenge his flurry of references too quickly, allowing him time to polish his next aphoristic retorts. Talented, widely read, he remained, intentionally, a clever dilettante in a land of professionals, an autodidact amid professors, a rude Saxon baiting stuffy Prussians, and he took pleasure in toying with all those in authority, maneuvering himself into positions that left them looking like vultures around a corpse. Thomas Mann's infamous remark about Wagner also fits Müller: "[his] art *is* dilettantism, monumentalized and lifted into the sphere of genius by his intelligence and his enormous will-power."[15] Strangely enough, despite his rigorous intel-lectualism, the almost hermetic concentration of his prose and verse, and his merciless Teutonism that travels so poorly, I think a part of Müller would like to have been a naive painter like Robert Wilson or a tactically naive, exuberant poet like Vladimir Mayakovsky – both of whom were also drawn to the theater and both of whom he admired. It was his and Brecht's bad luck, given their shared dream of achieving a purgative, regenerative naiveté in the theater, to have been born cerebral Germans.

And it was precisely this cerebralism, Müller's proclivity and memory for the details of every slight he ever suffered, personally or as a self-appointed proxy for socialism, that led him to talk so much more than was good for his plays and theater ideas. Many another artist – Tristan Tzara and Andy Warhol, for instance – spent a lifetime regarding the world aloofly as "material" and never invited the sort of criticism that Müller did with *War without Battle*, a book from which it is impossible to tell what integrity means to him. The objects of his admiration are so scattered and conditionally described that they end up seeming like another collection of false limbs. He admires the directors Ruth Berghaus and Benno Besson for finding ways around censoring authorities [147, 202], the director Fritz Marquardt for being the son of a farmer [251], the scholar Gerhard Scholz for his "fury of association" [125]. He describes as a "point of honor" his breaking a contract with Suhrkamp Verlag over its refusal to print a photo of Ulrike Meinhof [295], and he lauds the honesty of the worker-hero Hans Garbe because it embarrassed Party functionaries [150]. When he quotes one of his own characters' bold assertion of his "right to . . . cowardice" [201] (a formulation similar to his later response to the Stasi revelations: "there is a human right to cowardice" [16/187]) and then, a few pages later, decries "the birth of mannerism [in the GDR theater] from the spirit of cowardice" [207], the effect is risible.

"In fifty years it won't be important when and where I behaved like a swine; it'll be important whether I wrote like a swine or not," said Müller in a 1995 television interview with Frank Schirrmacher.[16] For the sake of argument, we can agree. It remains to be seen only how well *War without Battle* stands the test.

So, again, who was Heiner Müller? Decidedly, biography will be of slight help to anyone whose reason for asking is his work – and this is true even if the warm-hearted journalism about him after his death is taken into account. On a personal level, as his friends point out defensively, Müller was indeed kind, soft-spoken, and unpretentious: "he was a vulnerable person [who] tried to protect himself behind masks" (Christa Wolf);[17] "Never did I see his face distorted, never was he loud . . . he wore no masks" (Rosemarie Heise).[18] Where his work is concerned, however, such remarks are all but irrelevant. The sublimation and channeling of his violence and cynicism into writing and thinking was total, and the main reason he can still be an object of continuing interest years after the primary context for his writing disappeared (the GDR) is that, in the histrionic arena of that writing, he *was* his masks – as he said himself.

The foregoing biographical discussion notwithstanding, then, this book does not attempt to unmask him but rather to illuminate his work and thought *by way of* his carefully constructed alter egos, the personae based on other authors and cultural–historical paradigms within which he created. Müller is certainly not the only artist to have depended on alter egos for creativity – the Portuguese Fernando Pessoa (1888–1935), for instance, whom Müller admired, published under forty-four different names, each with a distinct voice and point of view – but he is the first I know of to ask to be read primarily through them, through the fact of them. In a paradox that says as much about his era as about him, he has the dubious distinction of being the first artist of lasting significance to ground a historical identity and claim to originality specifically on dependence and indebtedness – the first "strong poet" (to adapt Harold Bloom's term in *The Anxiety of Influence* to drama; Müller wrote lyric poetry but was not a strong lyric poet) to draw his strength largely from what Bloom means by "weakness":

> My concern is only with strong poets, major figures with the
> persistence to wrestle with their strong precursors, even to the
> death. Weaker talents idealize; figures of capable imagination
> appropriate for themselves. But nothing is got for nothing, and
> self-appropriation involves the immense anxieties of
> indebtedness, for what strong maker desires the realization that
> he has failed to create himself?[19]

Loyal admirers may object that I have overstated my case, that Müller most certainly did "create himself," with a particular style and collection of thematic obsessions that were internationally recognizable and uniquely his. My response is that the famous style (the dense, lapidary poetry combined with busy stage imagery, for instance) was never constant – particularly when one takes productions into account, a crucial point for an author who was also a director and theater theorist – and that the obsessions amounted to wardrobe, reusable drapery for interchangeable figures beneath.

Individual works of Müller's may indeed fit neatly into one of Bloom's strategic categories ("revisionary ratios") for the "misreading" attitudes of the durably strong – particularly what he calls *apophrades*, or "return of the dead [poet]" and *tessera*, "completion and antithesis . . . so reading the parent-poem as to retain its terms but to mean them in another sense, as though the precursor had failed to go far enough."[20] Müller's general relationship to past art, however, was based on a conviction that the artistic self could indeed be appropriated without what Bloom calls the "immense anxieties of indebtedness," or "melancholy at [one's] lack of priority,"[21] for he saw the artist's task as not merely issuing from an immersion in past history and culture (the pearl-diving of Walter Benjamin) but as actually subsumed by such immersion. Müller:

> He who is identical with himself might as well have himself buried, he doesn't exist anymore, isn't moving anymore. Identical is a monument. What we need is the future and not the eternity of the moment. We have to dig up the dead again and again, because only from them can we obtain a future.
>
> Necrophilia is love of the future. One has to accept the presence of the dead as dialogue partners or dialogue-disturbers – the future will emerge only out of dialogue with the dead.   [18/31]

Every text Müller wrote was, in some fashion, dialogue with the dead. Although he never attended a university, he was one of the most erudite dramatists of the century, conceiving most of his texts in direct response to other literary works. What distinguishes him from the century's many other master allusionists (say, Borges or Eliot) is the way he went about assimilating his sources in order to establish dialogue with them. His typical practices were: (1) to adopt the manner of the source author entirely, style, tone and all, occupying the corpus like a vampire or virus in order to explode it from within, or (2) to set up a source author or composite of several authors as a broad paradigm, a nexus of ideas drawn from fable and fact, and then embarrass it with similar occupation – these exploding or embarrassing processes coming to full fruition only in the public arena of production. The ideal result in both cases was a critique of the source artist's historical existence, not just of particular attitudes, manners, or opinions but of the original art's very basis for communication. History being a perennial bloodbath, all previous creators were, to him, guilty shadows with whom the living had a bloody obligation to grapple.

The risks involved in these practices were enormous. Most readers, especially in Müller's youth, recognized only his appropriation and not the subversive intentions behind it. "That's just too much Brecht!" wrote author-editor Stephan Hermlin to him in an early rejection note [0/79]. In 1972, the philosopher Wolfgang Harich jested (in a text in which he also hailed Müller as a "Mozart of adaptation") that his life's work would have to be bound under the title "Heiner Müller: *Collected Works, Partly from Sophocles, Shakespeare and Kleist.*"[22] And in the late 1970s, Müller stood trial for plagiarism, or so he claimed in his autobiography – the translators Adolf Dresen and Maik Hamburger considering his version of *Hamlet* too close to theirs. Hamburger's version of this story is considerably different; he says the matter never came to trial, the Leipzig judge refusing to issue even a temporary restraining order barring the Volksbühne from continuing performances – but it is nevertheless revealing that Müller *wanted* to be seen as the object of a plagiarism trial.[23] Sartre's comment about Genet applies also to Müller: "everything that he chooses to tell us about himself, is both true and false."[24]

More importantly, though, any writer who lives by mimicry gambles everything on being seen as a first-rate mimic. Brecht epigones were common in the 1950s GDR, but it took steely nerve for a writer in his late twenties to imitate not only Brecht's style and tone in such early plays as *The Scab* and *The Correction*, but also Brecht's precise manner of characterization, scenic structure, and script format. Brecht himself was Müller's main model for such "copying," having coined the term *Kopien* for his own practice of regarding texts by others as inducements to work rather than as private property.[25] (Examples stretch from the 1918 *Baal*, a reaction to Hanns Johst, to the 1953 *Turandot*, a reaction to Gozzi and Schiller; two of Müller's volumes are titled *Kopien 1* and *Kopien 2*, and all his other volumes could be similarly titled.) Mayakovsky, too, was confronted with accusations that his poems for children were derivative and replied that imitation was his compliment to the other authors. At any rate, all these models shrink beside the audacity of a case like Müller's *Mauser* (1970), a rebuttal in *Lehrstück* (learning play) form to *Die Massnahme* (*The Measures Taken*), the greatest of Brecht's *Lehrstücke* and a play that represents him at his highest powers of formal inventiveness and political pugnacity. Failure to write anything less than a text of comparable stature would have meant utter disgrace for the younger author.

The connection between Brecht and Müller deserves a book in itself, and I begin with this subject partly because the indebtedness is deeper and more absolute than in any of the other pairings discussed. Chapter 2 does not contain everything there is to say about the Brecht–Müller relationship, though, which underlies this entire study; all the subsequent chapters could be legitimately subtitled "Müller as Brecht." The chapter-head pairings are a way of isolating subtopics in a subject that could easily explode to unmanageable proportions. There may be readers who insist that I have missed the forest for the trees by not allowing myself to succumb to the explosion. This is a calculated risk. I can only hope that my readings prove them wrong. Each chapter focuses on one play or group of plays that the paradigm of a given shadow-figure seems to me especially suited to illuminate; but no paradigm is the only one applicable to the texts discussed through it, and no text for close examination is the only possible choice for that chapter. Also, because Müller became as much of a *Theatermann* as a literary man in his later career, the earlier chapters deal more with questions of dramatic literature, the latter more with issues of theatrical performance, including some of Müller's work as a director.

Hence: despite its general title, the central focus of chapter 2 is Müller's critique of the Brechtian *Lehrstück*, which I see as the basis of all his subsequent innovations, the main example being the play *Der Horatier* (*The Horatian*, 1968). The focus of chapter 4, titled "Müller as Mayakovsky," is Müller's variation on Socialist Realism and the difference between his youthful artistic temperament and his later one in works such as the 1983 adaptation of *Wladimir Maja-kowski Tragödie* (*Vladimir Mayakovsky: A Tragedy*). "Müller as Artaud" focuses on the Death-of-the-Author myth, postmodern ideas of exploded identity, and *Hamletmaschine* (*Hamletmachine*, 1977). And "Müller as Wagner" concentrates on *Germania Death in Berlin*, the "synthetic fragment's" relation to the *Gesamtkunstwerk*, and Müller's utopian dreams of a "theater of the future." There is no need to list every topic. These longer chapters alternate with shorter ones on subjects and relationships meriting further investigation. I hope my list of shadow figures is representative, but I also realize that it is not exhaustive; another critic might have written an equally fruitful study using Kafka, Lessing, Seghers, Jünger, Sophocles, Benn, Eliot, Dostoevsky, Nietzsche, or others.

An inherent danger in my approach is that readers unfamiliar with Müller but well informed about one or more of my comparative figures will expect the same level of factual reference with those figures that I give to the main subject. At the risk of redundancy, then, let me clarify that only what each figure meant *to Müller* is relevant to this study. Other than Brecht, Müller had no literary "fathers." The remainder of his massive and virtuosically wielded stockpile of sources was drawn from spiritual "brethren" with whom he moment-arily affiliated himself and then discarded – annihilated, as it were, like the numerous warring brothers in his narratives. He used and cited them partly because they were, in an essential, character-building sense, dead to him; for only then could they serve as the sort of whimsically manipulable, or edible, ghosts his mature texts re-quired. As he once said: "To know [the dead], you have to eat them. And then you spit out the living particles . . . [Reading is] an absolute luxury. Eating literature is faster" [19/67, 71]. Because Müller exclu-sively "ate" rather than "read" literature, at least from the 1970s on, because he thought and spoke in large, sometimes crass generaliza-tions, he invited the use of literary-historical paradigms that would be superficial in other circumstances. Negligence lies not in using those paradigms but in failing to explain their meaning to him and their value as exegetical tools.

Many in posterity may dismiss Müller out of hand, as happens with Brecht today, because he was, as the dramatist Freya Klier put it, "a Titan in Arts, yet a dwarf in life."[26] Many others, I suspect, will eventually see him as akin to Alfred Jarry, a willfully mischievous self-sacrificial joker who marked the collision of two epochs with a deadly serious "act" that he never dropped. The literary manifestations of Müller's "act" will be dusted off whenever his sort of equivocation and fence-sitting are again felt to be current (e.g. in times of weakening totalitarian rule). Long-term speculation aside, however, I see Müller's significance for the theater of his age – and we are still coping with the epochal collision to which he reacted – as concentrated in the following points.

1. By replacing the "closed" form of the Brechtian parable with "open" dramatic forms based, in Hans-Thies Lehmann's words, on a surreal "montage dramaturgy . . . in which the reality-level of characters and events vacillates hazily between life and dream and the stage becomes a hotbed of spirits and quotes outside any homogeneous notion of space and time,"[27] Müller redeemed Brecht's notion of theater as a forum for examining history, for making the processes of history appear changeable. In an era saturated with information that spins an illusion of universal democratic zeal, Brecht's genre of explicitly didactic drama grounded in datedly disruptive montage structures has lost even the limited ability to achieve *Verfremdung* (alienation – the making available of alternative choices in interpretation and action) that it once had (see chapter 2). Ours is "an age of ghosts," continues Lehmann, which calls for a dramaturgy of ghostly democracy; "with media-reality and the domination of 'digital appearances' the real existence of many beings has become ever more dubious. The spheres of the indefinite are expanding."[28] Müller's reaction was to utilize the postmodern indefinite (rather than simply surrender to it like the majority of writers hyped as postmodern) as a new means of articulating and offering audience access to multiple meanings anchored at almost all times in specific historical inquiry. And this is what distinguishes "dialogue with the dead" from authoritarian monologue in dialogue form.

2. Müller presents a subversive model of a flagrantly bookish intellectual finding a wide audience as a playwright, contrary to two and a half millennia of tradition. All great dramatists have been

thinkers and not merely the feelers they are often seen to be – as Eric Bentley and others remind us – but even among the most well-read (such as Shaw or Sartre) none has worn his reading on his sleeve like Müller. This attitude amounted to a petulant political position, I believe, undergirding the very black humor in which he cast most of his thought; as Thomas Mann once wrote, "Irony *woos*, even if secretly; it seeks to win for the intellect, even if in vain."[29] Nothing could be more threatening than this position in the anti-intellectual arena of the United States – nothing, not Communist ideology, sophistry, or protean evasiveness. Add to that a disastrous choice of an American translator and it becomes obvious why Müller has been neglected in the land of his friend and collaborator Robert Wilson.[30]

3. With Samuel Beckett, Müller provides one of the most compelling visions we have had of the need for theater in the face of overwhelming dominance by mechanical media – the need for it as a marginal alternative (see chapters 9 and 10). The Berlin Wall having been, among other things, a "time-wall" dividing the "slowed-down" East from the "accelerated" West, he thought, its disappearance meant the sudden subjection of "defenseless" masses to the "machine-world," the final deliverance of humanity into "the marriage of man and machine" [17/42, 18/18, 39]. Advertisements to the contrary notwithstanding, the marriage has never been harmonious and will invariably end with the annihilation of the inefficient partner. (As an East German, he begrudged himself a measure of hysteria about these matters, as Beckett allowed himself to be seen as a backward recluse though he worked in radio and television and roused himself on behalf of numerous public causes.) Even the guarded sanguineness of Walter Benjamin in "The Work of Art in the Age of Mechanical Reproduction" is not for this apocalyptist, who sees with his trusty lens of negativism a clear opportunity for theater and art in general: to establish "islands of disorder" amid seas of exploitative efficiency, moments of "humanized" braking amid the blind acceleration of technocracy.

4. The quintessential adaptability of Müller's theater texts, particularly those from 1970 on, has itself filled a controversial but very real need for a generation of theater directors, who have often sought not merely good plays on which they might leave a lasting

stamp (as Reinhardt or Meyerhold did) but infinitely tractable texts they could turn and mold entirely to their own purposes like verbal clay (see chapter 10). This directing tradition involves a paradoxical demand for geniuses of absence, authors whose words are strong and immovable like engraved tombstones but who *seem* to leave behind no proprietary claims. The disingenuousness of the whole debate about authority in the twentieth-century theater – directors have long held all the cards – has everything to do with Müller who, true to form, stood firmly on both sides of it. One internationally prominent director told me when I began this study that every era gets the culture it deserves, and ours deserved Heiner Müller.

A final word on my relationship with him. I first met Müller and, at his encouragement, began arranging appointments with him in the late 1980s – a period when demands on his time were at a peak – and our association began in frustration as he cancelled or cut short a dozen meetings over six months. The interview-essay that I published about that experience in *American Theatre* (February 1990) is only the first chapter of a longer tale, however. Müller went on to meet me, without apparent reluctance, on numerous other occasions, showed an interest in my work, and kindly provided information when I requested it. Though I know he was somewhat wary of me, as I was of him, this study is anything but the denunciation he may have suspected. Nor is it the exaltation some of his advocates may hope for, which holds equally little interest for me.

There is a great deal of excellent German criticism on Müller and a smaller amount of equally fine work in English; I have found the writings of Hans-Thies Lehmann, Genia Schulz, and Norbert Otto Eke, as well as Gerhard Fischer's book of essays from the 1994 Müller Symposium in Sydney, especially useful. I have not always been able, however, to engage with the important debates among these and other Müller-watchers to the extent I would like because of my prime aim: to introduce Müller to an Anglophone public largely unfamiliar with him. If my book succeeds in convincing some of the previously dubious to look, or look again, or clamor for fresh translations, I will consider myself fortunate.

2 Müller as Brecht: *The Horatian*

> The way people have of looking hurriedly at things from the
> opposite point of view, so as to impose their opinions indirectly,
> is called dialectic, in other words, heads I win, tails you lose,
> dressed up to look scholarly . . . Dialectics is an amusing
> machine that leads us (in banal fashion) to the opinions which
> we would have held in any case.   (Tristan Tzara[1])

At some point shortly after the shock of the *Resettler* affair of 1961 – a
decisive experience of rejection by paternalistic institutions (the
Communist Party and the Writers' Union) of which he had striven to
be worthy – Heiner Müller seems to have made a crucial decision, in
his drama, to face the point Tzara raises directly rather than sweep it
under the rug as did Brecht and most of the century's other Marxist
playwrights. The changes in Müller's writing following that first
Stalinist denunciation clearly indicate his final disillusionment with
what critics at the time called "closed" dramatic forms, self-pro-
claimed "dialectical" plays about the problems of characters caught in
the "contradictions" of building socialism, which closed (or answered)
questions about possible spectator action in the name of opening
them to discussion.

Müller's playwriting before this point, anything but party-line
Socialist Realism, will be examined in chapter 4. This chapter focuses
rather on the pivotal play *The Horatian* and on the central series of
decisions Müller made in the 1960s to repudiate dialectical parables,
conventional dialogue, and numerous other techniques that he
thought cut off possibilities of interpretation for spectators,
propagandizing and fostering ideological obedience rather than

original thinking. Much later, he would coin the term *Verschleierung*, or veiling, to describe the sort of excessively definite, and hence manipulative, directorial choices that similarly curtailed interpretive possibilities in performance. The conception of a theater more "democratic" than the one that had dominated Western culture since the late Middle Ages, however, probably his most significant practical legacy, had its roots in his reaction to similar theoretical ideas in the Brechtian *Lehrstück* during this period when Müller had no immediate access to productions.

As mentioned in chapter 1, Brecht is Müller's primary influence, a figure that stands behind all his other alter egos and tactical masks. His ideas about Brecht certainly changed over the years, but there was no time after the 1950s when he was not consciously imitating, apostrophizing, or criticizing him. Brecht epigones were common when Müller first arrived on the GDR theater scene – some of the more prominent were Helmut Baierl, Peter Hacks, and Hartmut Lange – but the fervent, keen, and intensely personal nature of Müller's identification was entirely his own. The two authors had only a few superficial contacts during the five years when both lived in Berlin (1951–6), once when Müller applied to become a *Meisterschüler* at the Berliner Ensemble. "Thank God that went wrong," he said four decades later. "The thank God is of course a later recognition" [0/82]. Müller nevertheless adopted some of the most conspicuous features of Brecht's personality as his own: the cigar-smoking, leather-jacket-wearing *roué*-demeanor, the quiet voice that ensured attentive listeners, the proclivity for (in Peter Thomson's words) "cultivating coldness," and the "unbending confidence in his own rightness."[2]

This identification ran very deep and sometimes had bizarre consequences, such as Müller's habit of answering interview questions with quotes from and anecdotes about Brecht, accurate and not, that blurred the distinction between Brecht and himself. The more he was interviewed in the 1980s and 1990s, the more the Brecht quotes passed unacknowledged, as if he presumed that his interlocutors were as intimate with the works as he, or that if they weren't they deserved to be deceived about origins. *War without Battle* describes a select writers' workshop that Müller attended in 1951 at which author-cum-politburo-member Johannes Becher was asked whether one could learn from Brecht, and answered: "No, under no circumstances. Brecht is a great dramatist, an important poet, but that's an endpoint, from there nothing goes further" [92]. Müller seems to have taken the remark as a slap at himself and maintained a determination to carry the flag throughout his career: "I always presuppose Brecht" (1976); "I started where Brecht left off" (1982) [14/33, 129].

The most important point is not that Brecht provided Müller's main model for an artist's behavior ("Brecht was the example that one could be a communist and an artist – without or with the system, against the system or in spite of the system" [0/112]), but that Müller's basic ideas about what theater art was supposed to accomplish were taken more or less intact from Brecht. In a 1948 meeting with students in Leipzig, Brecht said: "What this land needs is twenty years of ideology-destruction . . . a theater of scientific generation of scandals" [0/123]. The comment offers a rare *late* glimpse at his puckishly subversive side, which attracted Müller more than any other and which was much more in evidence before 1933 than after the war.

Müller in 1990: "What interests me in Brecht is the evil, which he himself very much concealed in his later years – or at least permitted Weigel to conceal. But the evil is the substance in Brecht" [17/63]. "Evil" in this sense is, for instance, the willingness to follow one's Mephistophelian passion to tear things apart without necessarily bothering to reassure that they will come together again, as in the first *Baal*. "Evil" is the will to construct a tinderbox emotional structure and take pleasure in watching it infuriate others, as in *The Measures Taken*, or a general carelessness about obedience to revolutionary authority and selfless commitment to the collective, as in *Trommeln in der Nacht* (*Drums in the Night*) and *Im Dickicht der Städte* (*In the Jungle of Cities*). This sort of "evil" is the operative framework for Müller's reaction to the *Lehrstück* – a reaction based on a nostalgia for an atmosphere of ideological unpredictability in which ideas exist to be criticized. As Müller famously said in 1980: "to use Brecht without criticizing him is betrayal" [19/133].[3]

Lehrstück is probably the most widely misunderstood concept in Brecht's theory among Anglophones. This is largely because the German scholarly books dating from the early 1970s that explain it –

Brecht's explanations were scattered piecemeal over three decades in program notes, unpublished jottings, and occasional journalism that had to be tracked down and collected after his death – have never been translated. In recent years, it has become fashionable among some Anglophone Brecht critics to blame Martin Esslin for the widespread misunderstanding. Writers such as Elizabeth Wright and Roswitha Mueller have summarized the German scholarship, they say, partly as a means of correcting the impression Esslin left in his 1959 book *Brecht: The Man and His Work* that *Lehrstück* was predominantly a heavy-handed form of ideological indoctrination.[4] Esslin (who translated *Lehrstück* as "didactic play";[5] Brecht preferred "learning play") was presumably negligent in not having anticipated Reiner Steinweg's pioneering book on the subject thirteen years later, which clarified Brecht's intentions for the first time, and was also presumably responsible for Brecht's opportunistic promotion of these plays as *Schaustücke* (plays for public performance) before and during his exile, that is, in a spirit that thoroughly obscured his original intentions.[6] The point is not a parochial matter of critical carping, because Brecht's compromises on this score were a primary impetus for Müller's reaction.

Originally, *Lehrstück* did not refer to authoritarian didacticism but rather to a group of plays (mostly written between 1929 and the mid-1930s) intended to teach those who were acting them, a form of self-didacticism for "producers" rather than "consumers," containing a whiff of socialist utopia, if not precisely the unobstructed interpretive "democracy" Müller was to propose. The idea for the genre grew out of the revolutionary hopes Brecht invested in the Berlin working classes during the turbulent period before and after the 1929 stock market crash, as well as the cultural atmosphere of *Neue Sachlichkeit*, which popularized the value of *Gebrauchskunst*, or art emulating the functional utility and efficiency of machines. Another source was the work of the Latvian actress Asja Lacis, whose postrevolutionary experiments with children's theater in Russia had been the subject of an essay by Walter Benjamin, and who introduced Benjamin to Brecht. The closest Brecht came to a manifesto or comprehensive statement of rules for this genre was a short, somewhat imprecisely written document (about half of which is quoted here) entitled "On the Theory of the *Lehrstück*," probably written in 1937 but unpublished until 1967:

> The *Lehrstück* teaches by being played, not by being seen. In principle, spectators are not needed for the *Lehrstück*, although they can of course be utilized. It is basic to the *Lehrstück* that the people playing can be socially influenced by the execution of certain attitudes, the adoption of certain postures, the repetition of certain speeches, and so forth. In this regard, the imitation of highly viable patterns plays a large role, as does the criticism of those patterns, which will be carried out through well-considered, altered modes of playing . . .
>
> Aesthetic standards for the formation of characters that pertain to performance plays [*Schaustücke*] are inoperative in the *Lehrstück* . . .
>
> The form of the *Lehrstück* is strict, but only so that elements of [the players'] own invention and current manner can be more easily inserted . . .
>
> Concerning manner of playing, the instructions for *Epic Theater* apply. Study of A[lienation]-effects is indispensable . . . The intellectual mastery of the whole play is absolutely necessary. It is not advisable, however, to conclude instruction about it before actual playing . . .
>
> In the *Lehrstück* an immense variety is possible . . .[7]

Here are the basic principles: players need not be professional actors; they are preferably non-actors who know little about theater and who end up questioning their real-life identities, beliefs, and routines in the course of acting in a *Lehrstück*. Participation in choral staging, for instance, would give them first-hand experience of collective identity: hence the multiple Lindberghs in *Der Flug der Lindberghs* (*The Flight of the Lindberghs*, 1928–9) and the multiple Agitators in *The Measures Taken*. On a more mundane level, specific acting experiences – e.g. policemen committing fictional crimes, bureaucrats burning prop-files – would allow participants to return to their lives more sympathetic to others and hence also better prepared for membership in a collective. And this preparation, moreover, would not be merely an intellectual "training" for "the kind of

athletes of the mind that good dialecticians should be."[8] Like Meyerhold, reflexologists, and behaviorist psychologists, Brecht believed
that the mere imitation or copying of appropriate gestures and expres-
sions could bring about desired mental states. (The appeal of writerly
Kopien to both Brecht and Müller no doubt enhanced their interest in
such learning by behavioral copying.)

Repeating a point Brecht himself insisted on up to the last year
of his life, Steinweg writes that "the *Lehrstück* is Brecht's most
revolutionary type of play," its radicalism more far-reaching than that
of Epic Theater in theory.[9] Other points touched on in the numerous
documents he unearthed include: the use of music to encourage group
participation and make learning pleasurable; the exchanging of roles
mid-performance to allow true sharing of experiences; the identification of collective artmaking as an explicit goal (*Lehrstücke* were
similar to "meetings," Brecht wrote later; Hanns Eisler compared
them to "political seminars"[10]); the priority of process over product;
and a general preference for the unfinished in the name of experimentation. This last point is especially interesting in light of Müller's later
fascination with fragments per se, and although direct influences are
few, there are many other affinities between *Lehrstück* theory and the
postwar avant-garde throughout Europe and the United States. Unfortunately, Brecht's enforced absence, after 1933, from places with any
hope of producing the socialist conditions necessary for *Lehrstücke*
put an abrupt halt to his radical experimentation with them. The
theorizing and playwriting continued, and he took up some ideas
again, with unsatisfying results, in Berlin after the war. By the 1960s,
however, the field was open for an artist such as Müller to reconceive
the genre in the GDR.

The Horatian is the middle text in what Müller calls a three-
play *Versuchsreihe* (series of experiments) that "presumes/criticizes
Brecht's *Lehrstück* theory and praxis" [6/68].[11] Written in 1968
shortly after Warsaw Pact forces occupied Czechoslovakia and ended
the Prague Spring, the text has been thoroughly overshadowed by the
first and third plays in the series which, for different reasons, are more
famous and more frequently produced. Its *Lehrstück* roots notwithstanding, the Sophocles adaptation *Philoctetes* (1958–64) has almost
always been seen as a powerful allegory about Stalinism in which

strong professional actors are showcased in unchanging roles. And *Mauser* (1970) is a polemic against particular thematic points in *The Measures Taken* that has proven as incendiary as its source. Precisely because of the stature and *Schaustück* stage histories of these other texts and their sources, the relatively short, dense, and disarmingly lucid *The Horatian* is a better example for my purposes.

All three of Müller's *Lehrstück* "experiments" deal with the theme of "necessary" killing that is also at the center of Brecht's *Lehrstück* plots – the issue of *Einverständnis* (informed agreement to loss of life or self or to other drastic action in the interest of the collective) being less central in Müller's less humane dramatic worlds. *The Horatian* is not, as its title implies, a polemical response to Brecht's *Die Horatier und die Kuriatier* (*The Horatians and the Curiatians*, 1935), the most schematic of his *Lehrstücke* and probably his play intended for the youngest audience. Müller does echo and alter specific lines in that work, but the underlying polemic in *The Horatian* is much more generalized, focusing on the handling of the genre itself, on ways the *Lehrstück* might be adapted to more sophisticated uses than those possible with plays like *The Horatians and the Curiatians*.

The original source for both authors is a Roman legend told by Livius and adapted by Corneille in the play *Horace*, and Müller stays much closer to these origins than Brecht, giving the tale as follows. The cities of Rome and Alba, facing imminent invasion by a common enemy, the Etruscans, decide to resolve a dispute over dominance between them not by open warfare, which would "weaken victor and vanquished" alike, but rather by single combat. Through a lottery, a Horatian is chosen to fight for Rome and, for Alba, a Curiatian who happens to be engaged to the Horatian's sister. The Curiatian is overcome and, despite his pleas for mercy, is killed by the Horatian, who is borne home as a hero. His sister, distraught with grief over her lover's death, cries: "Give me back what was in these clothes." The Horatian stabs her, saying, "Go to him, whom you love more than Rome" [6/46].

This eventful story fills only the first two pages of the nine-page text, the rest of which is a highly idiosyncratic trial-play (like *The Measures Taken*) dealing with questions of how Rome must respond to the dilemma of a man who has killed in its name both with and without "necessity." Some Romans shout "Honor the victor," others "Execute the murderer," and the city is forced once again to settle an internal conflict quickly so that its external enemy does not find it divided and weak. In the course of a troublesome debate, the richly ambiguous details of which provide the stuff of the play's metallically steady poetry, the people's court decides that the Horatian should be both honored as hero and executed as murderer – *Einverständnis* in this case being the group recognition that the valuable warrior must be sacrificed. (The justice thus meted out recalls the Duke of Brandenburg's treatment of Kleist's title character in "Michael Kohlhaas": remedying injustice by the Elector of Saxony, the Duke awards Kohlhaas financial recompense for the wrongs done him, then has him beheaded for his crimes committed in overzealous pursuit of justice.)

Müller's attraction to the Horatian–Curiatian legend is part of his lifelong artistic fixation on the divided Germany and the splitting of the Communist left after 1919 – a fixation also channeled, in later plays, into his characteristic theme of warring brothers. The self-destructive actions in the name of self-preservation before a presumably common external enemy also refer to events in Prague and, more distantly, to his imposed status as outsider within the GDR in 1968. Even when all this external information is understood, however, what principally allows the play to shimmer beyond its immediate circumstances is Müller's quiet repudiation of the chief paternalistic assumptions underlying Brecht's *Lehrstück* plots. Rather than focus on actions whose moral significance is already decided – Brecht's undecided characters and supposedly suspenseful scenes do not affect at all the "decided" nature of parables such as *The Horatians and the Curiatians*, *Der Jasager* (*The Yes-Sayer*, 1929–30) and *Der Neinsager* (*The No-Sayer*, 1929–30) – the action in *The Horatian* is *about* the difficulty of assigning unambiguous moral significance to its events.

Hans-Thies Lehmann writes:

> For Marxist art the contradiction between good deed and terror
> by the revolutionary power is a topos. . . Müller shifts the
> accent: not the initial problem of superfluous violence itself but
> rather the *speaking* about it proves to be. . . the real object for
> learning.[12]

To be sure, Müller is still present, as present as Brecht, one might say; in the end, "the voice of the people is itself the voice of the author of Marxist art," as Lehmann writes, "the voice of a consciousness with the all but impossible task of dealing with the identity of victor and murderer in the particular case of Stalin."[13] But Müller finds ways to delay the sense of his presence, subduing his teacherly voice until the final lines by means of several strategies that create a feeling of open-endedness. Moreover, the presence of that voice, when it *is* felt, is wholly different from Brecht's because its mood is aporetic, containing doubts about the legitimacy of Stalinist violence, the malevolence of the external threat, and even (less distinctly) the benevolence of technology (a recurrent theme in Brecht's *Lehrstücke* since the earliest *The Flight of the Lindberghs*).

With this last point I am thinking of Müller's language, which combines what Esslin calls the "functional . . . austere . . . [and] severely factual"[14] manner of Brecht in his *Gebrauchskunst* phase with a relentless pounding rhythm that leaves the impression of a world caught in a sinister machine. ("Give me the sleep of the machine" [6/66], says the mentally exhausted executioner in *Mauser*.) Machines eventually become a negative obsession for Müller, seen, for instance, in the robot president in *Gundling's Life . . .*, the Hamlet Actor in *Hamletmachine*, and, by implication, the apocalyptically ruined landscapes in those works, *Verkommenes Ufer* (*Despoiled Shore*), *Der Auftrag* (*The Mission*), and others. As the passages translated below demonstrate, the rhythm in *The Horatian* also recalls liturgical cadences – so does the language in *Mauser* – which gives the people's heroic efforts to rescue itself with dialectical reasoning a subtle anti-religious undertone.

Müller's main strategy for sustaining open-endedness, though, is abstention from dialogue. He writes the work as a single block of versified text undivided into different speakers – also originally a Brecht idea (from the *Fatzer* commentary) which Müller puts to shrewdly original use. Under most circumstances, the combination of a third-person point of view with an unchanging past tense would immediately activate questions about the narrator's identity, but *The Horatian*'s mimicry of the epic lends the speaking voice what Theodor Adorno called "epic naiveté." This is a tactical quality of

Urdummheit ("primal stupidity," the anthropologist K.T. Preuss' word) that creates a provisional trust in readers and spectators, evoking the tradition in which a narrowly circumscribed purview, a "rigid fixation on [an] object," is automatically accepted as a "positive" path to metaphorical riches.[15] Müller's imagination may have been sparked by contrivedly naive children's dramas like *The Horatians and the Curiatians*, but this is no naive children's drama, even if he once thought so.[16] He employs "epic naiveté" as a form of journalistic objectivity, keeping the action's outcome in doubt and keeping the voice from betraying moral preferences regarding that outcome until the end.

Writing the play as a large text-block could also be seen as a possible solution to the problem of limited learning opportunities in *Lehrstücke* that Brecht had already noticed in 1931. Even in utopian socialist performance circumstances in which no audience was present and a *Lehrstück* was performed only for the benefit of those producing it, he said, the learning process would be dependent on an exchanging of roles that possibly required multiple meetings or performances, since only the actor portraying the "asocial character" is really in a position to learn (e.g. the Young Comrade in *The Measures Taken* or the Merchant in *Die Ausnahme und die Regel* [*The Exception and the Rule*, 1930]).[17] The play in which Müller first seized on this issue directly is *Mauser*, to which he appended a note stating that "the given distribution of the text is a variable scheme, the means and degree of the variants a political decision that must be made case by case" [6/69]. Despite a contrasting note to *The Horatian* stating that "The playing follows the [text's] description" [6/54], Müller treated the line assignments as fully fluid in that play, too, when he directed it in 1988. That production, moreover (which is discussed further below), made especially clear that questions about whether the murderer/hero is an asocial character – and if so whether he is the only one – are meant to remain unanswered for most of the action.

The Horatian is more sophisticated than most of Brecht's *Lehrstücke* primarily because of its poetry and the structure of its argument. Throughout the action, Müller deals with notions of balance, rhythmic and ideational; he knows, as does Brecht, that sustained, perfect balance makes for dull drama, but unlike Brecht (and like Beckett) he thinks there is dramatic value in flirting with dullness.

> And the wreath-carrier said:
> His service cancels his guilt
> And the ax-carrier said:
> His guilt cancels his service
> And the wreath-carrier asked:
> Should the victor be executed?
> And the ax-carrier asked:
> Should the murderer be honored?
> And the wreath-carrier said:
> If the murderer is executed
> The victor will be executed
> And the ax-carrier said:
> If the victor is honored
> The murderer will be honored.
> And the people looked upon the indivisible one
> Doer of different deeds and said nothing.   [49]

Müller employs repetition and near-repetition partly in order to harness the emotional power of antiphonal chanting, the assumption being that, in performance, roles will be exchanged and lines such as those just quoted will be distributed among choral groups, as his "Note" to the play recommends. The model for such an arrangement is the famous Control Chorus in *The Measures Taken* – a pliant, adaptable, singing tribunal, sitting in judgement on a murder, whose function as a collective pool into which performers can disappear and reappear later as different characters makes it difficult for spectators to fix hatred on a singular culprit. Music was always central to this concept for Brecht, but an inevitable problem with it was (as he and Hanns Eisler discussed without solving[18]) that the choral effects thus created were invariably quasi-religious, based in strong emotions difficult to control, and could easily lead to mindless mass reactions. Müller confronts this heritage of choral emotionalism, turning it on its head, as it were; he leaves no narrative room for his masses to react irrationally but rather uses the clockwork-like sequence of their responses to chart the Roman people's mechanistic progress toward grim *Einverständnis*.

Three fundamental questions are raised – how should the Horatian be judged? what should be done with his executed body? how should he be remembered? – and each receives a similar response.

> And the people answered with one voice
>
>   . . .
>
> There is the victor. His name: Horatius
> There is the murderer. His name: Horatius
> Many men are in one man.
> One triumphed for Rome in single combat
> The other killed his sister
> Without necessity. To each his own.
> The wreath to the victor. The ax to the murderer.   [49–50]

> What should become of the victor's corpse?
> And the people answered with one voice:
> The victor's corpse should lie in state
> On the shields of the men saved by his sword
>
>   . . .
>
> What should become of the murderer's corpse?
> And the people answered with one voice
>
>   . . .
>
> The murderer's corpse
> Should be thrown to the dogs
> So that they tear it to pieces.   [51–52]

> How should the Horatian be remembered?
> And the people answered with one voice:
> He should be known as the victor over Alba
> He should be known as the murderer of his sister
> With one breath his service and his guilt.
> And he who speaks of his guilt and not his service
> Should live among dogs as a dog
> And he who speaks of his service and not his guilt
> He also should live among dogs.   [53]

Significantly, everyone agrees that the killing of the sister was a murder; the hero alone is guilty of confusion on this point due to his loyalty to the state, as in *Mauser*. This *Volk*, which invariably ends up speaking "with one voice," even though its factions disagree, is anything but mindless or over-emotional. Far from the ignorant, easily manipulable mobs found in Brecht and Shakespeare ("Bid them wash their faces / And keep their teeth clean" – *Coriolanus*, II. iii.67–8), it is extremely sharp, like a composite raisonneur, and is eminently capable of understanding concepts such as "collective threat" without the help of prop-centered demonstrations like those from which all Brecht's *Lehrstück* choruses must learn, as I will explain, the Control Chorus included. In Müller's *Lehrstücke*, actually, internal learning (i.e. by characters and choruses as opposed to performers and spectators) is increasingly irrelevant.

To illustrate, in *The Horatians and the Curiatians* Brecht makes use of a Chinese theater convention by which one actor represents an army, or a large unit of one. At one point, the Horatian archer wounds his superior foe by planting himself where the rising sun blinds his opponent, but he then suffers heavy losses when the sun (an actor-operated spotlight) progresses across the ridiculously symmetrical valley to the benefit of the Curiatians. The Horatian chorus learns its collective lesson – that natural forces will be loyal allies only to those who do not become self-satisfied with their cleverness in enlisting them – only by dint of this explicit and redundant demonstration. Müller seems to remark on the condescension of such demonstrations himself when he alludes to Brecht's unresonant refrain about object permanence, "Many things are in one thing,"[19] with his own faintly Pirandellian line, "Many men are in one man" [49]. ("No man is another man" [51], adds the narrator later, when the Horatian's father offers to die in place of his "indivisible" son and is rebuffed.) Müller too could be said to harp on a somewhat platitudinous point: that wisdom is won simply by holding two contradictory concepts in one's head simultaneously. Ultimately, though, his obsession with balance in *The Horatian* is revealed to be a strategic frame for contemplation – by performers, readers–spectators, and fictional Romans – of the unbalanceable.

No god descended from morality plays, from Marxist–Leninist

heaven or anywhere else, guarantees anything for the humans in *The Horatian*, and in the end only the illusion of perfect balance remains because the "one man, indivisible" must die in order to answer both sides of the people's neatly balanced judgement. His death is the price this conspicuously unanimous collectivity must pay to ensure that its "words remain pure":

> But he who speaks of his guilt at one time
> And speaks of his service at another
> Talking out of two sides of his mouth
> Or differently for different ears
> His tongue should be torn from his head.
> For the words must remain pure. Because
> A sword can be broken and a man
> Can be broken, but the words
> Fall into the gears of the world irrecoverably
> Making things clear or unclear.
> Lethal to humans is the unclear.
> And so, not fearing the impure truth, awaiting the enemy
> They set a provisional example
> Of pure differentiation, not hiding the rest
> That wasn't resolved in the course of ceaseless change.   [53]

The nature of the "impure truth" is the open question as the play ends. In didactic limbo hangs the still faintly sanguine implication that there is no future for socialism without truthfulness, without "looking history in the whites of the eyes" [13/141], to use a Müller formulation from another context. Müller seems to want to criticize political doublespeak and historical falsifications in the spirit of George Orwell, but phrases such as "tongue should be torn" and the very finely wrought roundness of his critique, in essence a *formal* flirtation with "pure truth," give the game away. Some of his formulations of "impure truth" are as harshly absolutist as what he ostensibly criticizes:

> half an example is no example
> What isn't completely pursued to its real end
> Walks crabwise toward nothingness in the reins of time.   [52]

It is this tension between the pure and the impure that makes *The Horatian* not only a self-conscious exercise in (and meditation on) dialectics but also a tale of individual shipwreck that has the patina of tragedy.[20] With scrutiny, the story even yields up vestiges of the sort of retributive dramatic justice Müller went to great lengths to circumvent. Left unresolved by the ending, for example, is the question of whether the Roman people (or, figurally, the German or Soviet people) suffer from some common pathology, erupting to the surface in individuals like the Horatian, that led it and will continue leading it to these sorts of crises. Its fairness and dialectical rationality notwithstanding (a rationality necessitated by the pressure of the external threat – the common Etruscan enemy?), perhaps the people's ready acceptance that the Horatian killed the Curiatian with "necessity" but his sister "without necessity" is not entirely healthy – an enlarged reflection, in aseptic political terms, of the tropistic loyalty shown by both soldiers before they fight and the cruel excess and native aggressiveness of the Horatian moments later.

> He is/You are engaged to your/his sister
> Should the lots be cast again?
> And the Horatian and the Curiatian said: No
> And they fought between the battle lines
> And the Horatian wounded the Curiatian
> And the Curiatian said with a weakening voice:
> Spare the vanquished. I am
> Engaged to your sister.
> And the Horatian cried:
> My bride's name is Rome
> And the Horatian shoved his sword
> Into the neck of the Curiatian, so that his blood fell to the earth.
>
> [45]

With typical effrontery, Müller plants a bold symbolic question mark concerning the benevolence of this Roman justice: the lictors guarding the Horatian make repeated use of "fasces" – drawing a parallel between fascism and the contemporary regimes being mythologized. The overriding mood in the end, however, is one of tragic loss (loss of simple notions of right and wrong, among other things) combined with a faintly uplifting sense that the collectivity, having preserved itself, brutally, has at least the chance to apply its lesson "of pure differentiation" in future efforts to avoid brutality.

For all his efforts to resist parable, then, Müller's story in *The Horatian* can function, albeit complexly, as an illustration of a moral lesson. The play is truly and importantly transitional in this sense between *Philoctetes*, which makes all but no challenge to parable, and *Mauser*, whose narrative "knot" is utterly peripheral. (It lacks a consistently objective narrative position or stable time-plane and depicts a frozen historical situation; in David Bathrick and Andreas Huyssen's words, it contains "no teleological moment."[21]) Müller's doubts about the parable form actually date back at least to 1958, when he attempted (at Paul Dessau's request) to expand Brecht's incomplete *Die Reisen des Glücksgotts* (*Journey of the Happiness God*) into a libretto. Explaining his reasons for abandoning that project in a text published in 1975, Müller writes:

> The first difficulty (impossibility) was the character of the
> Happiness God. Stationary characters (gods monuments types)
> are useful as catalysts when experience has overtaken history.
> Fossils on top of which wisdom can settle, which serve as
> explosives when called forth through progress. When the
> overtaking process happens the other way round they no longer
> work the same way. And that applies also to their playing field,
> the parable. It becomes marginal. It has a (sinister) future: when
> the chances are missed, what was a plan for a new world begins
> differently anew – as dialogue with the dead. In science fiction,
> which trivializes catastrophes into punch lines, it circulates as a
> trivial form. The positive: on the background of world history,
> for which communism (equal opportunity) is a requirement, the
> dialogue stands for the freeing of the past. Anticipation results
> in handicraft [*Kunstgewerbe*], which is to art what cosmetics is
> to surgery.   [4/7]

The comment about history having "overtaken" experience is opaque, but Müller's general feeling that, in his time, both parables and "stationary characters" are necessarily "marginal," or worse, is clear. He speaks later in the text of writing during a "transitional period" when the function of literature is undergoing important changes that render "monuments" such as a god-character useful only for "building material": "My reality in 1958 seemed to me both no longer and not yet representable as closed in that way" [4/8].[22]

These statements contain the kernel of a self-justification for what is often seen as Müller's highbrow abstruseness. Reacting to a Brecht text, he states categorically that nothing is to be expected from thought so "crude" ("*plump*," Brecht's word from *Dreigroschenroman* [*The Threepenny Novel*], famously dignified by Walter Benjamin) that it makes a mockery of dialectics in the eyes of intelligent observers like Tzara. Benjamin wrote in 1935:

> There are many people to whom a dialectician means a lover of subtleties. In this connection it is particularly useful when Brecht puts his finger on "crude thinking" which produces dialectics as its opposite, contains it within itself, and has need of it. Crude thoughts belong to the household of dialectical thinking precisely because they represent nothing other than the application of theory to practice: its *application* to practice, not its *dependence* on practice. Action can, of course, be as subtle as thought. But a thought must be crude in order to come into its own in action.[23]

For Müller, exactly the opposite is the case: a thought must have a certain complexity in order avoid misuse through bad faith or slavish mental habits that treat reality as unchangeable; only then can it "come into its own in action." His difficult texts are like "messages in a bottle,"[24] Müller once said, echoing the elitist description of Benjamin's friend Adorno for his own texts. Ours is no longer "a healthy world" in which metaphors can stand unequivocally due to universal agreement on the structure of reality. Thus, being "both no longer and not yet" ready for "crude thinking," we can use the closed form of the parable merely as "handicraft," producing at best a simplistic sort of dialogue with the dead and at worst "sinister" forms of audience manipulation.

That, at least, is the way it seems from the standpoint of the *Happiness God* fragment and most of Müller's writing in the following decades. The problem is, to distort a famous Oscar Wilde quip, most truths about this artist are such that the opposite is equally true. He did indeed reserve some of his harshest critical words for the fact that, as Nicola Chiaromonte once put it, "Brecht's dice are loaded and are meant to be."[25] In a 1980 text treating the revisions to the *Fatzer* material between 1927 and 1932 as a paradigm for Brecht's whole career, Müller spoke of "the shadow of Leninist party discipline"; with its descent into the parabolic, "the sketch begins to dry up into morality" [19/132]. There was something hollow about that harsh judgement, though, especially in the context of *Fatzer* – a 400-page collection of fragmentary dramatic writing that Müller claimed was "the best thing that's been written for the stage in this century and the best of Brecht."[26] Müller's high opinion arose mainly because Brecht had used this text "as a field for experimentation" [14/50] in the spirit of *Lehrstück*, its primary characteristic being variety of technical means: that is, part block text, part conventional dialogue, part choral exchanges involving shared roles, part critical commentary, and more. But in 1978, given access to the material in the Brecht archive for the purpose of assembling a script for professional production in Hamburg, Müller fashioned it into a fully logical, chronologically organized parable called *Der Untergang des Egoisten Johann Fatzer* (*The Downfall of the Egoist Johann Fatzer*), replete with critical choral interludes in the "classical" *Schaustück*-style of *Der kaukasische Kreidekreis* (*The Caucasian Chalk Circle*, 1944–5), *Leben des Galilei* (*Life of Galileo*, 1938–54) and *Mutter Courage und ihre Kinder* (*Mother Courage and Her Children*, 1939).[27] Chiaromonte notwithstanding, Müller could never begrudge Brecht his cheating; for his own lifelong effort was to try to cheat better.

The Dadaist Richard Huelsenbeck once put the same point another way:

> [Brecht's] insincerity is apparent in the fact that his workers are always right and his capitalists always wrong. However, insincerity and talent are not only not incompatible, they sometimes also determine one another. If an artist wants to avoid being a victim of his times, he has to have (today more than ever) a certain Machiavellism to get something for himself and for others.[28]

All other personal and stylistic similarities understood, this is, I think, the most significant point of linkage with Müller and the key to what he means by the "evil" in Brecht. An admirably "evil" artist is not bound by theory or ideology, his own least of all, since these are "material" like everything else, even if he happens to believe in them passionately. Such an artist's finger is on the political pulse of his public (impossible for Brecht in exile, thought Müller), and only that changeable circumstance – not abstract ideals like self-consistency or loyalty to a Hegelian view of historical progress – determines when he will pick up and drop a particular material or working method. Hence, Müller can state categorically in a 1977 open letter to Reiner Steinweg, "I think we have to take leave of the *Lehrstück* until the next earthquake" [6/85], and then, with the same equanimity, he can tell the interviewer Gregor Edelmann in 1986: "This *Lehrstück* playmodel is becoming current again" [14/189]. (His five-part text *Wolokolamsker Chaussee* [*Volokolamsk Highway*, 1984–7], the context of the comment to Edelmann, was written in *Lehrstück* block-form, as were many sections of *Anatomie Titus Fall of Rome* [*Anatomy of Titus Fall of Rome*, 1984].)

Two equally illuminating examples are the two professional German productions *The Horatian* received in the late 1980s, both of which used recordings of the distinctive, deadpan monotone voice of Müller to narrate the story. In the 1988 version from the Schauspielhaus Bochum, the director, Reinhild Hoffmann, was a well-known tanztheater (dance-theater) choreographer, and an important issue in tanztheater has always been the subordination of text to movement. As Müller once wrote about the related work of Pina Bausch: "History occurs as a nuisance, like mosquitos in summer" [19/106]. In this case, alas, with the singular, recognizable voice of the author seizing the audience's best attention while speaking his text from beginning to end, the movement was rather the nuisance – a ritualistic solo dance involving a "blood trail" made of red smocks, dragged sacks containing dirt and swords, and a long banner bearing the colors of the German flag.

By contrast, in Müller's own production at the Deutsches Theater in Berlin, also from 1988, tanztheater was not an issue and the voice recording was even more paternalistically directive. Originally suggested by the actress Johanna Schall, who was unsatisfied with the size of her role in Müller's production of *The Scab*, this version of *The Horatian* was developed as a prologue to that play, and Müller defended its modest production values on the ground that he didn't want to upstage his main event. (Rehearsal diary notes published after the opening indicate that a more expansive vision involving multiple choruses was discussed and discarded.[29]) In any case, the final staging involved two visually contrasting actors – Schall close-shorn and serious in a black, blood-smeared raincoat, Ulrich Mühe clownlike in whiteface and loosefitting, white clothes – representing various alter egos of the single characters, as well as opposite aspects of the single *Volk*. They moved stiffly, marionette-like, about the stage and occasionally engaged sensuously with each other and various props: red pot, hatchet, wreath, apple, sword, helmet, child's doll. All was tightly staged, refreshingly unformulaic, and emotionally compelling – until the final few minutes, when Müller's voice took over from the actors after the line "How should the Horatian be remembered?", finishing the text, so it seemed, *for* them. The implication was that only he and not the involved parties could act as judge, could draw the dialectical conclusions in the ending. That is, *Lehrstück* was reduced to *Schaustück* wrapper, then punctuated with the voice of an ideological overseer – "Leninist disciplinary" revision indeed.

In light of the contradictions inherent in Brecht's and Müller's experiments with the *Lehrstück* (and in light of the one strenuous critical effort recently made to trace "postmodern theater" in general to an original *Lehrstück* spring, surrounding the genre with glorifying nostalgia[30]), it may help to recall the case of Eberhard Wolfgang Möller, author of *Das Frankenburger Würfelspiel* (*The Frankenburg Dice Game*), which was the Nazi *Thingspiel* performed at the opening of the 1936 Olympics. *Thing* is an archaic German word for a form of judicial people's assembly in the Middle Ages, and *Thingspiel* was the name given to a form of outdoor mass performance, a historical story framed by a trial, planned in the early years of the Third Reich as the Nazis' distinctive, monumental theater form. Möller rose to the top of the heap of those competing to develop this genre partly because, having closely studied Brecht's *Lehrstück* experiments (a source he underplayed with his colleagues), he was full of interesting ideas on how to involve the public in performances. *The Frankenburg Dice Game* was originally conceived to include passages with which the stadium-size audience would speak and sing along with the actors, as well as processional marching with flags (in the tradition of Communist agit-prop!); the audience, as surrogate *Volk*, would serve as collective judge of the historical events depicted.

Several changes were instituted before the play's opening. Propaganda Minister Goebbels, fearful that audiences would find the religious and socialist associations in the speaking choruses too obvious and too appealing, ordered a nationwide ban on them (which Möller disregarded). And Möller arranged for the verdict in the play to be passed by a panel of seven judges (led by Hitler himself – the plan in Berlin, abandoned at curtain time), leaving spectators little responsibility beyond generating pathos with occasional singing.[31] Möller's experience illuminates Müller's, then, not only because both of them, under pressure, supplanted communal cooperation with authoritarian direction from above, but also because Brecht's participatory *Lehrstück* techniques were so readily adaptable to National Socialist purposes.

In thinking about Müller's trajectory as an artist, it is vital to remember that *Lehrstück* praxis is itself morally neutral and extremely malleable and that Müller thrived on this moral malleability. He used *Lehrstück* techniques and developed his own innovations around them partly because they were rooted in the utopian dreams of others but did not require similar commitment from him. He made use of the genre extra-morally, if not, as he once suggested, apolitically: "I would never say that I am a political author, as far as intention goes. I have never been that, I believe" [15/170]. During this whole period in the 1960s, and certainly afterward, it was very much an open question whether Müller stood with Koch or Fatzer or both in the great debate at the heart of his beloved *Lehrstück, Fatzer*:

KOCH
Our lot is so bad, Fatzer, that
Nothing less than the whole world can help us.
Therefore a plan to help us has to
Help the whole world.

FATZER
Everything that happens after us
Is as if
It didn't happen.[32]

As the 1970s arrived, it became clear that the transition from the eternal GDR artist's question – who is the enemy? – to the eternal Western artist's question – what is the subject? – was natural and seamless for Müller. And among the traits that crucially distinguished him from Brecht is that he never bothered to hide it.

3 Müller as Kleist: *Volokolamsk Highway, Gundling's Life Frederick of Prussia Lessing's Sleep Dream Scream, Mauser*

> Kleist is something strange. The strange is actually what one
> wants to be.   (Heiner Müller, 1994 [16/230])

If it is true that good dramatists tend to inhabit all the roles in the conflicts they invent, and that, as stated above, Müller was always something of a rude Saxon baiting stuffy Prussians, then it is also true that his baiting would never have had any potency had he not also cultivated a Prussian within. To have lasting impact as a provocateur, one must include onself as a target, and for Müller that meant first of all identifying a part of himself that his public could recognize as pan-Germanic. This is the crux of his connection to Heinrich von Kleist, a connection that also offers a window on feelings – such as his intense pain of exclusion – that otherwise remained buried beneath impenetrable veils his whole creative life.

Kleist was the paradigm of the insider become outsider for Müller. Scion of a noble Prussian military family that was too ashamed of him to tend his grave for a century after his suicide, Kleist functioned in Müller's work as the figure of a Germany that habitually went to war with itself in protracted throes of self-definition and as the mirror image of the Saxon Richard Wagner (dealt with in chapter 8), who also arrived at zealous nationalism but from the opposite position of self-perceived outsider clamoring for admittance. In less dispassionate terms, Müller's attachment to Kleist seems to have opened a channel to the strong emotions surrounding the string of enforced separations in his life – e.g. from the community of "decent folk" in the Third Reich, from his parents, from the East German Communist

44

Party, and from the Writers' Union. Kleist is one of the few alter egos through which Müller allowed himself to express melancholy, apparently trusting the Prussianness of the mask to clothe his momentary nakedness and protect him from sentimentality.

A century and a half apart, both Kleist and Müller grew up in cheerless surroundings, developed damaged, alienated relationships to their families, and had similarly pensive, lugubrious demeanors. Both also experienced lifelong feelings of rootlessness (even though Müller lived most of his life in Berlin, the largest city in old Prussia). Comparing himself with Müller after his death, the author Lothar Trolle put the matter this way: "We aren't of the same guitar-nature as Brecht, who moved around and read his stuff to the guitar. More Kleistian, somewhat stubborn, gloomy guys. More inward-directed, sort of lonely dogs."[1] This temperamental point should not be pressed too far – Müller was not a manic-depressive and never entertained thoughts of suicide, for instance [13/172; 19/220] – but it does have bearing on his work.

Among Kleist's numerous distinguishing features was the remarkable economy of his material, a product of patient and severe self-editing that very much suggests Müller. Kleist's finished prose, like Müller's, rests on a small number of densely packed sentences that concentrate necessary information in succinct, deceptively matter-of-fact paragraphs. The effect of the concentration is different in the two cases; Kleist's stories build to a headlong rush driven by urgent questions of character psychology, whereas Müller's non-dramatic and dramatic texts are more ponderous, their momentum frequently broken as the mind pauses to fill intentional gaps. What the writers significantly share, however, is that each achieves an almost surreptitious buildup of extreme emotion in the course of relating what seem to be unadorned facts. "That is the very essence of Kleist," says one of his biographers, "on the one hand, romantic madness; on the other, the rigid bearing of a Prussian officer."[2] I will return to this coupling of rigidity and romanticism.

That Kleist had been a Prussian officer may seem irrelevant to Müller at first, but the link becomes clear in light of his obsession with war and military imagery. Like so many of Müller's dramas, *Penthesilea* (1808), *Hermannsschlacht* (*The Battle of Teutoburg*

Forest, 1809), *Prinz Friedrich von Homburg* (*The Prince of Homburg*, 1811), and the fragmentary *Robert Guiscard* (1808) are all war-plays, and all but one feature protagonists torn apart inwardly by the action. Neither author had any interest in anti-war propaganda per se. Quite the contrary:[3] Kleist (like Shakespeare) often used the stage to celebrate military valor, and Müller (like Brecht) used war scenes partly to direct attention away from individual psychology and toward broad movements of history. The significance of the shared obsession is that both authors, unafraid of potential charges of sensationalism, often employed war-related scenarios to indulge their taste for extreme cases; and Müller, perfectly capable of inventing his own, found several of Kleist's cases exceedingly useful.

One example is the fifth and final part of *Volokolamsk Highway* (1987), a *Lehrstück* block-text that is called *Der Findling* (*The Foundling*) after Kleist's story about an orphan who, taken openheartedly into the home of an Italian businessman, tries after he is grown to rape his wife and dispossess him like Tartuffe. The businessman kills him, is sentenced to death, and goes to his execution refusing absolution so he may continue his revenge in hell. In Müller's story, transformed into a war-related case, the father bears much more guilt from the beginning: a communist functionary unable to father children (his genitals were mutilated in a concentration camp) adopts an orphan after World War II and, during the protests against Prague in 1968, as his wife lies dying of cancer, betrays the grown boy to the authorities. Some time after his release from five years in Bautzen prison, the son narrates the tale in verse as a memory from West Berlin, a hellish place with "corpses in the cellar and money in the bank" [9/251] from which all of life (i.e. the GDR?) looks like a morass of putrefaction. The Kleist source notwithstanding, Müller is much more interested in the contagious process of the father's inner degeneration, begun by violence done to him – in how that made an entire world impossible for succeeding generations – than in the inexplicable or unrepentable nature of any specific crimes.

Another explicit reference appears in the most personal and sorrowful of Müller's works, *Gundling's Life Frederick of Prussia Lessing's Sleep Dream Scream*, a "synthetic fragment" from 1976 dealing with Prussia and the historical plight of the German intellec-

1. Setting by Jannis Kounellis for Heiner Müller's multitext evening *Mauser* at the Deutsches Theater, East Berlin, 1991. The action shown is of *The Foundling*.

tual. In this text, Müller uses Kleist as a character (or rather several) in a surrealistic, mimed scene entitled "HEINRICH VON KLEIST PLAYS MICHAEL KOHLHAAS":

> Despoiled shore (lake near Strasbourg). Kleist in uniform.
> Kleist-Puppet. Woman-Puppet. Horse-Puppet. Executioner's block.
>
> Kleist touches the face breasts hands genitals of the Kleist-Puppet. Caresses kisses embraces the Woman-Puppet. Cuts the head off the Horse-Puppet with his sword. Tears the heart out of the Woman-Puppet and eats it. Tears the uniform off his body, laces up the head of the Kleist-Puppet inside the uniform-jacket, sets the horse-head on top, slashes at the Kleist-Puppet with the sword: roses and guts gush out. Throws aside the horse-head, sets the wig (with foot-length hair) from the Woman-Puppet on top, breaks the sword over his knee, goes to the executioner's block. Takes the wig off, spreads the woman's hair over the executioner's block, bites open one of his veins, holds his arm, out of which sawdust trickles, over the woman's hair on the executioner's block. From the flies a gray cloth is thrown over the scene, on which a red spot quickly spreads.   [7/33]

Interestingly, in this case, too, the specific story referred to is somewhat off the point. "Michael Kohlhaas" is about a Brandenburg horse-dealer who, cheated by a Saxon Junker and unable to gain satisfaction by legal means, gathers a vigilante army around him to seek justice on his own. Since Kohlhaas cannot afford to be selective, the army contains some savage criminals, and terrible crimes are committed in the name of a righteous ideal, bringing Brandenburg (the state that became the core of Prussia) to the brink of war with Saxony. The later Kohlhaas is a man of action whose ability to act is envied by his creator, Kleist-cum-Müller, as part of the extended meditation on *Hamlet* during this period (discussed in chapter 6). The later Kohlhaas is also a terrorist trying to make his country live up to his ideal image of it, and on other occasions Müller associated Kleist generally with left-wing terrorism in West Germany in the 1970s, writing in one text of "Ulrike Meinhof, daughter of Prussia and late-born bride of another foundling of German literature who buried himself by Wannsee" [9/262].[4] These general associations and the horse's head, however, appear to be all Müller retained from "Michael Kohlhaas."

The scene in *Gundling's Life. . .* is a collage within a collage that ought to be read in the context of a fragmented play in which Kleist, the young Frederick the Great, and the playwright-critic Lessing (all objects of identification for Müller, he once said [0/269]) are played by the same actor. The Woman-Puppet seems to refer to Henriette Vogel, the woman suffering from uterine cancer with whom Kleist made a suicide pact and whom he shot moments before shooting himself on the banks of the Wannsee. The executioner's block refers to earlier scenes about young Frederick's friend Lieutenant Katte, with whom he tried to run away in 1758 and whose beheading his father forced him to watch – a traumatic, transformative experience after which Frederick became hard and militaristic like his father. And there are numerous other allusions, to Samuel Beckett, John Ford, Kleist's essay "On the Marionette Theater," other Müller texts, and more. Generally speaking, though, the scene is meant to read as one in a series of composite responses to what Wolfgang Emmerich calls the "Prussification" [*Verpreussung*] process at the heart of the play: the degrading and desensitization of the individual (intellectual) and the suppressing of his natural drives until he accepts the necessity of placing the needs of the state above his own, or accepts "the implantation of a [sadistic and unspontaneous] foreign ego" to accomplish the same thing.[5] This is a disassembly/reassembly process that resembles Brecht's main theme in *Mann ist Mann* (*A Man's a Man*) and, more to the point, Kleist's in *The Prince of Homburg*.

The Homburg-syndrome – J.H. Reid once called it the "Homburg-Machine"[6] – is really the central point of interest for Müller in Kleist. It is the key veiled allusion behind all the explicit allusions in the examples cited above and is the main object of "dialogue" in several other powerful Müller texts. The Prince of Homburg is a dreamy, impulsive, hypersensitive young officer who, unable to contain his emotion, charges against orders into a battle against the Swedes and wins the day for Brandenburg-Prussia. Rather than crown him a hero, the Elector of Brandenburg condemns him to death for insubordination, a sentence that brings the army to the point of rebellion. Urged to reconsider by his niece, whom Homburg loves, the Elector says he is welcome to his freedom if he can maintain that the sentence was not strictly just. The young man understands this appeal to absolute values as a test of his honor and, formerly terrified of death, suddenly determines to face it heroically: "Now, O immortality, you are wholly mine!"[7] At the last minute, he is pardoned in the context of a mock-execution, which Müller once called a "crude joke" that completes the process of "taming an outsider" [14/53].

Typically for Müller, the original is not nearly as crude as his revisions of it; one must remember that, for the purpose of assessing his work, it is largely immaterial whether his reading of a source text or author is entirely fair. Much of the point of his borrowing is, again, to lay bare what he sees as hideous historical processes beneath lyrically beautiful literary surfaces. In another scene in *Gundling's Life. . .*, for instance, Müller substitutes the adult Frederick for Kleist's Elector in a scene in which a Saxon Woman begs for the life of her husband, who is about to be shot as a deserter. The enlightened despot, quoting Shakespeare and others, says the man is welcome to go free if his wife can maintain that his life is worth the sacrifice of his, the monarch's, "posthumous fame" [7/22]. She declines; in Reid's words, "she cannot wish away the myth of Frederick the Great."[8] And the execution takes place as planned, with the Woman barely escaping strangulation by Frederick with her own veil.

In "Russian Opening," the first part of *Volokolamsk Highway* (1984), a Russian Commander awaiting the Germans in 1941 assumes the Elector's mantle. Stationed in the woods with dangerously fearful troops 120 kilometers from Moscow, the Commander, thinking that "only terror drives out fear" [8/244], fires a machine-gun into the river to test his men. Among a group whose reaction is to run away is a squad-leader who shoots himself in the hand, and the Commander orders him executed by his own squad for cowardice. "My order will be carried out / And if it's unjust they may shoot me" [247], he says, echoing similar words by Kleist's Elector. As with the Saxon Woman's husband, the man receives no eleventh-hour reprieve; Müller includes a dreamlike sequence in which the Commander imagines a joyful reprieve-scenario, but it is abruptly interrupted by his order to "fire."

2. King Frederick (Jörg-Michael Koerbl) demonstrates his enlightened despotism to Voltaire (Florian Martens) in Gundling's *Life Frederick of Prussia Lessing's Sleep Dream Scream*, directed by Helmut Strassburger and Ernstgeorg Hering, Volksbühne, East Berlin, 1988.

At that moment, he looks on with "something like pride" as the *Prussian* hardening of his *Russian* men (a quintessential Müller provocation) begins to turn "this heap of humanity" into "a batallion" [247]. The execution of strict justice is their "first step" on the "way from Moscow to Berlin" [249] – that "way" being the quasi-mythical Volokolamsk Highway whose end is supposed to be universal reconciliation under Communism but turns out to be the contagious dehumanization of Müller's *The Foundling*.

The ferocity of these other works notwithstanding, Müller's most brutal and disturbing engagement with the Homburg-syndrome is in *Mauser* (1970), a text never permitted publication or production in the GDR and the first that he chose to direct after the dissolution of that state. (Interestingly, Kleist's works, too, were forbidden for many years there, "under the verdict of Lukács," said Müller.[9]) Müller's main literary target in *Mauser* is Brecht's *The Measures Taken*, a play that (as Reid points out[10]) may itself be seen as a variation on the Homburg-syndrome: a Young Comrade accompanying other Moscow agitators on a mission to foment revolution among Chinese workers ruins the group's plans several times due to his individualistic impulsiveness. Wounded and unable to flee, he is asked to assent to his own death so he will not be captured and betray them again, and the action of the play consists of the other agitators' enactment of events after the fact in self-justification before a tribunal called the Control Chorus.

The title *Mauser* is a triple word-play: a noun that means both mouse-catcher and a bird's annual process of moulting, it is also the name of the pistol most commonly used in the Russian Revolution. The play tells the story of a man named simply "A" who is deranged by his task of executing "enemies of the revolution" at a critical point during the Russian civil war, launching into a fit of orgiastic killing. He too is asked to assent to his own death and, toward that end, is subjected to a repetitive, rhythmic litany of ideological statements by ambiguous entities such as "Chorus [A]" and "[A] Chorus" which blur his identity with the group's. These ambiguous headings and the recurrent issue of *Einverständnis* are both "copied" from Brecht's *Lehrstücke*. Unlike *The Measures Taken*, the Chorus judges A under the pressure of imminent battle (as in *The Horatian*) and not in leisure afterward. Originally named "M" (the initial of Mauser and Müller[11]), A is a figure of shifting identity (moulting, changing feathers) who catches and kills enemy mice until he is caught himself in the infernal, mechanistic mousetrap that he operated.

> You fought at the front in the civil war
> The enemy found no weakness in you
> We found no weakness in you either.
> Now you are yourself a weakness
> We dare not let the enemy find in us.
> You dealt out death in the city Witebsk
> To the enemies of the revolution by our command
> Knowing the daily bread of the revolution
> In the city Witebsk as in other cities
> Is the death of its enemies, knowing, the grass
> Must be ripped out so that it stays green
> We killed them with your hand.
> But one morning in the city Witebsk
> You killed for yourself with your hand
> Not our enemies not by our command
> And must be killed, yourself an enemy.   [6/55]

The unique severity of *Mauser*'s view of the Homburg-syndrome comes from the mechanistic nature of the trap in it, itself a legacy of the preoccupation with technology and production in the *Lehrstücke*. Müller makes clear from the outset that the action is a circular process. On his first day, A is ordered to kill his predecessor, B, who betrayed the revolution by releasing three farmers he was supposed to shoot, the Chorus' instructions to him near the beginning raising the momentary possibility that they are addressing not him (A) but his successor in a flash-forward: "Your work begins today. The man who did it before you / Must be killed before tomorrow, himself an enemy" [57]. Müller's language is also laced with words that have become fetishes, like *Arbeit* (work or job), *Auftrag* (task), and *die Revolution* – this language recalling the obfuscations of East German officialese and casting Lenin's famous equation of the Communist Party with a factory in an unflattering light. Here the vision is of production and death, production *of* death. An intimidated A refers to killing as "a job like any other" [60], and the Chorus in response seems to toy with him, first admitting that "Your job was bloody and like no other" [65], then refusing to release him from it, and finally condemning him with the pseudo-Leninist reproach: "you became one with your work / And had no consciousness of it any more" [67].

In Müller's view, A – like Homburg but unlike the Young Comrade in *The Measures Taken* (who escapes the problem by dying) – is a passionate, volatile character whose individuality is annihilated in an encounter with absolute values.

> Your revolution is made quickly, lasts a day
> And is choked off tomorrow.
> But our revolution begins tomorrow
> Triumphs and changes the world.   *The Measures Taken*[12]

> For your hand isn't your hand
> Just as my hand isn't my hand
> Until the revolution has triumphed *absolutely*
> In the city of Witebsk as in other cities.
>
>   *Mauser* (my italics)   [58]

The crucial distinction is that Brecht, in 1930, is uninterested in the corrupting influence of absolutes, whereas Müller, reading Kleist a bit more deeply in the wake of Stalin and Hitler, cannot help but ask whether those who commit murder (such as Brecht's Agitators) and project an unbending militaristic bearing onto the world (such as the Mauser Chorus) may have disqualified themselves as potential agents of change toward a more humane world. This is a common question in postwar German drama, the central concern of Fritz Hochwälder's *Der Offentliche Ankläger* (*The Public Prosecutor*, 1949), Friedrich Dürrenmatt's *Der Besuch der Alten Dame* (*The Visit*, 1956), and many other works. Müller, however, sets it in what might be called a rigid Prussian frame by borrowing Brecht's impishly conceived prewar paradox – how can anyone know what a "human being" is before the revolution designed to remove "inhuman" social conditions has succeeded? – and pushing it to a cruel, logical extreme.

Wolfgang Schivelbusch once called *The Measures Taken* "the tragedy of *premature* humanity,"[13] a designation that makes sense only in the context of a protagonist, like the Young Comrade or

Homburg, who can *be* prematurely human. With its circular action and intentionally ambiguous dialogue indications, *Mauser* cannot be said to have such a singular protagonist. Part of what is so disturbing about the play is the absence of a fully human, and hence convincingly heroic, center on which audiences and players may fix their sympathies. In the Rotbuch edition of the work, Müller illustrated this point by appending an assemblage of photos by Ralph Gibson in which a cropped shock of hair and bare shoulder abut a cropped wrist and hand wielding a cocked pistol, creating a composite beast made only of weapon and minimal head. The assemblage reinforces the impression of extreme absurdity left by the text, which presents a presumably dialectical debate concerning human identity and human rights within a scenario so emotionally charged it leaves little space to think. A in orgiastic confusion offers an image of reification run amuck: "A human being is something into which one shoots / Until the human being rises from the wreckage of the human being" [64].

It is this conflict between the play's surface rationality and the unavoidable emotionalism it provokes, between Müller's icy equilibrium and the rage his scenario induces, that constitutes its real dialectic. Insofar as *Mauser* thus establishes a model for Müller's preferred audience–stage relationship one may indeed speak of a general Kleistian dynamic in his work. "In the execution of his suicide as in his writing, the wildest exaltation is mingled with the coldest awareness and calculation," writes Joachim Maass of Kleist.[14] The majority of Müller's plays from *Mauser* on (and some earlier pieces as well) mingle the same elements. His best poetic energy, like Kleist's, is devoted to keenly exploiting what Adorno once called "the metaphysical surplus of the German language," the tendency of its words to "say more than they say,"[15] resonating beyond the merely phenomenal – the main difference being that with Müller the resonance always seems tongue-in-cheek or excruciatingly bleak. "Into the dust with all enemies of Brandenburg!" is the chilling and aggressive reconciliation of "All" in the last line of *The Prince of Homburg*.[16] "DEATH TO THE ENEMIES OF THE REVOLUTION" [68], cries the entity "A [Chorus]" at the end of *Mauser*, leaving ambiguous whether A is consenting to his death or calling for vengeance against his murderers (who are, after all, his alternative, collective self).

Müller's preoccupation with things German, in particular Germany's long, violent path to unity, is not, as is sometimes said, merely a parochial "family" matter. As Emmerich points out, Müller sees the Homburg-syndrome as a metaphor for humanity's perilous and stubborn adherence to a pattern of instrumental, functional thinking: "Prussia as world condition."[17] Hence, when he writes at the opening of the volume *Germania Death in Berlin* that

> THE TERROR OF WHICH I WRITE DOESN'T COME FROM
> GERMANY IT IS A TERROR OF THE SOUL
> (Edgar Allan Poe)
> THE TERROR OF WHICH I WRITE COMES FROM GERMANY
>
> [5/8]

he is establishing his ground and declaring that Germany is a source of truths about the soul for him. Kleist, who once edited a weekly journal on German affairs called *Germania*, is not the only model of this world view for Müller, but he is a vital one – both because of *The Prince of Homburg* and because of the degree to which Müller admired his resistance to instrumental, functional thinking in a body of plays that mostly remained unperformed during his lifetime. "[My plays are] written for a theater which doesn't exist,"[18] said Müller on numerous occasions – an unacknowledged paraphrase of Kleist.

4 Müller as Mayakovsky: *The Scab*, *The Correction*, *The Resettler*

The erection of the Berlin Wall in 1961 cast a veil of obscurity over the cultural politics of East Germany in the 1950s that lasted twenty-eight years. Now nearly a decade beyond that, memories are especially hazy of the sixteen-year period (1945–61) when thousands argued the superiority of socialism on principle, in the face of an increasingly successful and visible consumer society in the West, when Berlin theaters vied for the hearts and Deutschmarks of spectators within a single, open metropolitan area. This was the atmosphere in which Müller began his work as a playwright: Berlin as an ideological battle-ground for the human soul where voices calling for epic theater vied noisily with voices suspicious of new, "decadent," Western theater (e.g. Wilder, Anouilh, Giradoux, Genet, Ionesco, and Beckett), and still other voices determined to recover part of the three decades "stolen" from the German Left (1919–49) by making Socialist Realism, already moribund in the Soviet Union, compulsory.

The young Müller negotiated this difficult, and frequently mined, terrain with a finesse appreciated by only a narrow circle at the time, eventually writing himself into a political corner that isolated him and gave him time to refine his critique of the *Lehrstück*. At his death, Müller was widely seen as the only GDR dramatist whose writing from the 1950s was still stageworthy, largely because of his own extraordinary 1988 production of his 1956 play *The Scab*.[1] Actually, a full picture of him in this period must account for a remarkable combination of soaring idealism and sterile compromise: a persistent mixture of serious idiosyncratic writing with serious propagandistic writing along with works in which he invested little or nothing of himself. The authorial paradigm I use to elucidate this

57

phase is the Russian poet and playwright Vladimir Mayakovsky. Contrary to this book's general pattern, however, I will not bring in this figure substantially until later in the chapter. The Müller who wrote the works leading up to the banned *Resettler* is an especially elusive creature outside the former GDR – partly because of his obscure and distant cultural context and partly because of the involvement of his second wife, Inge Müller, in some of his work – and I wish simply to clarify what he was doing before offering theories about it.

The early Müller plays *The Scab*, *The Correction* (1957, rewritten 1958), *Tractor* (1955/61), and *The Resettler* (1956–61) date from the period after Stalin's death when the Soviet Politburo, and after some delay the East German SED (the Communist Party) as well, called for a softer approach to the forced institution of socialism (understood during the Soviet era as the imperfect but necessary interim system before the arrival of world Communism). Some of the first few years of the GDR, founded in 1949, were indeed quite restrictive culturally, largely because of the "Fight Against Formalism in Art and Literature" declared in 1951, which resulted in (among other things) the cancellation of Brecht's project *Die Tage der Kommune* (*Days of the Commune*) at the Berliner Ensemble.[2] Because of that and the highly publicized suppression of the workers' rebellion of June 17, 1953 by the East German police and the Soviet army, it is not generally understood in the West that official GDR policies of the time leaned toward liberalization. The relatively lenient "New Course" (*Neuer Kurs*), a sort of latter-day NEP (New Economic Policy, the partial capitalism that Lenin introduced in the 1920s) – announced a week or so before the rebellion, too late to calm the populace – was a relaxation of economic planning that brought a corresponding openness in cultural policy.

As early as 1952, the Soviet Politburo member Georgi Malenkov had spoken of the dry, colorless, simplistic art that had resulted from the dominance of Andrey Zhdanov's notions of topical realism, and had encouraged new approaches to representing Soviet life, including satire.[3] The first Soviet revivals of Mayakovsky's satirical late plays, *The Bedbug* (1929) and *The Bathhouse* (1930), were mounted at this time, to critical and popular acclaim. The problem with introducing such relaxations in the GDR in the mid-1950s, however, was that cultural bureaucrats who led the "Fight Against Formalism" had already spilled huge amounts of ink ruing the shortage of good dramas and stories about everyday life in the new, planned society. Wholesale departure from topical realism was therefore unthinkable. The prudish, essentially bourgeois notions of acceptable art that would drive official policy for decades were already entrenched.

The spirit of the Malenkov thaw did open new avenues of opportunity for young GDR dramatists, but not unrestricted ones. Only those committed to socialism, of course, had a hope of production or publication. And any new influence by avant-gardists like Mayakovsky had to be within the "psychologist" forms of Socialist Realism that he despised. (It is curious indeed that a revival of *The Bathhouse* was permitted in 1959 in East Berlin and that it received generally favorable reviews.[4]) But playwrights could now experiment, for instance, with the dialectical methods of Brecht, and otherwise depart from the structural models offered by early GDR dramatists such as Friedrich Wolf and Gustav von Wangenheim, whose work the later East German playwright Peter Hacks once described as "completely satisfied with just putting the new [working] class on the stage; they portrayed them at their most silly and banal, and the only message was that this new class had a monopoly on virtue."[5] When Müller writes in his prefatory note to *The Scab* that

> the play does not attempt to present the battle between the
> Old and the New – which can't be decided by a playwright –
> as resolved with the victory of the New before the final curtain;
> it tries to bring the battle to the new public, which will
> decide it   [1/15]

he is thinking of precisely this sort of primitively tendentious, early GDR drama.

Müller's more sophisticated argument with Brecht along these lines has already been discussed. What is often forgotten is that his attitude toward drama that (in H. G. Huettich's words) "[stacked] the deck of historical contingencies"[6] first developed in the context of the *Aufbaustücke* (reconstruction plays). They constituted his main competition when he began. The crude boosterism of Wolf and Wangenheim aside, his reaction was scarcely less critical to much more nuanced writing such as Erwin Strittmatter's 1953 *Katzgraben: Szenen aus dem Bauernleben* (*Katzgraben: Scenes from the Farmers' Life*) (an episodic work depicting a small town's gradual acceptance of socialist ideas over many years – the main competitive target of *The Resettler*) and Helmut Baierl's 1961 *Frau Flinz* (a counter-play to *Mother Courage* that features an implausible deathbed conversion) – both Berliner Ensemble projects. The point is, one sees plainly in retrospect that, even while making use of officially sanctioned forms and accepting Party criticism of his work in the late 1950s, Müller abhorred drama that underestimated the intelligence of spectators. He was determined, at his best, to be fair to the "new public."

That public, we now know, consisted almost exclusively of an urban intellectual and artistic elite, following the longstanding pattern of bourgeois theater. At no point in its 41-year history did the theater in the "Workers' and Farmers' State" ever attract significant numbers of industrial workers and farmers to its doors, but that was not always for lack of trying. In 1956, for example, when *The Scab* was written, an effort was under way to respond to a widely publicized, official request from the workers of the People's Brown Coal Factory in Nachterstedt. "There are still not enough books in which our authors treat, artistically, the new developments in our factories and our lives," the workers wrote in 1955. "Write works in which our people can recognize themselves."[7] This apparently authentic grassroots appeal, known as "The Nachterstedt Letter," from a group whose literacy and awareness of socialist issues astonished nearly everyone, was remarkable partly because of its underlying assumption that authors were properly addressed as service workers in a service cooperative. This assumption touched deep wounds of romantic alienation, even in writers previously cool to topicality. Müller was among those who sprang to answer the challenge with Mayakovskian enthusiasm, apparently viewing it as a chance to prove not only that he could write good topical drama but also that the "new public" could handle greater literary sophistication than had been assumed.

The Scab – scheduled for performance together with *The Correction* in 1958 before the latter was forbidden – uses the story, already legendary by 1956, of the GDR's first "Stakhanovite" industrial worker-hero, Hans Garbe, an employee of a Siemens-Plania factory where Inge Müller had once worked. Garbe risked his life in 1949–50 to rebuild a broken industrial kiln there before it was fully cooled down, preventing an embarrassing delay in the state's Five-Year Plan and saving Siemens-Plania nearly a million Deutschmarks (by his own conservative reckoning). To his colleagues, however, Garbe was not a hero but rather a *Lohndrücker* – the play's German title – literally one who depresses wages by working too hard and devaluing the labor of others. The American epithet "scab" conveys well the disdainful tone of the German, though it should be understood that a *Lohndrücker* is not necessarily in conflict with a union.

Garbe was the intended subject of Brecht's first topical drama about the GDR, which he never finished despite having at his elbow extensive research into the oven incident compiled by his assistant, Käthe Rülicke. Müller was also assisted by similar "field research" compiled by Inge, whom he originally credited as co-author of *The Scab* and *The Correction* and with whom he traveled for a lengthy visit to the industrial complex Schwarze Pumpe, where *The Correction* is set. (The Nachterstedt "service call" was followed by a rash of hastily arranged "field trips" to the provinces by East Berlin authors.) In *War without Battle*, Müller disclaimed not only Inge's co-authorship of these plays – "I wrote [*The Scab*] alone, that is, by myself at my desk" [143][8] – but also the importance of her research, saying he knew the workers' argot and environment intimately from his own youth. As I will explain, even if this claim is taken at face value, it does not discount Inge Müller's significant contribution.

Müller once said that the primary reason he was able to make the Garbe material into drama was that, unlike Brecht, he realized that its proper focus was not the protagonist-hero, whose exceptional actions could serve only the crudest of agitational purposes, but rather the circumstances those actions provoked in the workplace. Hence the impersonal titles *Scab, Correction, Resettler, Construction Site,* which indicate (in line with the *Lehrstück* ethos) that the dramatic subject for the "new public" should not be a person but a process, the benign and malign channeling of productive energies in German society rather than the good or bad fortune of a worker-Everyman, a worker-Faust, or a worker-Coriolanus. (Brecht's attempt to adapt Shakespeare's play dates from 1951.) In fact, the "hero" of *The Scab* has a Nazi past and is aggrandized by the action only once, in a diminutive, passing moment when he takes a brick that was thrown at him and builds it into the kiln rather than saving it as evidence.

In an interview published in the program for his 1988 production, Müller discussed this issue in terms reminiscent of Emile Zola (who also made research "field trips" comparable to the East Germans').

> That's the misunderstanding over a play like *Lohndrücker*, that people continue to see politics and ideology where really it has to do only with the behavior of lab animals who have to conduct themselves under certain conditions that they didn't set themselves and can alter only within narrow and relative limits. And every ideological view of that is a false view and prevents people from seeing what's really there.

As in Naturalism, "what's really there" in the play is presumably free from ideological disfigurement because Müller has had the courage to face squarely the results of his empirical observation. The old, still compelling dream of scientism almost succeeds in distracting us – with Müller as well – from Zola's counter-truth that any artwork, even the most photographically naturalistic, "will always be only a corner of nature as seen through a certain temperament."[9]

The gritty, rugged industrial milieu in *The Scab* is thoroughly convincing, language and all, even if it isn't naturalistic; nevertheless, the play calls to mind the issue of temperament before its first scene is over. Here is an encounter between two workers in a bar from the end of that scene, one of whom expresses hostility to socialism (the cynically attractive Stettiner is a former Nazi, we learn later):

> STETTINER: *a cigarette in his outstretched hand* Come here.
> GESCHKE: The whole way for a cigarette? No.
> *Stettiner lights another cigarette, grinning*
> GESCHKE: Half way. All right?
> *Stettiner grins. Geschke takes three steps toward him, stands still. Stettiner smokes.* Two steps I'll give you. *He does it.*
> *Pause.* Have a heart, Stettiner.
> STETTINER: Two cigarettes.

GESCHKE: I said, half way.

STETTINER: Two cigarettes.

Pause. Stettiner throws down a cigarette for Geschke and goes off. Geschke picks the cigarette up, puts it away, and goes off too. [1/16]

This sequence is, among other things, a fillip at the purists of Socialist Realism since it ends in symbolism, though that provocation is lost to later audiences. More important, the questions it raises symbolically are all extremely touchy politically: how should German socialism deal with the problem of worker incentives? What are the implications for socialism of blindly exploiting the same motivation the Nazis did – that is, the famed German ethic of efficiency? This is the provocative manner in which Müller wants to consider the Garbe material. He has all but no interest in writing a conventional drama, replete with Scribean suspense, about whether the kiln is finished properly and safely, which was the preference of Party ideologues. "The story of the circular kiln is well known" [15], he writes curtly in his prefatory note; his "teacherly" concern is the way such tales manipulate and trivialize.

The play's episodic fifteen-scene structure is already a harbinger of collage, a habitual technique for him later on – as are the structures of *The Correction* and *Tractor*. *The Scab*'s scenes are chronological, but each seems to exist primarily not to advance the plot but rather to frame some sensitive image or quandary, usually leaving unclear what the author's attitude is toward it. A young man, glancing around to see if anyone is watching, rips down a poster that reads "SED – Party of Reconstruction" [16], after which tired workers trample it. Is the trampling accidental or malicious? Actors and directors may decide but the author does not. Balke (the Garbe character) inspires a "big laugh" among his belligerent colleagues when he says, in response to complaints about the price of butter, "We have to make the butter cheaper" by "working better" [18]. Is the laughter ignorant or wise? Again, the text is ambiguous, passing on responsibility for making that political decision to readers, spectators, and producers. When Müller includes questions of Nazi collaboration in this game of studied neutrality he raises the emotional stakes for

3. Heiner Müller's production of *The Scab* at the Deutsches Theater, East Berlin, 1988.

others, but his own attitude remains restrained. "They would have shortened my head if [the facts of sabotage in our munitions factory] were revealed without me" [28], explains Balke to the new Party Secretary, whom he once denounced as a saboteur. "Maybe," retorts the Secretary "coldly," a moment Müller froze and repeated several times in his thoroughly nonrealistic production.

Müller's goading impulses aside, this is the sort of epic technique, designed to frame discrete social and historical dilemmas for dialectical consideration by "the new public," that Walter Ulbricht and the GDR's chief theater critic, Fritz Erpenbeck, had actively discouraged, labeling it "didactic teaching theater." The issue was formulated at the time as a choice between "the good new" and "the bad new": Friedrich Wolf's aesthetic versus Brecht's.[10] It was one matter to emulate the recently deceased and idolized Brecht by applying his methods to the 8-year-old Garbe story in *The Scab*, quite another to question Party policies with those methods in a contemporary circumstance, which is what Müller did in *The Correction: A Report on the Building of the "Schwarze Pumpe" Combine.*

This play is set in 1956 at what was then the GDR's largest industrial complex and a subject of boasting for Ulbricht. Produced for radio in 1957, its broadcast was forbidden; produced for the stage along with *The Scab* at the Maxim Gorki Theater the following year, performances were banned after the dress rehearsal – after which Müller rewrote it based on the criticisms received. The play, then, exists in two versions, which I will call *Correction 1* and *Correction 2*, the second of which he later repudiated: "The correction of *The Correction* is interesting only as a document" (1992) [0/145].[11]

Both versions deal with the dilemma of a functionary named Bremer who is sent to work at Schwarze Pumpe, in his blunt words from *Correction 1*, "because I hit a Nazi in the face who held a post at the National Front" [47]. Appointing him foreman of a worker brigade, the Party Secretary says, echoing a central theme in *The Scab*: "You'll have difficulties. Socialism won't be built with socialists alone, not here, not elsewhere, least of all here" [1/47]. A Party member since 1918, Bremer finds that his strong socialist integrity is a liability on the job. He refuses a demand by his men, for instance, to misrepresent their output in order to circumvent production "norms" that they perceive as unreasonable, continuing to refuse even after they beat him.

When a foundation crumbles because of his brigade's negligence, Bremer, unaware of the negligence, accuses the bourgeois engineer who drew the plans; "foundation," here and elsewhere in early Müller, is an allegorical reference to the basis of the GDR.[12] After the workers admit the truth – that, in order to save time, they failed to remix concrete that had begun to dry out (their wages are based on output per pay period) – the Party Secretary demotes Bremer and forces him to "correct [his] error" [57] and apologize to the engineer. A laconic final scene – entitled "The *Einverständnis*" in homage to the *Lehrstück* – implies modest historical progress when a young brigade member named Heinz B. tells Bremer that he wants to join the Party: "If [the foundation] collapses again I'll break your skull" [59], says the former foreman to his new comrade.

From the opening view of industrial work as punitive to the view throughout of the Party opportunistically upholding class divisions, *Correction 1* is as risky and provocative as *The Scab*. ("I sat in a concentration camp for eight years," says Bremer to the condescending engineer. "All that time you stuffed your bellies and designed bombers for Hitler as arms specialists" [55]. Interestingly enough, all former concentration-camp prisoners in early Müller are communists, never Jews; like most GDR authors he was convinced the "Jewish question" had nothing to do with him.) Both plays pose sharp and troubling questions about worker-incentives under socialism, about assimilation of former enemies for the sake of "reconstruction," about paranoia regarding sabotage. *Correction 1* also contains its own proto-collage structure that asserts epic-theater values over Zdhanovian realism by establishing multiple perspectives on events. It alternates scenes in dialogue with long monologues (a central feature of Müller's dramaturgy from this point on) in which characters reflect on the main plot and offer autobiographical reflections with historical resonance.

The tone of both plays implies that Müller is using the pretext of objective observation to air public secrets – such as the increasingly sensitive topic of *Republikflucht*, fleeing the GDR, which comes up several times in *The Scab*, couched in sarcasm. Again, though, one of his primary concerns is obviously plausibility; if the compulsory dramatic style is to be realism, he thinks, then it ought to be a realism that audiences recognize and believe. Several times, *War without Battle* touches snidely on cases of unrosy realities being unacceptable to the authorities as realism. In 1958, for instance, Müller was paid to travel to Klettwitz to write a radio play about a brigade dealing with a collapsed construction bridge:

> and then I heard sinister stories about gloomy developments, sabotage, Stasi, all sorts of things. It was no longer possible to write anything realistic about it. That was hopeless. So I then composed a hymn, totally abstract. That was the first text of mine to be favorably mentioned in the Party magazine *Einheit*, because I had located myself on the path toward Socialist Realism.   [144]

The same year, Hans Garbe happened to be present during a discussion of *The Scab* with local Party functionaries, who condemned the play for its "false picture of the working class, insult to the working class, distortion of socialist reality." Müller describes Garbe's response:

> "Well, Comrades, I'd like to say, it was much worse even than that." Then he told awful stories. How he was nearly bumped off for his activist deed not only by his colleagues but also by the Party Secretary, how the Party had interfered with him and all sorts of things; compared with that the play was harmless. The functionaries were awkwardly affected and ignored the disturbance.   [149–50]

This is the Müller of 1992, who seems to forget during large portions of *War without Battle* how many assiduous efforts he made to placate such functionaries, including the "abstract" hymn praised in *Einheit* and *Correction 2*. *Correction 2* was a response to feedback he had received during two discussions, one with workers at Schwarze Pumpe, where a sympathetic functionary had arranged a presentation of the banned radio production, one with Party officials after the Gorki Theater dress rehearsal.[13] It opens with a prologue introducing the characters and their political attitudes in doggerel couplets rather than with the earlier brusque exchange containing Bremer's line about why he is at the combine: "I hit a Nazi in the face. . ." Since he is a foreman to begin with, the Party is not portrayed as tyrannical in punishing him and since he no longer explicitly objects to working with former Nazis, he is not guilty of what Party officials had called intolerable "sectarianism."

In general, *Correction 2* is purged of all emotional flashpoints of the kind Müller would soon make his trademark. He had already begun using them in *The Scab* and *Correction 1*, points that draw spectators into his dispassionate dialectical rationalizing: for example, Balke's confrontation with the man he denounced during the war. Bremer is no longer a former concentration-camp inmate, and the engineer is no longer demonized as an unfeeling, self-serving bourgeois. Indeed, anti-socialist people and ideas are kept from gaining ascendancy even momentarily, as if Müller's response to the additional accusation of "depressiveness" was to present a façade of cheery optimism that he could not fully believe. The blunt, truncated quality and multiple perspectives of *Correction 1* are relinquished in favor of explanatory transitional material within and between the scenic units, elaborating on the workers' personal struggles. More snide interjections appear in the group scenes for the sake of polemical points. In general, the work has a sophomoric, exaggerated air that becomes positively stifling in the final scene when the conversion of Heinz B. is crassly juxtaposed with the firing of a former Nazi.

As already mentioned, this is far from the only example of artistic compromise on Müller's part. From the poem celebrating Lenin that he wrote as a favor to Paul Dessau around this same time, to his 1969 collaboration with Party functionaries on the genially harmless, fawningly Party-loyal play *Waldstück* (*Forestplay*) in an attempt to loosen travel restrictions on his third wife (the Bulgarian Ginka Tscholokowa), to his 1989 consent that a scene be removed from a production of *Germania Death in Berlin* so that "German comrades" would not be offended when the show toured in Moscow, he proved himself open throughout his career to compromise at the cost of artistic quality.[14] Indeed, this sort of readiness in him to sacrifice his integrity, even to make unethicalness into an ethic (like Genet), is what poses the heaviest obstacle to explaining why his work is of continuing interest. With his eye constantly on history and his texts rooted in more literary sources than could ever be exhaustively traced, he risked everything on others' willingness to put their ethical questions about him historically: for example, were Shakespeare and Sophocles really nobler than him simply because they wrote about nobler values?

The cases of *Correction 2* and *The Resettler*, to which I will return, are especially interesting because they occur early enough to be considered formative experiences. And the question of how the young idealistic Müller became an artist ethically comparable to Genet is behind the connection I wish to pursue with Mayakovsky, who also never objected to the idea of supplying state propaganda – indeed, 90 percent of his poetic output served that purpose. He objected to incredible propaganda that encouraged narcotic mental habits and promoted distrust between the people and its leaders.

It ought to be understood at this point that my thesis about his early writings would not have sat well with Heiner Müller, who disapproved of separating his work into periods or phases. "Periodization is colonial politics," he said on one occasion [13/95]. And on another: "I could write a play like *Hamletmachine* tomorrow and the day after tomorrow one like *The Scab*. This idea of periodization is complete nonsense" [15/96]. The fact is, though, he never did write a play "like *The Scab*" (i.e. a topical drama about the GDR attempting to improve on officially sanctioned forms) after *Hamletmachine* (1977), or after *The Resettler* for that matter, nor did he publish or circulate any "synthetic fragments" before the 1970s, or *Lehrstück* experiments before 1964. The dates of completion and public circulation of nearly all his works (some admittedly compiled from material begun decades earlier) certainly do break down into distinct periods, but, for his own reasons, he wanted others to believe that his temperament, the spirit in which he made his art, was consistent over a lifetime.

Anyone reading *War without Battle* in isolation from his early work would come away with the impression that, even as a callow "*Bub*" in the 1950s (Helene Weigel's word for him then [0/183]), he was already a lone, cynical guerilla-artist hardened by long culture wars and expert at protean modes of survival. His multifarious efforts to deprive his works of subjective centers from the *Lehrstück* experiments on, employing disguised, pluralized, and otherwise problematized voices, contributed to this elusively monolithic image, as did his directing projects in the 1980s and 1990s, which fragmented early texts and recast them within image-centered *mises-en-scène* that recalled Robert Wilson's. All of this makes it difficult to characterize his distinctive, singular voice in the 1950s. The value of the Mayakovsky paradigm, for me, is its ability to cut through this smoke-screen, revealing hidden or forgotten aspects of a Müller who had never yet been outside Germany, who still sought a balance between earnestness and sardonicism, and who experienced real ambivalence concerning the relationship of his own revolutionary integrity to his state's cultural policies.

The actual poet Mayakovsky – as distinct from the paradigm – was one of Müller's most powerful and early influences. Müller began reading him as part of his ravenous postwar ingestion of literature in the late 1940s and early 1950s, and his plays and lyric poems through the 1960s are replete with Mayakovsky quotations and paraphrases. It would be a simple matter to apply the model of *Kopien* that I have applied elsewhere and thus trace the progress of Müller's art through the uses he makes of the Russian's. *Correction 2*, for instance, ends with an enthusiastic tribute to Mayakovsky's "Left March" (a notorious, militant poem from 1918 containing the line, "You have the floor, Comrade Mauser!"[15]):

> Left and left in step with the Five-Year Plans
> We tear the new world
> From the withering old one.   [1/80]

The Construction Site (1963–4), by contrast – a densely metaphorical play about efforts to sidestep obstructive central planning written during Müller's internal exile – places other Mayakovsky quotes in ironic contexts. A clownish character named Bolbig, for instance, mocks himself by saying "I'm a cloud in trousers" [1/106] (the title of a 1914–15 lyric), and the Party Secretary Donat later asks rhetorically, "Have you read Mayakovsky? 'For you / I have licked away consumptives' spittle / With the rough tongue of posters'" [108] (a paraphrase from the disconsolate and fragmentary "At the Top of My Voice,"

Mayakovsky's last important work before his 1930 suicide, in which he spoke of the "petrified crap" of the current day and complained that "agitprop sticks in my teeth"[16]).

In 1983, Müller published an adaptation of the two-act play *Vladimir Mayakovsky: A Tragedy* (1913), an inexhaustibly strange, fiercely tristful work – Pasternak said admiringly that he "had never before heard anything like it"[17] – consisting of monologic dialogue spoken by multiple fanciful alter egos of the poet-hero. This grave yet ludicrous text, originating in a futurist tradition that never had currency in the GDR, is a pre-revolutionary expression of a deeply romantic poet's extravagant hopes and anxieties about post-revolutionary life. Typically, Müller appropriates or "displaces" the work in time so that his own hand and era lay bare its original assumptions about history, bringing on a collision of world views. The play appealed to him, he said, because it was malleable, "still proto-plasm," and because it "gives the feeling that it's all over for good with wholeness";[18] he obviously savored the suggestion that the revolution had become so stuck in his time that poets longed nostalgi-cally for disillusionment of an amorphous pre-revolutionary kind. The adaptation is also remarkable for highlighting the locus where Müller's poetic techniques had long overlapped those of Mayakovsky: e.g. their mutual habit of yoking emotionless human and industrial images for strident emotional effect ("The locomotive wheel snuggles up to my neck" [11/145]).[19]

Mayakovsky's (Kleistian) depressiveness notwithstanding, nu-merous other affinities between him and Müller are salient by the 1980s as well. For instance, Mayakovsky wore plain street clothes to portray himself in his *Tragedy*, just as Müller did when portraying himself in numerous performances. Both authors wrote magisterially about their trips abroad, eager to provide criteria by which others could appreciate the decadence of Western cultural and political values; both were inveterate self-quoters, and both wrote autobio-graphies that were criticized for not being fully serious. Both were also skillful manipulators of publicity and had similar penchants for shocking and scandalous statements driven by black humor and tac-tical cynicism, which earned them enemies and drew accusations that they were sympathetic to dictatorial terrorism: "I like to watch little children die" (Mayakovsky);[20] "A Molotov cocktail is the last bourgeois educational experience" (Müller) [14/53]. Indeed, both authors may have truly had some sympathy with Stalin's violent tactics.

Nevertheless, if we are speaking of the young Müller, this congeries of similarities must be considered part of the smokescreen referred to above. Because Müller could not have fully embraced avant-gardist forms such as *Vladimir Mayakovsky: A Tragedy* and remained a player in the early GDR theater, the pertinent comparison is rather the public image or paradigm "Mayakovsky" and the way it functioned as a touchstone for the socialist credentials of Eastern bloc writers from 1930 to 1989. Mayakovsky always had admirers in the West during the Cold War (Eluard, Aragon, Neruda, and Benn to name a few), but only in the East did he acquire the stature of a paradigm, providing a peculiar example of canonization as both "optimist" (the view of cultural functionaries) and "pessimist" (the view of writers such as Yevtuchenko, Becher, and Hermlin). The power of this paradigm over both Müller and the saturnine, unrecognized poet who shared his name and life for thirteen years would be difficult to exaggerate.

In the West, Mayakovsky has long been seen as a thwarted avant-gardist, more truly "left" than the purported leftists who administered the Russian Revolution and a brave champion of, say, Meyerhold's "theatricalist" aesthetic over the officially sanctioned "psychologist" one. (These were scrimmage terms from the 1920s theater in Moscow.) That image existed in the Cold War East as well, but it was less freighted with pathos there, since readers were capable of accepting the revolutionary zeal of a talented satirist as relevant to their lives. Stalin himself complicated Mayakovsky's Eastern reputation with his grim rehabilitation in 1935: "Mayakovsky was and remains the best and most talented poet of our Soviet epoch. Indifference to his memory and his works is a crime."[21] After this blessing, he was force-fed to Soviet readers in school curricula, books, and magazines; his countenance and name were immortalized in statues, streets, and parks throughout the country – an enshrinement by philistinism that would have repulsed him. The enshrinement was what the Russian author of a 1994 article in *The Times Literary Supplement* had primarily in mind in declaring: "Vladimir Mayakovsky is now perhaps the deadest Russian poet of the twentieth century."[22] The statement is reminiscent of similar historical dismissals of Müller in journalistic articles following the fall of the Berlin Wall.[23]

What was most relevant to the young Heiner and Inge Müller, however, was the split within Mayakovsky himself (about which he wrote in many texts, including a 1915 article entitled "About the Various Mayakovskys"), which in turn reflected a split in the Eastern image of "Mayakovsky"; for the Müllers saw this split in different ways. On the one hand, Mayakovsky was the leftist artist who provided a role-model of devotion to the revolutionary state – an especially potent image for Germans since, as a Russian, he could celebrate a successful revolution rather than brood over a failed or externally imposed one. On the other hand, Mayakovsky was seen, and occasionally saw himself, as a case of strangulated individual exuberance, not a victim of public denunciation, like, say, Pasternak, but certainly someone whose pathos was interesting as a topos.

According to the critic Fritz Mierau, it was the contagiousness of that pathos, coming from a poet whose life story ended with a bullet in his head, that most troubled Heiner Müller and other German writers (such as Stephan Hermlin and Georg Maurer) who shared Brecht's distrust of sentimentality in the postwar era. These writers' anxiety about Mayakovsky's martyrdom, fed by their general questioning of heroes and heroism inherited from Brecht, led to their artificially hardened view of Mayakovsky as an "anti-Rilke": the Party-faithful propagandist and satirist seen as a corrective superego to the wounded, heaven-storming romantic.[24] Inge Müller by contrast – who committed suicide in 1966, suffering from alcoholism and depression aggravated by the hardships of internal exile – was unafraid of pathos of any sort and was unconvinced that Rilke or his paradigm needed mitigation. For her (a Party-faithful Communist until the *Resettler* affair), Mayakovsky was an even more crucial influence than he was for Heiner; the frames of some of her poems consist exclusively of strings of altered quotations and paraphrases from the Russian.[25]

One might begin to reconstruct the Müllers' argument on this subject by examining this pair of similarly titled poems, Heiner's from

1956, Inge's undated. Heiner Müller responded to a query about their order of composition with the remark: "mine was earlier (that happens too)."[26]

MAYAKOVSKY	MAYAKOVSKY
	After Cloud in Trousers
by Heiner Müller	by Inge Müller
Mayakovsky, why	Still there are those
The leaden endpoint?	Who lick the thrashing hands
Heartache, Vladimir?	Dig in!
"Did a lady	No kidding, it happened!
Shut him out	(You will soon turn like a squirrel
Or	In the rotor of laughter)
Open up to	Someone
Another?"	Lost a few teeth in a fight.
Take	Why
My bayonet	The leaden endpoint?
Out of your teeth	Heartache, Vladimir?
Comrades!	Forest. No voice.
Blood curdled	Silence.
Into medal-tin.	A muddle, friend and foe . . .
The walls stand	Everywhere
Speechless and cold	On the swamp-path
In the wind	On the stony road
Clatter the flags.	With blood and brains
	We drench
	The body of the planets
	And stamp
	In cadence
	Don't forget! for us!
	(Under Pontius Pilate
	The wind of the grenades
	Tears the cassock
	The flesh.)
	No German
	No Russian

Not China
No Black
It was Mayakovsky
Who flays the living.
The legs rise again
Running.

Neither poem is the writer's best work, but they make for fruitful comparison because of the shared theme and because they employ the same strategy of using Mayakovsky's own words against him, so to speak, thus creating a dialogue with the dead martyr about the demoralizing effects of his martyrdom, about dialectics, and (in Inge Müller's case) about the artistic value of immersing readers in images of horror. Heiner Müller is responding to specific lines in "Backbone Flute" (1915) (e.g. "More and more often I think: / it might be far better for me / to punctuate my end with a bullet"[27]), Inge Müller to specific lines in that poem, "Cloud in Trousers," and "War and the World" (1916) (e.g. "Have you seen / a dog lick the hand that thrashed it?!"; "Nero! / I say! / D'you want a show . . . You'll spin in a squirrel-wheel of laughter to see 'em / when I trouble your dust to tell of it."[28])

Heiner Müller's poem depends far less on knowledge of its allusions. It has a gelid tone similar to that of Brecht's "Epitaph for M." – "The sharks I dodged / The tigers I slew / What ate me up / Was the bedbugs"[29] – and is sharply focused on the ramifications of Mayakovsky's suicide. (Since it was a point of embarrassment for the Soviet Union, this event was reported in newspapers the world over, explained in many cases as the result of a failed love affair – all of which Müller treats as common knowledge.[30]) Readers who do know "Backbone Flute" can more easily understand that the "leaden end-point" is meant to be taken grammatically and historically, as a complaint about loss of faith in dialectical argument and progress, and that Mayakovsky himself connected the loss of a lady's love with suicide in a grand conceit of self-crucifixion. However, the voice of Heiner Müller's poem itself, particularly when read in the context of the *Lektionen* ("Lessons"), the 1956 grouping to which it belongs, suffices to communicate that the speaker sees his responsibility as maintaining a cool, *verfremdet* air in the face of certain "lessons" about literary martyrdom that still hold considerable power over him. Müller:

BRECHT

Truly, he lived in dark times.
The times have grown brighter.
The times have grown darker.
When the brightness says, I am the darkness
It's spoken the truth.
When the darkness says, I am
The brightness, it doesn't lie.   [1/82]

OR BÜCHNER who died in Zurich
100 years before his birth
Age 23, from want of hope.   [83]

"Mayakovsky: After Cloud in Trousers" is, by comparison, a hermetical exchange, all but opaque to those who do not have the Mayakovsky sources at their elbow. It is part of a series of poems in which Inge Müller appropriates the Russian's words and confessional manner as a way of infusing herself with his revolutionary steadfastness.[31] Hers is an intimate engagement in which the conflated traumas of suicide and war (World War I for Mayakovsky, World War II for her) are always still occurring, and the "leaden endpoint" is consequently a caesura in an ongoing fight. In emulation of "War and the World," Inge Müller wants to use a long, grotesque battle narrative to sing of universal (collective) guilt for humanity's sufferings, but her voice continually disappears into the severe attenuations of the lines she quotes, and ultimately suffocates before finding a melody. (Compare her verses to this lucid passage from Mayakovsky, for instance: "Forests. / Nothing the silence challenging. / Bodies mixed without distinction or succession. / Only the nights and ravens / fly past, scavenging, / all in black, in monastic procession."[32]) For my purposes, what is most interesting about the poem is that the romantic ego in it, while unquestionably alive, is presented as too weak (too billowy, like a cloud) to imagine itself as a martyr or savior anymore – "Dig in!" she says to the dog that licked the thrashing hand in "Cloud in Trousers." The final image of a human fragment rising "again" (legs only – the reference is to a reanimated, flayed corpse) bespeaks an approach-avoidance reaction to Mayakovsky wholly different from Heiner's – purposefully unprotected, hyper-exposed, recklessly open to whatever vestigial strength and faith might still be absorbed from the martyr.

The point is that, because Mayakovsky was a trope for intellectual exuberance in general in the 1950s GDR, a name for the nexus of questions surrounding the issue of romantic heroism, he could also be an argumentative tool or mask in this sort of quasi-private debate. Inge Müller (whose work was publicly recognized only posthumously, partly because of Heiner's brighter star and partly because she kept much of it to herself) wrote poetry in order to survive debilitatingly horrific war experiences – her most important influences being Mayakovsky, Paul Celan, Sylvia Plath, Sergei Esenin, and Georg Trakl, all spiritual kinsmen to Rilke and all suicides. She used Mayakovsky within a sensibility that might be called *"abglanzbeladen,"* a Celan formulation meaning laden with reflection[33] – reflection on horror, wartime memories that always threaten to become lethal emotional eddies – and she is far from alone in this general attitude.

Heiner Müller, for his part, was an ambitious young playwright trying to impress the Brecht epigones in and around the Berliner Ensemble with his innate understanding of *Verfremdung*, and for him such a reflective sensibility in his wife and sometime collaborator must have been irritating.[34] Like the other authors discussed by Fritz Mierau, Heiner did his best to contain "Mayakovsky" within certain limits, e.g. as representative of the dream of the unified self, the impossible model of the integrated leftist artist who satisfies both himself and the working class (his presumed "new public") politically and aesthetically, and hence never *needs* to regress into a lonely genius, crying for mystical communion with the ignorant masses. Heiner, too, had painful war memories, but he refrained from giving most of them literary form for decades, probably regarding Inge's indulgence in hers as a desperate refuge or trap, if not a therapy. Biographical theses about this couple will always be risky, but any reader of both their texts from the late 1950s and early 1960s would be drawn to wonder whether the cool, emotionally distant persona for which Heiner is now known may have been developed as a means of distancing himself from attitudes and behaviors akin to "Inge's Mayakovsky."

Particularly for those familiar with the avant-gardist texts that later won him world fame, among the most fascinating aspects of Heiner Müller's early work is that he is not yet entirely convinced of his famous leather-toughness. There is still ambivalence in him concerning, among other things, the official pressure to employ an "optimistic" (read: sentimental) voice for the sake of buttressing socialist morale – as the cases of *Correction 2* and *The Resettler* best demonstrate.

The Resettler, Müller's longest play (eighty-four pages), was the first one written entirely without assistance from his wife, he said [0/158].[35] Its full title, *Die Umsiedlerin, oder Das Leben auf dem Lande*, literally means *The Resettled Woman, or Life in the Country* (a deliberate variation on Strittmatter's *Katzgraben: Scenes from the Farmers' Life*) – the particular word used for "resettler" being a provocation in itself. *Umsiedlerin* (female) and *Umsiedler* (male) are epithets, still in current usage, for people of German ancestry from the eastern regions of the former Reich forcibly resettled in East and West Germany after the war because they were no longer wanted in what were supposed to be the "socialist brother-lands." The character referred to in the title actually plays a very small part in the action, and Müller retitled the work *Die Bauern* (*The Farmers*) for production and publication in the mid-1970s, in deference to Party officials concerned about awakening memories of the 1961 scandal. (Recall from chapter 1 that he was expelled from the Writers' Union due to this play, its amateur cast interrogated, and its director sentenced to hard labor.) Significantly, he always used the old title *Umsiedlerin* when speaking of the work, and that title communicates well his mischievous mood when composing it.

The bulk of the text dates from a two-year, open-ended workshop (1959–61) that Müller engaged in with the director B.K. Tragelehn and students at the Hochschule für Okonomie in Berlin. This school was the main training center for future Party leaders in agricultural planning and was the sponsor of an ambitious extra-curricular theater program that had already produced *The Scab* and *The Correction*. Müller himself confessed that part of "the fun" of the project "consisted in our being bad boys who left shit on the teacher's desk" [0/162], but it is also true that the extreme official reaction after the dress rehearsal was due to unlucky timing. The premiere was scheduled as the opening event for the International Student Theater Week on September 11, 1961, which meant that final rehearsals took place during the building of the Berlin Wall, begun on August 13. Much of what was taken as pointed dissent and conspiracy to embarrass the regime in a high-visibility circumstance was actually written two years before: for example the line "It could happen that the grass between us suddenly becomes a national border . . . you're standing in Russia without taking a step, I in America" [3/71].

Müller said in *War without Battle* that he wrote in this workshop "with the feeling of absolute freedom in dealing with the material; even the political was just more material. It was like being on an island" [161–2]. But island or not, material or not, actual politics was a part of the work from the beginning. Based on his promise to write about the life and milieu of German farmers, he had been living on a stipendium from the Cultural Ministry since 1957, and, as Marianne Streisand points out, the amount of financial and material support the workshop received was unusually large for a nonprofessional project.[36] Furthermore, Müller would have been acutely aware at the time that his elite "island" circumstances, to say nothing of his episodic dramatic technique (de-emphasizing protagonist and plot), were at odds with the new national policy known as "The Bitterfeld Way": an aggressive enforcement of priorities similar to those called for in the 1955 "Nachterstedt Letter," which insisted that literature ought to be a mass activity and professional writers ought to exist only to tell stories from workers' perspectives. ("*Greif zur Feder, Kumpel!*" – "Grab a pen, buddy!" – was one of the mottos from the advertising campaign.)

The background of *The Resettler* is the two major East German land reforms of 1945 and 1960. The first of these, administered by the Soviets, dispossessed all farmers who owned more than 100 hectares (247 acres), as well as all war criminals, and divided their land in lots of 5 hectares (12.4 acres) among smaller farmers, farm-workers, and *Umsiedler*, all of whom became known as "new farmers." One problem with this practice was that those who previously owned less than 100 but substantially more than 5 hectares, now called "middle farmers," found themselves at a tremendous, unfair advantage (e.g. an owner of 95 hectares and one or two extra plow animals had the means of turning his poorer neighbors into sharecroppers). The second reform, carried out by the eleven-year-old GDR, and thus recent history in 1961, completed the process of full collectivization widely feared during the preceding period and disputed among German communists. Most of the play takes place between 1946 and 1950, when the "contradictions" of the first new agriculture policy were most obvious.[37]

Immediately after the war, the first reform was intended to make ownership of land a buffer against starvation and an incentive to productivity, but it soon became clear to the newly enfranchised that their 5-hectare farms could never be economically self-sufficient. The state applied gradual pressure to band them together as collective farms, like the Soviet kolkhozes, all the while denying that it was doing so, which only made the farmers distrust the government as it was trying to win their sympathy.

The play opens in 1946. Bürgermeister Beutler, until recently a lowly dairyman, is conducting unfelt and ridiculously brief ceremonies to distribute the small land parcels. "Middle farmer" Rammler enters and offers the use of a plow-horse to the "new farmers" in return for half their crops.

> *Flint [the Party Secretary] raises the flag.*
> *Enter Rammler.*
> FLINT: You want to cut out a slice from the land reform, kulak? Be happy you have three hectares too few for the expropriation. Three hectares richer, you'd be as poor as a junker.
> RAMMLER: Do I know what a kulak is? I'm a German. Your hand, Flint. None free? No one'll carry your bridal train for you, so you have to hold it yourself at the victory party, and the advertisement too?   [3/23]

Inasmuch as a central story exists, it involves the struggles of the "new farmers" to survive without succumbing to this centuries-old form of economic enslavement by the likes of Rammler. Flint and other convinced socialists struggle to overcome cynicism about the new system and the entrenched beliefs about the need for ruthless self-interest. Hope enters the play in the form of two tractors, gifts of the Soviet Union, made available to the "new farmers" in a central lending station called MAS (*Maschinenausleihstation*), but disappointment soon follows when the boorish tractorists accompanying the machinery turn out to be former Nazis who work for bribes of food, sex, and money. Rammler, it should be added, is an anti-Semite whose bigotry again calls attention to the absence of Jews in Müller's drama and consciousness. Aside from occasional depictions of insensitivity toward them such as Rammler's, Müller simply never mentions Jews in this period, and throughout his career he was comfortable in the typically East German belief that Jews and their disastrous experience in Germany were entirely the other Germany's concern.

Müller creates a panorama of incisive character portraits. Beutler, for instance, is a creature so habituated to opportunistic dissembling and bootlicking that he cannot understand privilege and position in any other terms. At one point, he extorts money from a desperate bürgermeister on the run from the police, then turns the man in. At another point, he sides with the tax collector and "middle farmer" Treiber against "new farmer" Ketzer, seizing the poorer man's horse, after which Ketzer stabs the animal and then hangs himself.

> KETZER *turns his pockets out, they're empty*: My bankbook.
> DEBT COLLECTOR: *takes a third paper out of his briefcase*:
> Then it's confiscation.
> KETZER: I still have a shirt on my body. Here! What do I need a
> shirt for. *Takes the shirt off, throws it at the debt collector.*
> And seven layers of skin underneath; you can still take six off.
> When the frost comes I'll set my cottage on fire, small but
> mine. That warms you up. You want to confiscate? Stamp your
> seal on the ground and floor you presented me with. The Lord
> gave and the Lord took away. *Throws clumps of earth.* You like
> the taste of free soil? Plug up the shingles. *Takes apart his roof,*

throws the shingles. What do I need a roof over my head for?
The rain tickles the dead.   [27]

Another portrait, just as cynical but perversely attractive, is a resettler named Fondrak who abuses his pregnant companion Niet (the original title character), refuses to work, and responds with a sort of homespun, alcoholic nihilism to Flint's repeated attempts to rekindle his self-respect by offering him the dead Ketzer's farm.

> FLINT: You owe me an answer, Fondrak.
> FONDRAK: I have other debts. Myself for instance I owe
> A beer since yesterday. Flint, what would you prefer:
> One catholic more or a small
> Investment? Another hour of thirst
> And I'll sign my soul over to the priests.
> You want that, Flint?
> FLINT: My offer still stands.
> And when you have land, you also have beer.
> FONDRAK: Mixed with sweat, which turns my stomach.
> FLINT: If your sweat doesn't taste good, drink water, Fondrak.
> FONDRAK: A beer and before you stands a communist, Flint.
> FLINT: A parasite is before me.
> FONDRAK: You misunderstand me.
> Show me a mousehole and I'll fuck the world.
> I'm a spiritual man, Flint, beer is soul
> The soul raises the human over the animal
> Work throws him back beneath the beast again.
> *Stops a farmer walking past.*
> Take him for example. Is that still a human? He can't even open
> his hand anymore, crooked. *Demonstrates it.* His hunchback,
> too. Ten years more and he'll walk on all fours again like his
> ancestors in Darwin. Work is a crime against humanity. The
> human is born into life; I want to get drunk in freedom; I shit on
> the land. To each according to his ability, says your newspaper.
> And according to his need. You know my need; you know my
> ability. Is your newspaper lying? A beer or I'll report you, Flint,
> for enemy propaganda.   [78–9]

The provocation of *The Resettler* really lies in the recklessly honest tone of passages like this one, the glee Müller takes in wringing every last detail out of the hypocrisies he sees around him. He writes with an emotional expansiveness uncharacteristic of him and never seen in his work again, exploiting every class-baiting opportunity his scenario could offer, filling speech after speech with a venom whose personal edge is unmistakable. The careerist figure of Beutler alone was enough to make Party officials in the audience cringe (as was Mayakovsky's similarly opportunistic bureaucrat Pobedonosikov in *The Bathhouse* three decades before). Beutler's continual threats to use his official power for personal retaliation, along with Flint's obvious nostalgia for violent quick-fix solutions, were largely responsible for the "dark" vision of the GDR as a tyrannical dictatorship to which Party officials objected in the inquisitional hearings afterward. "Comrade Mauser is on speech-restraint, Flint" [64], says the District Secretary at one point, laughing.

Still, if *The Resettler* is Müller's most eloquent, candid, and warm-blooded work, it also has jarring credibility problems. As Matthias Braun explains in his study of the scandal, Müller thought of himself at the time as improving not only on the dated original model of *Katzgraben* but also on the more recent genre of "socialist agro-drama," a movement inspired by the "Bitterfeld Way" that never won much respect even in the GDR because of its endemic plot contrivances, prepackaged theses, and preordained outcomes.[38] (Examples are Fred Reichwald's *Das Wagnis der Maria Diehl* [*The Gambit of Maria Diehl*, 1959], Helmut Sakowski's *Die Entscheidung der Lene Mattke* [*The Decision of Lene Mattke*, 1959], and Erwin Strittmatter's *Die Holländerbraut* [*The Dutchman's Bride*, 1960] – all of which feature the problems of newly emancipated women in farming situations.) The truth is, though, *The Resettler*, particularly in its final scenes, is scarcely less schematically optimistic than these deservedly forgotten "agro-dramas."

The moment after the dispossessed farmer exits with a rope around his neck, for instance, another farmer enters and calls out, "Tractors are coming, Ketzer" [29], demonstrating that socialist manna will come to all those willing to wait for it. After a tractorist is wounded in a mine explosion, Niet binds his leg with a sheet that, she is told, she must pay for, demonstrating that compassion may never be expected from profit-minded employers, only from naturally humane workers. When Rammler and Treiber, in need of a cheap laborer, try to bribe Fondrak with beer, they end up fighting each other, demonstrating that the selfishness of "kulaks" will eventually lead to mutual annihilation. Most flagrant of all, the essentially static fifteen-scene text suddenly transforms into an action-based suspense-drama in Scene Thirteen, when an improbably wise District President, who does not acquire his Solomonic moral authority from within the play's world, drops in on an assembly, replaces Beutler with Flint, and dispenses some of the most heavy-handed poetic justice yet seen on the GDR stage. (He agrees temporarily to an impertinent suggestion that the tractors be given to two farmers by lot. This creates unhappiness. The farmers are convinced for the first time that the collective MAS is indeed an improvement over the exploitative old system.) The final scene, set ten years later in 1960, shows the fruit of Flint's persuasion as the last "kulak" finally joins the collective farm.

The Resettler, in other words, is the document of a collision of inner tendencies that the young Müller had far more trouble reconciling in himself than he wanted his public to believe later on. Part of him wanted credit for being "totally cheerful," as he said about the workshop – "We . . . found what we were doing so genuinely socialist" [0/162]. And he was willing to risk what he knew to be fairy-tale utopian plot contrivances to create that impression. Another part of him longed to give dramatic expression to what was complex and ambiguous in GDR reality, ignoring the obvious preference for the exclusively straightforward and easily assimilable on the part of those in control of purse-strings and censorship.

The greatest irony of the affair is: he was so candid about the Party's tactical hypocrisy in *The Resettler* that no one noticed he didn't disapprove of it. His Party representatives were painted so sympathetically, even sentimentally, that the real functionaries in the audience were too disturbed to compliment him on the success of his realism: "Politically, they'll beat you to death, because you apologize for them," said Hacks to Müller at the hearing expelling him from the Writers' Union [0/168]. Inge Müller thought that he had purposely sought out issues to embarrass those in power. Hanns

Eisler, also present at the Union hearing, voiced the opposite complaint that he had euphemized, making the GDR's "contradictions" appear less destructive and intransigent than they really were.[39]

These differences of opinion were rooted in the author's internal conflict; for the Müller of *The Resettler*, like the Müller of *Correction 2*, did not yet fully understand that his greatest strength lay in writing cynically, or at least ironically, in arranging socially corrosive comedy around the likes of Fondrak, Rammler, and Stettiner, in deflating sentimental bubbles – in writing *against* generally accepted standards of "right" and "normal," whether communist or capitalist. It's as if a man who could not stomach religion had nevertheless tried to become part of a congregation in order to assail his co-religionists' piety.

This man, in this period, was a Mayakovsky *manqué*, a brash, young author who would be a dedicated team player, who deeply wanted to be, if only the team would accept his unique support in even the ambivalent manner that the Soviets accepted Mayakovsky's. Müller actually seems uncertain whether earnest exuberance ought to be a part of his artistic persona up to the writing of *The Construction Site*, and the accompanying ambivalence about utopia in his writing, about whether concrete visions of it are worthwhile, does not completely disappear until he rejects Socialist Realism categorically and releases his own horrific war memories, carefully fragmented, in such partly surrealistic plays as *Germania Death in Berlin* and *The Battle*.[40]

What is unique and fateful in all this is that Müller ultimately comes to regard this *manqué*-persona as positive. During the years after the *Resettler* affair, he turns so severely against sunny idealism and anything that might be construed as sentimental attachment that he ends up making a fetish out of their opposite, cool disconnection. If only in the interests of humanizing a figure who did so much to appear inhuman, then, we do well to remember that he is less a clever Machiavel in the 1950s than a young firebrand hungry for recognition but forced to dance delicately round the issue of literary heroism. Before he becomes an international avant-gardist, he is caught, like so many Soviet bloc artists, in what might be called the Mayakovskian dilemma: the process of working to eliminate the conditions that make romantic heroism necessary transforms the artist into a romantic hero. The attachments Müller is soon to establish with Artaud, surrealism, and the rest of the Western avant-garde are, among many other qualities, byproducts of the curiously straightforward solution he finds to that dilemma: make the artist repulsive.

5 Müller as Shakespeare: *Macbeth,*
Anatomy of Titus Fall of Rome

[Shakespeare] is the human being I feel the closest to.

(Heiner Müller, [19/210])

Müller's devotion to Shakespeare was long and intense. It began with a schoolboy fascination with *Hamlet,* and it informed every phase of his career as a professional writer. English was the only foreign language he could use actively, and his published works include modern-German translations of *As You Like It* (1967) and *Hamlet* (1976), a play based loosely on *A Midsummer Night's Dream* (*Forestplay,* 1969), and adaptations of *Macbeth* (1971) and *Titus Andronicus* (1984) that amount to original plays. *Hamletmachine* (1977), the work that launched his international fame, was a byproduct of the *Hamlet* translation. A 1988 essay–lecture entitled "Shakespeare a Difference" is one of his most revealing theoretical writings. The variety of these texts is itself evidence of how many different meanings Shakespeare had for him over a lifetime. Two points nevertheless seem more important than others: Shakespeare served as a fount of fresh dramatic ideas during several difficult transitions in Müller's career, and Shakespeare stood in his mind as an important ally in his ongoing arguments with Brecht.

Müller spoke often about the reasons for his affinity with Shakespeare. He said that they both lived and worked in similar "transitional" periods, under a similar "pressure of experience" attributable to upheavals in language and politics at the close of one epoch and the dawn of another [14/148]. Shakespeare also shared with him an obsession with history and drama, history as drama, and the need to flatter absolute authority while indulging his fascination with the psychology of the powerful. Like him too, Müller thought, Shakespeare based the bulk of his works on existing sources. (Such borrowing was, of course, common practice in the English Renaissance; as Harold Bloom writes, "Shakespeare belongs to the giant age before the flood, before the anxiety of influence became central to poetic consciousness."[1] Müller nevertheless perceived an impulse toward "summation" in Shakespeare's use of sources, a "falling back on everything old" as that "old" was dying, that he thought paralleled his own [14/148; 15/135].) Recalling Goethe's remark that Shakespeare's plays could be fully experienced only when read, not when performed, Müller cited this "utopian" potential as yet another similarity with his often dense and complicated work [14/150].[2] When one reads the texts of Müller's adaptations, however, all these factors quickly recede in the face of his obviously practical, immediate uses for Shakespeare.

Like so much else in his work, Müller's major Shakespeare adaptations – *Macbeth*, *Anatomy of Titus Fall of Rome: A Shakespeare Commentary*, and *Hamletmachine* (discussed in chapter 6) are by far the most substantial[3] – began at a point where Brecht left off. Like Brecht and the many GDR writers who took their cues from him, Müller refused to revere any classical text on principle and sought to establish benevolently destructive relationships with canonical works that he thought euphemized or disguised barbaric historical realities. "A classical literature is first of all literature of a class," he said in 1975 [14/23]. Moreover, classical texts in general had lacked political bite in Germany, Müller felt, at least since the adaptation work of Schiller and Goethe at the Weimar Court Theater:

> The non-appearance of the bourgeois revolution in Germany made possible and at the same time necessitated Weimar classicism as an annulment of the positions of Sturm und Drang. Classicism as substitute for revolution.   [13/140]

Where *Macbeth*, and to a lesser extent *Anatomy of Titus*, depart from the model of Brecht is in refraining from what Müller called the "trivializing" practice of seeking one-to-one correspondences with "day-to-day politics" [0/125, 204]. "Shakespeare was for me also an antidote to Brecht, to the simplification in Brecht," he wrote in *War without Battle* [0/265]. Building on, among other things, Shakespeare's Senecan violence and horror, Müller altered plays with an eye more toward their general historical assumptions, the qualities in them that calcified people's atttitudes toward classicism. Only through recognition of an original work's strengths, he thought, and not through reduction, could one hope to explode the bourgeois compact that sees classics as harmless forms of rebellion.

Müller once stated that his purpose in *Macbeth* was to react critically to "the Shakespeare play that I liked the least," engaging in a "line by line" debate with the Bard through translation, alteration, and elision.[4] Judging from the text, what apparently bothered him most about the original was its assumption that political violence could be fruitfully seen as a temporary aberration, or a psychological anomaly, in a socio-political structure that excludes the lower classes from power. The world in this *Macbeth*, like that in *Anatomy of Titus*, never possesses any political health or divine order to which it can be restored by return of a rightful monarch. Müller's Duncan, a bloodthirsty tyrant who appears atop a throne made of corpses, is displaced by another bloodthirsty tyrant, Macbeth, who then contends with crassly brutal and ambitious adversaries himself. "My best enemy whom I forgot to slaughter" [8/223] is Macbeth's description of Macduff, who is seen at one point cutting out the tongue of an insufficiently cowed servant. In the end, as Macduff is slaughtered in turn, the newly crowned young Malcolm cries, "Did I say I want that. I wish I were in England" – after which the witches indicate the start of yet another cycle of killing by greeting him as they did Macbeth near the beginning: "Hail Malcolm Hail King of Scotland Hail" [239].

The power struggle is depicted as the perverse privilege of a feudal aristocracy that pursues its clan warfare in spite and at the expense of a hostile but defenseless peasantry. When the play opens Duncan's army is repelling a rebellion of Scottish peasants as well as an opportunistic attack, in the wake of the peasants' defeat, by the King of Norway, assisted by the renegade Thane of Cawdor. The peasants never pose a serious threat, are treated as an annoying distraction from the real battles among the aristocrats, and throughout the play their suffering is used as black comic background. The sounds of peasant-prisoners being drowned in a nearby swamp, for instance, accompany Duncan's regal declaration that Malcolm is his heir. A peasant in the stocks outside Macbeth's castle is later seen as "a skeleton with shreds of flesh" [207]. And Lady Macbeth, disturbed by "noise" outside from a peasant reportedly behind on his rent, demands "to see him bleeding, to prepare my eyes / For the painting that the night will bring us" [192] – one of numerous references to scenes of killing and torture as "paintings." The peasants' agonies, it seems, are part of a bloody landscape that will remain hideous as long as art is a reflection of the pre-human values of this "prehistorical" elite.

What was most scandalous about the text in 1971, and is still most startling, is its flat and coarse idiom. The linguistic mundaneness is crucial to the creation of a milieu in which killing and torture have become everyday phenomena. For instance, hearing of Macbeth's soldierly exploits on his behalf in the opening scene, Duncan does not say anything like Shakespeare's "O valiant cousin, worthy gentleman!" but simply *"Guter Macbeth"* – "Good Macbeth." And his reaction to the news of victory a few moments later is not "Great happiness!" but rather *"Das nenn ich Glück"* – "That's what I call luck" [184–5]. Like everyone else, the witches are blunt and to the point, a single, crude line from them – "Aren't you hot for King Duncan's crown, Thane" [188] – substituting for Banquo's entire speech in Shakespeare distrusting "the instruments of darkness." All polite manners, sincere endearments, and pretensions to nobility are treated as superfluous, and all potential sources of pathos, moments of hesitation, and reflections about scruples not necessary to the plot are removed.

As in the past, Müller also uses the text to deflate East German jargon, focusing, for example, as obsessively on the word "work" (*Arbeit*) as he did in *Mauser*, this time satirically. (Recall that *Mauser*, written the previous year, could not be produced or published in the GDR and was virtually unknown there throughout the 1970s.) "He's at work," says Lady Macbeth when her husband is off slitting Duncan's throat [198]. "I recommend the work to you warmly" [211], says Macbeth to Banquo's murderers, one of whom then says about a corpse: "even dead he's working for his cash" [214]. Most caustic of all is this sequence following the Porter's comic monologue that delays his opening of Macbeth's castle gate:

> MACDUFF: Should I nail you to the gate, gate-keeper.
> *Does it with his sword.*
> LENNOX: I want you to find your legs, arm-stump. Run.
> *Cuts off his wooden leg. Both laugh. Macbeth.*
> LENNOX: We had to give your gate-keeper a few
> Pointers, Lord. He limps against the clock.
> MACBETH: Thanks for the work.
> LENNOX: We liked doing it.
> MACBETH: Work is work.
> MACDUFF: Work we like to do isn't.   [202–3]

After the play premiered in Brandenburg in 1972 (Müller says he supplied the text under the aegis of a new translation to a theater that had already announced "Shakespeare's *Macbeth*" in its season schedule [0/260]), this scene was cited by several East German critics as evidence that Müller lacked respect for peasants.[5] He had failed to endow them with any redemptive seeds of humanity, it seems, as he supposedly had in earlier plays like *The Resettler*.

The political climate at the time this work was conceived is an important factor in its attitude and initial reception. In 1971, the student protests in West Germany and West Berlin had been going on for three years, those in the United States for seven years. The Vietnam War was anything but over, and a spirit of rebellion against parents and elders prevailed in the East as well as the West. Erich Honecker had just taken over the reins of the East German government, and, partly because of this atmosphere, many were poised to test his mettle. The crudeness of *Macbeth* should be seen partly in this context, as should the correspondences with "day-to-day politics" that it does contain: for example, the language issues just mentioned, a general fear of speaking openly about government, and one veiled reference to the Berlin Wall ("Scotland's King builds a fortress against Scotland" [220]). The work's strong effect in no way depends on this sort of correspondence, however, and even in 1972 it proved to be provocative outside the GDR, when a production in Switzlerland enraged local critics. It remains stageworthy and ripe for translation today.

Taken as a whole, *Macbeth* is much more powerful than the brief quotes I have given may imply. Over the course of its twenty-three scenes, the amassed vulgarity takes on its own cumulative gravity that counterbalances the intentionally tasteless humor and leads the mind to grim recognition of the author/adaptor's conviction that his world simply has not earned Shakespearean radiance. The seriousness of Müller's laughable, medieval/modern Gehenna originates in Shakespeare's shadow, in the way the later author provides just enough eloquence to spark recognition of and longing for all that his era refuses to inspire or sustain. Macbeth on childlessness and historical futility: "I want to tear this race out of the future. / If nothing comes from me, then nothingness will come from me. / Who's there" [210]. The play (along with *Germania Death in Berlin* [also 1971], which remained unpublished and unproduced for six years) introduces what will be Müller's characteristic aesthetic through the 1970s, his famous vision of drama as a sort of Brechtian Grand Guignol in which bloodied and bloodthirsty puppet-like creatures try to become human beings by escaping from the string of gruesome, fragmentary dramas called "history." The work is also important because it sparked the first high-profile *critical* assault on him in his country.

This small "paper war" [0/261], as he called it, was begun in the main East German literary periodical, *Sinn und Form*, by the prominent philosopher Wolfgang Harich – himself a man of fascinating Mülleresque contradictions whose arrest in 1956 figured fictionally in Müller's last play, *Germania 3* (published 1996). Harich's digressive and redundant 11,000-word article, "The Runaway Dingo, The Forgotten Raft" (1973), was really an elaborate attempt to hide shock and disgust behind an ostensibly knowing dismissal. It is worth recalling, though, because it documents some of the fears Müller's work tapped at the time among the ruling class. Harich, a passionate Communist, had spent more than eight years in prison (seven in solitary confinement) for publishing a reform program for the GDR that included German reunification, democratization, and abolition of the Stasi, yet the prudish and paranoid ideas in his article (*not* the prose) could very well have come from any of the innumerable Party bureaucrats anxiously observing then that the Berlin Wall was not impervious to Western cultural trends.

Harich denounced Müller as "pessimistic" and "reactionary," condescendingly declaring that if he "persisted in [this] dreadful erring" he would end up "barely reparable."[6] Complaining bitterly about Müller's "*Banalisierung*" of Shakespeare's language, Harich called him a "would-be archaist" who employed a "cannibal vocabulary" to the disgrace of his past adaptations (*Philoctetes* [1958–64], *Oedipus Rex* [1965], and *Prometheus* [1967–8]).[7] "An artwork of the highest order born of the spirit of the Renaissance" was transformed "into a modern reprise of Schopenhauerian philosophy" whose "profoundness" and "demanding refinement" was expunged by a sensibility "uncultured, common, of the sewer."[8] Unable or unwilling to conceive that Müller's own experiences within the GDR might have figured importantly in *Macbeth*, Harich fulminated about the Western "porn wave" (Bernd Bartoszewski's production in Brandenburg included nudity) and "cruelty wave," and insisted that "Müller lets himself be dragged along not only by films like *The Devils*, *Straw Dogs* and *A Clockwork Orange* . . . [but also] gives this filth the opportunity to feed parasitically on Shakespeare's poetic strength."[9] Müller, who could not secure a visa even to attend the Swiss premiere of *Macbeth*, had not yet seen these films. Not that a valid case could not have been made at the time for him reaching toward the West. Formulating it persuasively just required a more circumspect critic than Harich.

Interestingly, Müller's advocates in the GDR also had blind spots regarding *Macbeth*. Martin Linzer, Friedrich Dieckmann, and Anselm Schlösser, for instance, all suggested that he was using the history of medieval Scotland to criticize American actions in Vietnam.[10] Dieckmann appended a West German metaphor, calling the character Malcolm "a sort of Adenauer."[11] And Wolfgang Heise praised the play for (unlike absurdist dramas such as Ionesco's *Macbett*) encouraging "the overthrow of all social conditions in which the human being is a degraded, oppressed, forsaken, contemptible creature" [Marx].[12] All these critics and others overlooked the more immediate comparison with Stalin's Soviet Union and the Eastern European governments modeled on it, preferring to analyze the play chiefly as an allegory about proto-capitalism in the eleventh century. Only in the West were parallels drawn between Müller's entrenched feudal elite and isolated Communist leaders whose ruthless self-preservative actions made an eventual revolution against them inevitable.

By the time Müller returned to Shakespearean adaptation in 1984, he was a very different writer, one who could travel freely, see whatever he pleased in the Western cinema and theater, and who had little inclination to disguise critique behind classical metaphors that cultural apparatchiks were unable to understand – a widespread practice in the GDR of the 1960s and 1970s, as it also was in the Nazi era among authors of Germany's "inner immigration." (Müller in 1988: "I don't need to adapt *Macbeth* anymore; I can write everything about Stalin now" [15/136]). By the mid-1980s, he had written *Hamlet-machine*, *The Mission*, *Quartett* (*Quartet*), and numerous other works that treated time and space as fluid and regarded the idea of discrete, dependably individual characters as absurd. Perhaps more important, he had acquired experience as a director that gave him an opportunity to test such "utopian," *Lehrstück*-based ideas in the theater. Though at first some saw Müller in this period (largely because of *Hamlet-machine*) as bent on frustrating the procedures of institutional theaters, that was not a tenable theory for long.[13] His productions of the early 1980s – two stagings of *The Mission* and a 1982 co-production of *Macbeth* with Ginka Tscholakowa – were not only crucial to his development but extremely influential within the GDR.

The dominant visual background for the 1982 *Macbeth* consisted of three drab, multi-storey walls that unmistakably resembled a dreary inner courtyard in Prenzlauerberg, the rundown neighborhood that was East Berlin's artists' quarter.[14] To this were added a telephone booth, an anomalous mannikin, music from The Doors ("This is the end, my friend . . ." familiar then from the 1979 film *Apocalpyse Now*), and a host of elegant visual effects such as a banquet table made of enormous, gently draped cloths that dropped in the center into an abrupt, grave-like depression. These and other anachronisms brought Müller's unvarnished world(s) onto the stage, setting it (them) within a time–space that collapsed eleventh-century Scotland, the 1980s GDR, and the 1980s West into a continuous, bloody present.

As already suggested, implicit in the text all along was the idea

4. Dieter Montag (Macbeth 1), Michael Gwisdek (Macbeth 2), and Hermann Beyer (Macbeth 3) in *Macbeth*, directed by Heiner Müller and Ginka Tscholakowa, Volksbühne, East Berlin, 1982.

5. Recessed courtyard setting by Hans-Joachim Schlieker for Müller and Tscholakowa's production of *Macbeth*, Volksbühne, East Berlin, 1982.

that language in Müller's era was inadequate to the task of dignifying and aggrandizing the individual, as tragic poetry and other forms of lyricism were able to do in the Elizabethan era. The modern individual lacked worth and resplendence partly because language was degraded. Müller and Tscholakowa extended this point by physicalizing it, employing a multiple casting of roles that made the play's degraded language seem to facilitate the individual's disappearance. The Duncan who visited Macbeth's castle, for instance, was played by one of the witches, whose skulls were metallic blue and silver (implying machine-like evil); these actors later also doubled as Lady Macduff and Macbeth's soldiers. The wife of a disloyal lord whom Macbeth's soldiers flayed (while Macbeth recited a passage from Ovid – a scene not in Shakespeare) was played by the actress of Lady Macbeth. Indeed, it was impossible to keep track of all the doublings and triplings; forty-three roles were played by fifteen actors, most of whom wore signs on their backs bearing the names of the characters they were currently playing.

Most prominent of all, Macbeth himself was split into three figures or alter egos, played by three different actors who corresponded, according to Hans-Thies Lehmann, to the conflicting motives within him: "Macbeth the official carrier of power, statesman, Macbeth the private man with his sexuality, Macbeth the murderer and candidate for death."[15] The last of these was strapped to an electric chair at the back of the auditorium. Müller wrote in a program note (echoing a theory of terrorism by Jean Baudrillard that he had been reading, which saw terror as a leveling process that made bodies and values "exchangeable"[16]):

> The subject of the adaptation/production is the exchangeability
> of human beings. It plunges the individual into despair. The
> despair of the individual is the hope of the collective.
> Communism means the possibility of real individualizing,
> which is the end of exchangeability. Release of the human being
> from the emergency of his prehistory into the universe of his
> loneliness.[17]

These concerns – the individual cut adrift in a sea of (technological) anonymity; theatricality as an (Elizabethan) metaphor for the hyper-real or "simulated" condition of those in power (another Baudrillard thesis[18]); the use of richly enigmatic stage pictures to fill a vacuum left by inadequate or damaged language; theater as a form of terrorism in which important literary and historical figures are held "hostage" (Sue-Ellen Case's thesis linking Müller's Shakespeare work with Artaud[19]) – all prefigure *Anatomy of Titus*, the collaborations with Robert Wilson (which deserve a book in themselves), and the rest of Müller's magnificent directing work in the 1980s and 1990s. Moreover, these points are largely why he became the central figure in German theater and German theater scholarship during that period.

Like *Macbeth*, *Anatomy of Titus* began with a particular venue for performance. Müller had agreed to supply a prose translation of *Julius Caesar* to directors Manfred Karge and Matthias Langhoff for production in Bochum when the government of West Germany suddenly fell, under conditions that all involved thought could too easily be read into the play as facile metaphors. The Free Democratic Party under Hans Dietrich Genscher split from its coalition with the Social Democratic Party of Chancellor Helmut Schmidt to form a new coalition with Helmut Kohl and his conservative Christian Democrats. Müller: "Brutus Genscher and Caesar Schmidt, one just couldn't do that to Shakespeare" [0/323–4]. Müller then suggested replacing *Julius Caesar* with *Titus Andronicus* since, as he said, "I was already pregnant with it," and the directors agreed [0/324].

Unlike *Macbeth* and *Julius Caesar*, however, *Titus Andronicus* is not generally recognized as a masterpiece. It is one of Shakespeare's earliest works and is chock-full of gruesome onstage violence and contrived turns of plot that may have suited the sixteenth century but are utterly implausible today. Modern scholars have seen the magnificent Lear-like speeches of the title character in the last three acts as its main redeeming virtue, but this does not seem to be what most attracted Müller. Judging from his text, he was drawn mostly by the camp appeal of its splatter-movie gore (which has also been a point of access for numerous other twentieth-century artists such as Joseph Beuys, Friedrich Dürrenmatt, and Julie Taymor) and by the densely political nature of the action – the fact that, as H.T. Price once wrote, the play's "real hero . . . is the state . . . no particular person but . . . Rome herself."[20]

Titus is unlike all Shakespeare's other dramas in that it sticks to a strict Senecan pattern that precludes redemptive changes of heart and any other serious diversions from the central figure's single-minded pursuit of revenge, following the depiction of atrocious crimes against him. The play therefore could almost have served as a "copied" Müller work as is, if not for the return of divine order at the end with the crowning of Titus' last surviving son Lucius – again, credible in the Elizabethan era but hopelessly incredible today. Müller makes short work of this problem, reducing the moderating voice of Titus' brother Marcus to a small nuisance and making Lucius just as vicious, self-serving, and ungrateful as everyone else. Lucius tortures the tribune Aemelius who comes to arrange a parley with him, for instance, blithely breaks his oath to spare Aaron's son (*"Goths throw the dead child onto the table"* [9/220]), and then contemptuously dismisses the Gothic army that helped install him.

> LUCIUS: To you my gallant Goths our thanks
> You're released now back to your steppe
> Make sure they march off richly rewarded, uncle
> GOTHS: Maybe we'd prefer to stay in Rome
> LUCIUS: Swords enough has Rome to drive you off
> The Goth is a negro is a Jew
> Doesn't he have curly hair black skin thick lips
> And isn't he outside as he is inside   [222]

This passage indicates the general drift of Müller's other changes as well. He did not merely rewrite Shakespeare's story but rather rewrote it as a kind of dramatic surface for political graffiti, sprinkling the dialogue with anachronisms (nuclear arms, film, and television all figure) and interrupting it with frequent and extensive commentary ("A Shakespeare Commentary" is the work's subtitle). The commentary bleeds into the dialogue at times, with some passages written in *Lehrstück* block-form implying different speakers without indicating them. Mostly, it is separate from the dialogue and printed in capital letters, as if Müller had decided that screaming was now the only tone fit to address "the emergency of [man's] prehistory" referred to in his *Macbeth* note. In a note attached to *Anatomy of Titus*, he stressed that "the commentary as a means of bringing the reality of the author into play is drama, not description, and should not be delegated to a narrator" [224]. The insertions sometimes do substitute for exposition, but they usually function as a means of keeping contemporary historical and political associations constantly before spectators, an epic distancing effect to disrupt purely hedonistic consumption of the campy violence.

The opening passage, for instance, creates the atmosphere when the victorious Titus returns to Rome, bruited as a popular choice for emperor to the dismay of the feuding blood heirs.

> I
>
> A NEW CONQUEST LAYS WASTE ROME THE CAPITAL
> OF THE WORLD TWO SONS OF THE DEAD EMPEROR
> EACH FOLLOWED BY HIS BAND OF THUGS
> RAISE CLAIMS TO THE EMPTY THRONE
>
> . . .
>
> TITUS ANDRONICUS WHO FOR TEN YEARS
> HAS WARRED AGAINST THE GOTHS WHO PRESS IN
> FROM FOREST AND STEPPE TOWARD THE TROUGH OF THE CITIES
> DECIMATED BY WOLVES BAD HARVESTS STORMS
> THE MESSENGER WHO REPORTED THE VICTORY
> LIES ON THE STEPS WITH HIS LUNGS RIPPED OUT
>
> . . .
>
> THE CORRUGATED METAL OF THE SUBURBS ALREADY TREMBLES
> FROM MARCHING AND THE GUARDS ON THE TOWERS
> SEE THE COLUMN OF DUST FROM THE ADVANCING ARMY
> ROME AWAITS THE BOOTY SLAVES FOR
> THE LABOR MARKET FRESH FLESH FOR THE BORDELLOS
> GOLD FOR THE BANKS WEAPONS FOR THE ARSENAL.   [126–7]

Other passages contain political animadversion both more and less explicit ("PILLAGE[D] COLONIES . . . WILL KISS THE HOOFS OF THEIR HORSES / FETCHING HOME THE FIRST WORLD INTO NOTHINGNESS" [141]), textual interpretations that double as stage directions ("TITUS ANDRONICUS THE ANATOMIST / CAREFUL NOT TO DAMAGE HIS FLESH / CUTS THE THROATS OF THE GOTHIC PRINCES" [215]), and what amount to personal reflections by Müller ("THE POET SINGS HIS SONG KEEPS HIS HUMOR / THE HUMOR OF THE BUTCHER OR OF

DESPAIR . . . IN THE EPOCH OF TOURISM MURDER / IS MERCY SEEING MEANS KILLING PICTURES / IN THE GREY COAT OF MY NO MAN'S NAME / YOUR MURDERER WILLIAM SHAKESPEARE IS MY MURDERER" [152–3]).

Subtleties of the poetry aside, this formidable screen of intellectualizing is something of a diversion in the drama. As with *Macbeth* at the Volksbühne two years earlier, what most interested Müller, apparently, in creating this work was the supply of fresh *theatrical* ideas in Shakespeare that Müller's own *Lehrstück*-inspired experimental vision seemed ideally suited to exploit. Here is a section of his note to *Anatomy of Titus*, for instance, which describes at length what he sees as the work's measureless performance possibilities, recalling his note to *Mauser* quoted in chapter 3:

> [The commentary] can be spoken by a chorus; by the actor of the figure to whom reference is made; by the actor of another figure who either has or doesn't have a relationship to the one commented on. The expression of emotion can, as in the Japanese theater, be taken over by the commentator (speaker or chorus) . . . The repertory of roles (positions) that the commentary supplies (spectator voyeur overseer reporter previous speaker prompter party whip sparring partner hired mourner shadow doppelgänger ghost) is available to all who participate in the play . . . No monopoly on roles masks gestures text, the epic circumstance no privilege: to all the chance of becoming alienated from themselves.   [224]

In *War without Battle*, Müller said that *Anatomy of Titus* "was like a maneuver field [in which] an arsenal of forms could be tried out for later plays" [324], and it is indeed a shame that he did not write more plays in the eleven years left to him that made use of the arsenal. (*Bildebeschreibung* [*Description of a Picture*, 1984] is a remarkable exception, to be discussed in chapter 9, and Müller's later directing projects should also be seen partly as products of his Shakespeare work.)

The truth is, though, that *Anatomy of Titus* announces and celebrates an authorial burst that never really occurred, and, measured against its own aspirations, it is also a markedly weaker piece of writing than *Macbeth*. (It received only one German production in the 1980s after Bochum, whereas *Macbeth* received fifteen between 1972 and 1987[21] – not that Müller would have seen these statistics as a measure of anything, of course.) Part of its problems certainly originate with Shakespeare's limited ambitions. Müller seems constantly to be working to deflate through brutality and vulgarity what was never pompous or inflated in the first place. The portrayal of Lucius in particular reads as a petty effort to prove Müller can make Shakespeare's bloodiest play bloodier.

Most unsatisfying of all, though, is the commentary's efforts to frame the action as an allegory about the exploitation of the Third World by the First World. Recalling the references to Genet in *The Mission* (see chapter 7), the evil negro Aaron is "HIS OWN DIRECTOR" in "THE THEATER OF HIS BLACK REVENGE" [142] who, half buried and left to die, "GROWS IN THE EARTH" [222] at the end, foreshadowing his eventual figural return as barbarian masses that will overrun Rome and as dust that will cover it. Lucius, exiled by the Emperor and sent by his father to gather the Gothic army against Rome, is "A BASTARD OF HIS FATHERLAND A JEW" who must be "brainwashed" and learn "to whimper Gothic" [166]; and Titus, bereft of his right hand and all but two children, "LEARNS THE ALPHABET OF THE NEGRO" [189].

In the first place, the spectacle of a GDR author (with apartments in both Berlins at this point) completely excluding the communist Second World from even this sketchy description of the dilemma of the world's downtrodden is irredeemably hollow – especially considering his trumpeted scorn for "the people of the Federal Republic [who feel] innocent of everything."[22] In the second place, his sudden show of sympathy with Jews-as-universal-outcasts rings of tokenism after so many years of uninterest in Jewish history and silence about Jews. *Anatomy of Titus* "has to do with the relationship between writing and blood, alphabet and terror," he once said, explaining that Lucius' forced adoption of the Goth's "foreign alphabet" was like "the Bulgarian attempt to force Bulgarian names on its Turkish minority" [0/325]; he was apparently unaware of the most widespread instance of compulsory name-changing in European history, that of the Jews.

Müller, I think, was fully aware that his Shakespeare adaptations were at their strongest when drawing on the poetic splendor of Shakespeare – even if only negatively, by way of denial and withholding, as in *Macbeth* – and not when editorializing and straining after contemporary metaphors. The best evidence of this is his 1988 text "Shakespeare a Difference" in which he stated that the "pressure of experience" in his era exerted pressure on drama to reduce its dependence on metaphor, relying more on raw, recognizable, worldly forces that spectators could see battling "nakedly, without the drapery, the costume of ideas" [9/229]. Shakespeare had a "view of the ages," said Müller, meaning that without really analyzing or philosophizing about his historical moment, he nevertheless produced incisive, nearly literal documentation of the brutal power transitions and shifts in social affiliations accompanying the end of the Middle Ages: "The dead have their place on his stage, nature has a vote" [229].

What keeps a contemporary dramatist from doing precisely the same thing (talent aside) are the intervening centuries, "the long march through the hells of the Enlightenment, through the bloodswamp of ideologies" [227], which have changed our responsibilities both toward history and toward the canonical dramatists we admire.

> Shakespeare is a mirror through the ages, our hope a world that he doesn't reflect anymore. We haven't arrived where we live as long as Shakespeare writes our plays.
>
> . . .
>
> A Shakespeare variation: Macbeth sees Banquo's ghost, and a difference. Our task – or the rest will be statistics and an affair for computers – is to work on this difference.   [228, 230]

The difficulty lies in "work[ing] on this difference" without falling victim to the ghost's original power, in splattering fresh historical blood onto classical canvases without becoming enthralled with their glorious imagery. Müller's most memorable engagement with this difficulty was *Hamletmachine*.

6 Müller as Artaud: *Hamletmachine*

In a 1987 colloquium at the Freie Universität in West Berlin, Heiner Müller was asked to name any authors other than Brecht whom he considered significant influences. His polite response – "I'm sorry, but I have few influences" – drew first a laugh and then embarrassed silence from the audience of mostly professors and graduate students. Clearly, many found it difficult to take him at his word, his preference for "eating" rather than "reading" literature (discussed in chapter 1) having never been well understood in academia, or anywhere else for that matter. That preference, however, is key to an understanding of his relationship to Antonin Artaud, to all the shadow figures examined from this point on, and to *Hamletmachine*, which I think is the central text in his oeuvre. Especially when seen against its Artaudian underpinnings, *Hamletmachine* demonstrates better than any other text the tactical tergiversation and misdirection, the *half*-serious shadowboxing with forebears, that helped establish Müller as an international avant-garde star in the late 1970s.

Müller warned against overstressing his connection to Artaud.

> I don't think that there has been a direct influence. That is an invention of the feuilleton, as always. At some point I read Artaud, of course. But already before I had read Artaud or knew anything about him, there were things, simply due to a similar experience (or similar attitude to experience), into which critics then read an influence.   [14/152]

Nearly every dissertation and book-length study on Müller nevertheless contains a separate section, if not an entire chapter, summarizing Artaud's theories and establishing affinities that are then held to be fundamental.[1] Many of the affinities are true and significant. It is the claims to fundamentality that misrepresent Müller's facetious spirit and the way he made use of the Artaudian tradition as a game.

In any case, by the time Müller began traveling to the West, maintaining a residence and receiving numerous productions there in the 1970s, Artaud himself was already less important than the paradigm "Artaud" in the Euro-American theater. The name was a lodestar for a wide array of attitudes and practices, attributable to him and not, that questioned representation as such, circulated exaggerated reports about the death of the Author, advocated real or realistically simulated violence and sex onstage, and opposed rationality as a basis for stage communication. Artaud was a guru for 1960s youth in Western Europe and the United States, whose rebellions were watched with envy and awe by many in Eastern Europe (often on Western television in the GDR[2]), and with fear by others (recall Harich's fulmination against the Western "cruelty wave"). Almost regardless of Müller's own reading experience, then, the influence of Artaud's cult – and the incendiary mood suffusing the art it did directly affect – pervaded his working atmosphere during the early Honecker era.

Müller did acknowledge that he found Artaud to be "a very productive disturbance" because he forced "the European left," along with the theater artists who shared its aims, to question "its having always articulated and presented itself in rationalistic terms" [14/46]. This 1976 remark is particularly interesting in that it reveals a shift in Müller's thinking about audiences and also suggests that he himself sometimes sought release from the polemics in his writing. This search for release was especially strong toward the end of his life – "From naiveté comes the strength to assert fantasy as reality, as a component of reality. . . one is always hunting after dreams, trying to reach the same freedom as in a dream while dealing with particles of reality," he said in 1991 [18/25] – but its beginnings in the early 1970s are equally interesting. Having already challenged Brecht on dialectics in his *Lehrstück* experiments, he now reached for artistic techniques inimical to rationality, most importantly the language and heritage of surrealism, which SED ideologues had always dismissed as "decadent." (André Breton in the "Second Manifesto of Surrealism," written in 1930, three years after he broke with followers reluctant to become "fellow travelers": "I do not believe in the present possibility of an art or literature which expresses the aspirations of the working class."[3])

The longer Müller's isolation from East German audiences lasted, it seems – and he was denied production and publication until 1973, with only a few exceptions such as *Macbeth* – the readier he was to draw on sources like Artaud and surrealism for forms and approaches that could help him play to the West as well as the East. This broadening of sources began in his private notebooks, Müller said, long before either the publication of *Germania Death in Berlin* and *Hamletmachine* (both 1977) or the completion of the former play in 1971. This strategy was consistent with his previous work in at least one important way, as part of his desire (discussed in chapter 2) to reach audiences repulsed by Brecht's preachiness. (A typical Western view of the matter was Ionesco's: "all authors have tried to make propaganda. The great ones are those who have failed, who have gained access, consciously or not, to a deeper and more universal reality."[4]) Probably more important in the late 1970s, though, was Müller's increasing consciousness of fame and notoriety, his clear awareness that numerous theater artists – Peter Weiss, Edward Bond, Peter Brook, and Jerzy Grotowski, for example – had earned international recognition by fusing Brecht and Artaud in original syntheses.

Artaud was not simply a figure for surrealism to Müller. He knew the writings well, and alluded explicitly to Artaud texts in several works, including *Germania Death in Berlin*, *Medeaspiel* (*Medeaplay* [3/17]), and *Hamletmachine*. Müller also enjoyed viewing himself as something of a *poète maudit*, that is, as part of the glorified tradition of outcast and dissipated writers that include Artaud, Genet, Lautréamont, Nerval, and Poe – though that was a bit of an affectation since, whatever he may have meant by the "similar experience" referred to above, Müller did not suffer, say, the childhood meningitis, drug addiction, psychosis, or extended incarceration in an asylum that Artaud did. More generally and bookishly, Müller did write from a sense that the contemporary "subject" was diseased, a view influenced as much by Nietzsche and Foucault as by Artaud. In a one-paragraph essay written for an Artaud collection the same year as *Hamletmachine*, Müller connected this diseased "subject" with the broad critique of the "rotting" Enlightenment that would underlie his work through "Shakespeare a Difference" and beyond: "THINKING IS AMONG THE GREATEST PLEASURES OF THE HUMAN RACE, Brecht has Galilei say, before they show him the instruments. The lightning that split the consciousness of Artaud was Nietzsche's experience" [13/169].

All these areas of connection understood, the following analysis of *Hamletmachine* concentrates on another idea: the eradication of dramatic literature, or rather the displacement of drama by its means of enactment, theater. Most theater practitioners who have taken Artaud seriously have treated this idea as central to him. However, unlike Brook, Grotowski, and others who experimented with practical application of Artaudian theory, Heiner Müller was an author, and the apparent paradox of this, of an author producing dramas that map the failure of drama to take place, was partly a result of his not taking the Artaudian tradition fully seriously. This seems to me the point most deserving of scrutiny. The death of drama, like the death of the Author, was a myth to Müller, a double-edged fiction whose ambiguity and power over others he tried to harness on his behalf in the same way he coolly exploited Stalinist violence, East German politics, Teutonic myth, and much else, as "material."

From its first appearance in 1977, *Hamletmachine*, which contains a stage direction calling for the tearing of the author's photograph, was regarded as a moment of crisis in Müller's career, a reaction he could not have stage-managed more fittingly for his purposes. The title, for instance, arose as a reference to the mechanized art factory of Andy Warhol, whom Müller quotes in the work ("I want to be a machine"), and to the "Bachelor-Machine" of Marcel Duchamp [0/295]. "That was then interpreted: HamletMachine = H.M. = Heiner Müller. This reading I circulated with care," said the author in 1982 [14/115]. Similarly, while early interviews refer to *Hamletmachine* as an important endpoint in his career –

> From *The Scab* to *Hamletmachine* everything is one story, a
> slow process of reduction. With my last play *Hamletmachine*
> that's come to an end. No substance for dialogue exists
> anymore because there is no more history.   (1978) [14/54]

– later comments express contempt for any biographical interpretation of the text as a chronicle of authentic emergency. "If you
want, you could say that I'm always in crisis, I've always been in
crisis. Or never," he warned in 1989. "And parts of *Hamletmachine*
are quite old. Parts are from the 1950s."[5]

These warnings notwithstanding, it is obvious that *Hamletmachine* – nine pages of residua from the 200-page *Hamlet* translation
he prepared for Benno Besson in 1976–7 (see chapters 1 and 5) – refers
to the idea of identity crisis. And today we can see that its *sense* of
authentic crisis has helped make it one of Müller's most frequently
staged and analyzed works. It has acquired not only a substantial
literary reputation but also notoriety as a sort of dramatic practical
joke: a playscript conceived for "open" use by those who don't believe
in the viability of plays anymore, as well as a metaphorical examination of the crisis of the Marxist intellectual written by an intellectual who wishes it known that he may be neither Marxist nor in crisis.

Hamletmachine seems deliberately conceived to cause be-
wilderment among those interested in the taxonomy of dramatic
literature. Divided into five sections, like a Shakespeare play, it consists largely of long monologues by speakers of fluid or multiple
identity, its few stage directions and dialogue passages offering little
guidance for staging or interpreting the suggested structural connection to *Hamlet*. Packed with quotations and paraphrases from Eliot,
cummings, Hölderlin, Marx, Benjamin, Artaud, Sartre, Warhol, Shakespeare, the Bible, Müller himself, and others, often strung together
without connecting text, *Hamletmachine* tacitly renounces style but
nevertheless acquires something like a style due to the humor and
intelligence with which Müller applies the quotations and molds
Shakespeare's characters and other borrowed figures to his purposes.
It is dense with irony and posturing yet nevertheless gathers a sort of
sincerity in the course of protesting too much about its insincerity.
Müller:

> For thirty years Hamlet was a real obsession for me, so I tried to
> destroy him by writing a short text, *Hamletmachine*. German
> history was another obsession and I tried to destroy this
> obsession, this whole complex. I think the main impulse is to

strip things to their skeleton, to rid them of their flesh and
surface. Then you are finished with them.   [13/43]

This act of reduction was an attempt to smash a too-
compelling icon, but, like so many acts of its kind, it only generated a
new icon, the Hamlet Destroyer, trapping Müller in yet another
infernal circle. Unique and strange as it is, even *Hamletmachine*
cannot quite shake free of its roots in certain traditions, among them
Romantic closet drama, with its impractical stage directions and
central egos split into various characters, and the general Eastern
European tendency (seen in writers from Witkiewicz to Kohout and
Havel) to use Hamlet as a symbol for the modern intellectual's pre-
varications, hesitations, and rationalizations in the face of tyranny
and terror. There are also two famous German interpretations of
Shakespeare to which Müller was reacting, both of which treat
Hamlet as a type and his dilemma as a syndrome: Brecht's, which
views the character as "an idealist who becomes a cynic," and
Nietzsche's, which views him as "loath to act" because of an excess of
"understanding," "a surplus of possibilities."[6]

It is *Hamletmachine*'s very ladenness, its sheer referential
density, that makes it such an interesting case in the history of
attempts to break down what Artaud called "the formal screen" that
literary masterpieces "interpose" between artists and the public.[7]
Müller resisted such "idolatry" not by removing revered objects
(Artaud's displacement of drama by theater) but by accumulating and
magnifying them. This was his hypertrophied means of seeking "difference" from idols, as he later put it in his Shakespeare essay. Artaud
to André Gide in 1935:

> A character says a word under the impression that another
> word will come along and destroy it and, above all, under the
> impression of an ideal atmosphere that distorts it while
> focusing on it at the same time. . . I destroy the idea from fear
> that respect for the idea will only result in creating a form,
> which in its turn, favors the continuance of bad ideas.[8]

Having no interest in purifying himself in preparation for any
holy rite (Artaud's "ideal atmosphere"), Müller used sarcasm and

seriocomic ponderousness to produce yet another sort of topsy-turvy *Verfremdungseffekt* – one compatible with both logical thinking and surrealist manifestations of the marvelous. This time, however, part of his game was to build a trap for himself in order to walk into it, violating the Brechtian supremacy of reason and dialectics so that others could watch those factors rein him in anyway as he indulged his interest in politics and exercised his fervently ratiocinative mind. A comment of Alfred Jarry's in the epigraph to *Ubu Enchaîné* (*Ubu Bound*) pinpoints the dilemma: "We shall not have succeeded in demolishing everything unless we demolish the ruins as well. But the only way I can see of doing that is to use them to put up a lot of fine, well-designed buildings."[9] *Hamletmachine*'s point of departure is recognition of this quintessential avant-gardist impasse.

The first section, entitled "FAMILY ALBUM," begins: "I was Hamlet. I stood on the coast and talked with the surf BLABLA, at my back the ruins of Europe." [6/89]. Since no speaker is indicated, the identity of the "I" is an active question even before the memories give meaning to the section title. Situated in an apocalyptic future, the speaker implies he has renounced a family tradition and will recount his process of renunciation as if flipping through an album. What family? Which tradition? The Hamlet reference (as well as the self-quote from Müller's Artaud essay – "Read on the ruins of Europe [his texts] will be classic" [13/169]) suggests, with Nietzschean boldness, that all of European culture is in question (as it is in *Anatomy of Titus* and most of Müller's other works from this point on).

The "I" who was Hamlet continues with a dreamlike, past-tense narrative about his father's state funeral – an overtly provocative passage that presents sensitive political content in a surrealistic setting. (Müller said the scene was inspired by the case of Laszlo Rajk, a Hungarian foreign minister executed for treason in 1952 and, four years later, rehabilitated and given a state funeral.) Goosestepping councillors and "murderer and widow a couple" attend the procession for this "important cadaver" and "GREAT GIVER OF ALMS." Suddenly Hamlet pries open the coffin with his sword, which breaks, and uses "the dull remnant" to dispense pieces of the corpse, alms-like, to the crowd. Thus figuratively emasculated while attempting to nourish the masses with his "dead procreator['s]" remains, he joins in his own humiliation by shouting "SHOULD I HELP YOU UP UNCLE OPEN YOUR LEGS MAMA" as the murderer mounts the widow atop the empty coffin [6/89]. When the tense changes to the present and the "I" speaks insolently to the Ghost, everything preceding reads as background to his rebellion against Hamlet's traditional role as revenger: "What do you want from me. . . Old mooch. As if you have no blood on your shoes. What's your corpse to me" [90].

This rebellion immediately raises a question, however. Since Shakespeare's Hamlet is not a straightforward revenger but a hesitant revenger, how has the speaker truly departed from tradition? Like many other sons in Müller, the "I" has trouble breaking free from a paternal heritage that supports a violent status quo socio-political structure. Later parts of the text will suggest that Hamlet's father generally represents history seen as drama, history viewed as coercive because it organizes events teleologically like a dramatic script. (Indeed, the father and uncle are eventually fused as "Claudius/ Hamlet's Father," rendering the question of legitimacy irrelevant.) Escaping the mental hold of such scripts is far more difficult than simply perceiving their coerciveness, and Müller's Hamlet, like Nietzsche's, is disgusted by his inanition in the face of understanding.

> The truth once seen, man [Hamlet] is aware everywhere of the
> ghastly absurdity of existence, comprehends the symbolism of
> Ophelia's fate and the wisdom of the wood sprite Silenus:
> nausea invades him.   (Nietzsche)[10]

> I am
> A privileged man My nausea
> Is a privilege
> Guarded with Wall
> Barbed wire Prison   [96] (Müller's Hamlet Actor)

Unlike Nietzsche's Hamlet, however, Müller's responds to his condition, at least at first, by making perverse intellectual jokes. His humor is less subtle than that of Shakespeare's Hamlet, or that of the passage's other self-mocking ghost-figure, Antoine Roquentin in Sartre's *La Nausée* (*Nausea*) – a disenchanted historian. This Hamlet's jokes are typified by his self-designation "SECOND CLOWN IN THE

COMMUNIST SPRINGTIME" [89] and by the following lines which mix Nietzsche's grave wisdom of Silenus ("Ephemeral wretch. . . What would be best for you is . . . not to have been born, not to *be*, to be *nothing*")[11] with Hamlet's regret in Shakespeare ("The time is out of joint; – O cursed spite, / That ever I was born to set it right!" [I.v.189–90]), reducing all to a series of asinine quips.

> Here comes the ghost that made me, axe still in his skull. You
> can keep your hat on, I know you have one hole too many. I
> wish my mother had had one too few when you were in flesh: I
> would've been spared myself. They should sew the women up,
> a world without mothers.   [90]

This humor may not win the "I" sympathy or affection, but it does cast doubt on the literal meaning of everything he has said or will say. Perhaps, for instance, he is not remembering in an apocalyptic future at all, but rather imagining that circumstance of remembering at a desk in East Germany – his impulses toward political rebellion channeled into self-aggrandizing literary conceits for the umpteenth time.

Müller's "I," like Hamlet, is every inch a theater man, indeed he is later called "Hamlet Actor," and section one ends with a pointedly theatrical scenario whose first words are "Enter Horatio," not italicized as a stage direction. Here the Hamlet Actor plays author-director. Horatio, his "confidant," is told there is "NO PLACE FOR YOU IN MY TRAGEDY" and asked if he'd like to play Polonius, "who wants to sleep with his daughter" [90]. Then the scenario ends with a first-person narration of Hamlet raping his mother: "Now I tear the wedding dress. Now you must scream. Now I smear the shreds of your wedding dress with the earth that my father has become" [91]. A violent, resolute departure from the canonical *Hamlet*, it would seem, except that it is hypothetical, imaginary, a virtual rebellion carried out with mental puppets. Even the closing line – "let me eat your heart, Ophelia, which cries my tears" – is an envious allusion to the decidedly *un*hesitant overturning of social order in another play, John Ford's *'Tis Pity She's a Whore*.

According to some commentators,[12] serious determination enters *Hamletmachine* with Ophelia in the next section, whose title, "THE EUROPE OF WOMEN," indicates that the European family tradition ostensibly challenged in section one will now be viewed by females. (Müller, citing similar sentiments by Lenin and others, did say, a bit unenthusiastically, that women were a more likely source of historical renewal than men: "movement [toward revolution] begins in the provinces, and woman is the province of man" [0/295][13]). A quasi-historical locale is given, *"Enormous Room"* – the title of e.e. cummings' novel about a French interrogation center during World War I – and then Ophelia, or rather a composite figure called "Ophelia [Chorus/Hamlet]," delivers the following speech, which at first glance does seem to indicate a rebellion more absolute and unflinchingly violent than Hamlet's.

> I am Ophelia. The one the river didn't hold. The woman on the rope The woman with the arteries slit open The woman with the overdose SNOW ON THE LIPS The woman with her head in the gas oven. Yesterday I stopped killing myself. I am alone with my breasts my thighs my womb. I demolish the tools of my imprisonment the chair the table the bed. I destroy the battlefield that was my home. I wrench open the doors so that the wind can come in and the scream of the world. I shatter the window. With my bloody hands I tear up the photographs of the men whom I loved and who used me on the bed on the table on the chair on the ground. I set fire to my prison. I throw my clothes on the fire. I dig the clock that was my heart out of my breast. I go into the street clothed in my blood.   [91–2]

Still, it is important not to make too much of this speech's apparent coherence and straightforwardness. For one thing, it is no less stuffed with quotations than section one is: "The one the river didn't hold," besides its immediate application to Shakespeare's Ophelia, is a reference to Rosa Luxemburg from *Germania Death in Berlin* [5/78] with echoes of T. S. Eliot's *The Waste Land* ("Fear death by water. . ."), and the lines beginning "The woman on the rope" are allusions to Ulrike Meinhof and Inge Müller from *Gundling's Life. . .* [7/34] and *Todesanzeige* [*Obituary*, 5/32] – all three extremely problematic cases of victimization, the speech's unifying idea. For another thing, the *Lehrstück*-style designation "Ophelia [Chorus/Hamlet]" suggests that Hamlet and Ophelia may be opposing aspects of a single creative consciousness, game pieces or soldiers in a mental *Schlacht-feld*. In any case, clear-cut generalizations about the female rebellion are hard to make after Ophelia willingly reenters a coffin, naked, with Claudius/Hamlet's Father in section three and Marx, Lenin, and Mao appear as naked women in section four.

Ophelia and the Hamlet Actor are certainly bearers of clearly opposed attitudes and themes, but they are also victims of a common identity crisis and are allies in a common project to dismantle the representational frame of that crisis. That is why Artaud is such an important shadow figure in the text. Gestures like Ophelia's tearing of the "photographs of the men whom I loved" and the similar "tearing of the photograph of the author" in section four suggest that iconography, representation itself, is under attack as much as any male- or author-principle. Jacques Derrida writes:

> The theater of cruelty is not a *representation*. It is life itself, in the extent to which life is unrepresentable. . . Like Nietzsche. . . Artaud wants to have done with the *imitative* concept of art, with the Aristotelean aesthetics in which the metaphysics of Western art comes into its own.[14]

Ophelia's extraction of the clock, which has been seen as a symbol (traceable to Walter Benjamin) of the age of bourgeois productivity, may also be read in this context as a critique of time – time as a "frame" for reality, time seen teleologically as an agent of change and redemption that never arrive.

This point about the theater of cruelty must not be overstated because, as already mentioned, Müller is only half serious about it. That theater is the board, however, on which his Hamlet-game is played out. If Ophelia and Hamlet are not viewed as agents of therapeutic destruction and painful psychic healing in an Artaudian spirit, it is difficult to see how they differ significantly from the author-surrogates of unapologetically romantic forms such as closet drama and monodrama – and one obvious purpose of *Hamletmachine* is to resist precisely that sort of unquestioned egocentricity. The text's interruptive majuscule verse quotations, for instance, often seem to search outside the characters for some "irreversible and absolute determination" (Artaud)[15] prior to their fictional contexts:

"I'M GOOD HAMLET GI'ME A *CAUSE FOR GRIEF* / AH THE WHOLE GLOBE FOR *A REAL SORROW*" [89 – my italics]. That this search is doomed to failure, if only because the speaker (whoever he or she is) never breaks free from quotations, is beside the point. Quoting Andy Warhol, the Hamlet Actor later longs for a surrender to mechanized coldness – "I want to be a machine" [96] – but his wish is tinged with regret, as if another part of him longed for warm human contact. (The shamanic "warming" figure of Joseph Beuys, an artist Müller admired, comes to mind. One of Beuys' last pieces, *The End of the Twentieth Century* (1983–5), was an attempt, in Donald Kuspit's words, "to 'wrap' Andy Warhol in his warmth, which failed, because Warhol was irremediably cold – frozen, a black hole of nothingness in which everything disappeared."[16])

The Artaudian obsessions, as well as the equivocation about them, continue in section three, entitled "SCHERZO," with a different focus. Consisting almost entirely of stage directions, this brief section emphasizes visual and gestural languages over spoken language. (Recall Shakespeare's Hamlet's rumination on "words, words, words," as well as his self-castigating curse: "Why, what an ass am I! This is most brave, / That I . . . Must, like a whore, unpack my heart with words" [II.ii.611–14]). Notwithstanding Derrida's point about Artaud's resistance to representation in general, both Artaud and Müller express a preference for one representative mode over another, a compromise with mimesis that each justifies as the lesser of two evils. Adoption of an iconography that might undermine the dominion of words (logos, the patriarchal order) is preferable to continued acceptance of it or the total relinquishing of communication. And this new visual emphasis develops the sexual and political themes of *Hamletmachine*'s previous sections.

> *University of the dead. Whispering and muttering. From their gravestones (front desks) the dead philosophers throw their books at Hamlet. Gallery (ballet) of the dead women. The woman on the rope The woman with the arteries slit open etc. Hamlet regards them with the attitude of a museum (theater)-goer. The dead women tear his clothes off his body. From an upright coffin with the inscription HAMLET I step Claudius*

and Ophelia, dressed and made up as a whore. Striptease by
Ophelia.
OPHELIA: Do you want to eat my heart, Hamlet? *Laughs.*
HAMLET: *Face in his hands.* I want to be a woman.
Hamlet puts on Ophelia's clothes; Ophelia makes his face up
as a whore. . .   [92]

The throwing of books reduces classical education – a trope for the Enlightenment – to crude violence, and the riches of culture are presented as objectified females (the victims from section two) who demonstrate the beginnings of active agency when they strip Hamlet. (Recall Ophelia: "I shatter the window.") He, for his part, envies the women their object status, having apparently become overburdened with his intense subjectivity. Again, Müller is setting us up to believe that a new, matriarchal order of pictorial dominance is about to be born. Indeed, the described pictures are intensely compelling from the section's closing image (the breast cancer on a Madonna swinging overhead "radiates like the sun" – an allusion to Artaud's *Jet de sang* [*Spurt of Blood*]) to the final tableau in which a wheelchair-bound Ophelia, in the deep sea, is silenced by men wrapping her in gauze. But neither that snuffing nor the Hamlet Actor's malignant remark in section four that his "thoughts suck the blood out of the pictures" [93] suggests a sanguine future for the new order.

The opposing forces are, again, at an impasse, and only in section four, entitled "PLAGUE [*PEST*] IN BUDA BATTLE FOR GREEN-LAND," do we get a sense of Müller's point in asserting and reasserting this. To be sure, this section has just as many false limbs, calculated diversions and cul-de-sacs as any other. It presents a long scenario of rebellion by the Hamlet Actor, for instance ("I am not Hamlet. I'm not playing a role anymore" [93]), filled out with numerous specific time and place references (to 1956 Hungary and other pivotal moments in Communist history), but this rebellion turns out to be just as ambivalent, hypothetical, and ultimately futile as the one in section one. "My place, if my drama still took place, would be on both sides of the front," he says, adding later, "My drama didn't take place" [94–5].

The crucial distinction from the previous sections is in the introduction of a voice that claims to be the speaker-behind-the-other-speakers – the *real* author, the *real* Marxist intellectual after Stalin, in a realistic quandary – which sharpens the play's emotional hook.

> I stand in the sweaty smell of the crowd and throw rocks at policemen soldiers tanks bullet-proof glass. I look through the bullet-proof-glass folding door at the pressing crowd and smell my own nervous sweat.   [94]

Müller clearly has no more faith in the coherence or stability of this identity than he does in those of Hamlet, Ophelia, or any other character, but this ostensibly new central speaker does suffer from a deepened disgust and self-scrutiny that change the quality of the language. The borrowed stylistic conceits are replaced by simple, flat-footed moaning for a time ("I don't want to eat drink breathe love a woman anymore a man a child an animal'" [96]) and the infernal joking ceases as the voice works itself up to a frenzy of self-loathing (itself another crude reflection of Shakespeare, whose Hamlet delivers several self-loathing soliloquies).

> *Tearing of the photograph of the author.*
> I tear open my sealed flesh. I want to live in my veins, in the marrow of my bones, in the labyrinth of my skull. I withdraw into my entrails. I take my place in my shit, my blood. Somewhere bodies are crushed so that I can live in my shit. Somewhere bodies are dissected so that I can be alone with my blood. My thoughts are wounds in my brain. My brain is a scar.   [96]

One needn't deny any of the calculatedness of this passage – Müller is punning and quoting as much as ever (the German word for marrow [*Mark*], for instance, also means Deutschmark and trademark, and Benjamin said that all cultural artifacts are documents of barbarism) – to argue that it is the source of whatever grudging sincerity *Hamletmachine* possesses. Like Artaud conducting his Gnostic searches "within" in his prose-poems and theater scenarios, Müller sets up a polarized mental space in which mind and body are realms of good and evil, and the speaker is understood to be pridefully passing through a period of degradation and humiliation on the way to redemption and transcendence of the corporeal. His humiliation is a result of his inward gaze: he realizes, for instance, that his crusade against received culture has rejoined him with his patrimony. His ravenous reading and incessant wielding of references have made him into a new kind of master author whose identity is a pastiche of other identities (again a reminder of the disgust of Sartre's Roquentin upon discovering the "Self-Taught Man" reading alphabetically through the town library). His pride comes from his deeper knowledge (*gnosis*) that he is nevertheless on a path to eventual salvation, his descent into (postmodern) baseness preparatory and purgative – and that is really the unusual point for Müller.

Susan Sontag writes, with Artaud in mind:

> The self, or spirit, discovers itself in the break with "the world"
> . . . only when morality has been deliberately flouted is the
> individual capable of a radical transformation: entering into a
> state of grace that leaves all moral categories behind. . .
> someone who is saved is beyond good and evil. Founded on an
> exacerbation of dualisms (body–mind, matter–spirit, evil–good,
> dark–light), Gnosticism promises the abolition of all
> dualisms.[17]

Beyond good and evil. Like Sontag, Müller wants us to hear a Nietzschean echo, but only an echo ("For thine is the nothingness Nausea" [95]). Though he seldom admitted it, he dreamed of a "transvaluation of values" as much as Artaud – recall his ideal Shakespearean theater beyond "the drapery, the costume of ideas," for instance. Still, it is crucial to the peculiar tightrope dance of *Hamletmachine* that this dream be suppressed. Müller's speaker must yearn for a redemptive future but never describe or name it. He must register sincerity without specific desire, suggest belief without an object of belief, continue to imagine communal rather than individual redemption (*Lehrstück*-as-grail), if he is to keep his drama from "taking place," keep it from backsliding into what Derrida called "the theological stage."

> The theatrical practice of cruelty, in its action and structure,
> inhabits or rather *produces* a nontheological space . . .

> The stage is theological for as long as its structure,
> following the entirety of tradition, comports the following
> elements: an author-creator who, absent and from afar, is armed
> with a text and keeps watch over, assembles, regulates the time
> or the meaning of representation, letting this latter *represent*
> him as concerns what is called the content of his thoughts, his
> intentions, his ideas.[18]

As much as anything else, it is the fear of becoming an unambiguously privileged speaker like this "author-creator" that makes the Hamlet Actor step into the father's armor and take up his parade of masks again at the end of section four. At least his father is a ghost, a role, which many fear but no one really believes in.

The final words of section four are *"Ice age"* – the title of Tankred Dorst's 1973 play about Knut Hamsun, a Nobel Prize-winning author and unregenerate Nazi – and section five restores the humor and savoir faire of the previous pastiche, even as it implies that the real, effectual revolution must enter suspended animation for an eon or so. It begins with a capitalized quote from Friedrich Hölderlin, an author who was diagnosed as insane (like Artaud, Nietzsche, Hamsun, Hamlet, and Ophelia) and spent the last thirty-six years of his life in a tower, playing piano and flute, reading classics, and occasionally composing inconsequential verse:[19]

FEROCIOUSLY POISED / IN THE AWFUL ARMOR /
THROUGH MILLENIA
*Deep sea. Ophelia in a wheelchair. Fish wreckage corpses and
pieces of corpses drift by.*   [97]

Müller used "ice age" as a figure for Capitalism in *The Construction Site* [1/134]; here it indicates the return of a mythic space of permanent horror. Myth rushes in to fill the vacuum that the vacation of history has created. The speaker is timelessly both a traitor (the quotes contain references to Judas and the betrayal of the 1919 Spartacus uprising) and a dormant germ in the body politic, a female fifth column waiting silently for an advantageous moment to attack the patriarchy from within. During the "ice age," such "nontheological" resistance can appear in the world only as terror: "When she walks through your bedrooms with butcher knives you'll know the truth," is the last line, a quote from a Manson gang member.

In 1979 an interesting attack on Müller appeared in the West German journal *Literatur Konkret* that illuminates his uses of Artaud. "Heiner Müller's 'Endgames,'" by Michael Schneider, was partly an ill-considered attempt to update and dignify Harich's East German denunciation from six years earlier, discussed in the previous chapter. Citing *Hamletmachine* (as well as *Germania Death in Berlin* and *Gundling's Life. . .*) as certain evidence that the author himself was "in crisis," Schneider complained that he had "given up for good" the "position of Enlightener" and become preoccupied instead with "distorted, desperate hate-hymns to history."[20] This argument bears repeating today even more than Harich's because it stems from a misunderstanding still common among Müller's public. Schneider missed the essential point that Müller was not truly ill, not actually suffering anything like Artaud's "central collapse of the soul."[21] If he were, he would not have been able to maintain such strict control over *Hamletmachine*'s balancing act, carefully ensuring that every last hint of true conviction was specifically contradicted. His relationship to Artaud was tactical; he borrowed a complexion of authentic pathology to lure us into a diabolical literary-historical funhouse where he could administer his own version of cruelty: enforcing a "lidless stare" [9/227] at the grinding wheels of history and culture, art as "a thorn in the eye" [13/103].[22]

What Schneider did understand well was Müller's general avant-gardist ambition to resist marketing and easy assimilation by bourgeois theatrical institutions. He saw that *Hamletmachine*'s obdurately unconventional form was an attempt to create something undomesticable, but he thought that it failed.

> Where history is portrayed only in connection with universal terror and oppression . . . and where no possibility of radical action exists anymore, resignation is the only outcome, and even the spectator who once thought of himself as an active opponent of the prevailing circumstances has no choice but to sit there motionless, in masochistic enjoyment of his powerlessness in the face of history.[23]

6.   Heiner Müller's production of *Hamlet/Machine*, his own translation of Shakespeare's *Hamlet* combined with *Hamletmachine*, at the Deutsches Theater, East Berlin, 1990.

Conceding that *Hamletmachine* might have had some limited value in the East, which was "overfed for so long with 'positive heroes,'" Schneider pointed out that it was played and published only in the West, where its "historical-philosophical despair. . . fit wonderfully with the fashionable pessimism and coquettish nihilism."[24] Müller was transformed "with one blow into a star dramatist."[25] This point has validity. Written as an anti-masterpiece, the work won a place as a modern classic even before it was produced. How one reacts to that cooptation, however, depends on how "hard-line" one wishes to be in the push toward revolutionary upheaval in the traditional (bourgeois) theater.

Müller, for one, said he was repulsed by the coopting process, which he called "being taken into custody" (*Dingfestmachung* [14/ 56]). Reacting to the "fetishization" of the work's structural peculiarities (particularly the predominance of monologue), he deliberately set out in his next plays, *The Mission* and *Quartet*, to avoid "police identification" by reshuffling his technical "battle forms." [14/56–7]. These efforts notwithstanding, *Hamletmachine* was more provocative and challenging when it first appeared than its hasty canonization implies.

For instance, Theo Girshausen's book *The Hamletmachine: Heiner Müller's Endgame* contains copious documentation of a Cologne theater's cancellation of the world premiere two weeks before its scheduled opening in 1978. "*Hamletmachine* placed demands on a 'normally' functioning state theater that pushed its capacity for freedom and facilities to the limits," writes Girshausen.[26] The actors bickered among themselves and with the director (Volker Geissler) over conceptual points such as the reason for producing the play in the first place and the division of the group into a chorus and two protagonists (Hamlet and Ophelia); and the director clashed with theater administrators over his insistence that "it would contradict the intention of the text to direct it in an authoritarian manner" and over his seeming indifference to delivering a "finished" production by a set date.[27] Even when the work did reach the German stage in Essen the following year, it was anything but snug in its institutional context; according to one report, the final tableau was so frightening that some spectators rushed onto the stage to free Ophelia from her gauze bandages.[28]

More to the point, though, any director who understands *Hamletmachine*'s tactical use of Artaud will not necessarily wrap Ophelia in gauze bandages or follow any of the work's other stage directions for that matter. (Here again, Müller pushes a Brechtian idea – *mises-en-scène* that collide and contrast critically with playtexts – to an Artaudian extreme.) Müller disregarded almost all his own stage directions on the several occasions he directed *Hamletmachine*, as did Robert Wilson in his famous 1986 production in New York, London, and Hamburg. Remarkably, Wilson's staging was almost completely uncontingent on the play.

"I do not understand the text," said Wilson at a press confer-
ence during his Hamburg rehearsals.[29] Indeed, he did no research or
textual interpretation, as directors usually do, to identify or highlight
subtexts and themes, apart from a chat with the author he described
as follows.

> I came to Berlin to see Heiner before I went to New York and
> asked him whether he could say something to me about it. He
> said, "No, do it however you want." "Help me out just a little."
> (*laughs*) He said: "It shouldn't be longer than fifty minutes." I
> said, "Okay." Then I went to New York, worked for ten days –
> I had only three weeks – and brought all the action and
> movements onto the stage without thinking about the text
> and then laid the text over the movements and then began to
> fit the movements to the text.[30]

Affixing the text to a preconceived scenic structure was Wilson's way
of gambling that chance and his subrational understanding of the
work would create conjunctions between his aims and Müller's:
"usually you begin with a text and then think over which gestures to
take with it, but that way you usually fall into a trap."[31] The gamble
paid off, as it did in many similarly chance-based collaborations
between Merce Cunningham and John Cage. Wilson's scenic structure
– rotating the set a quarter turn after each section and repeating the
same action sequence with slight variations after each rotation – was
magnificently double-edged: fundamental changelessness given a
semblance of variety and progress through shifting perspectives. Juxtaposed with the Müller text, this quasi-mechanical repetition became a
picturization of time, history, and all the other teleological demons
associated with the Hamlet Actor's "drama."

It was the stillness of Wilson's production, broken only by
desultory sound effects (a distant animal howl, a simple piano phrase,
a machine-gun blast) and Müller's aggressive words, that so sharpened
its sense of entrapment by something immense and grinding yet
invisible. Faced with Wilson's disturbingly composed figures and his
obvious indifference to illustrating or even acknowledging the text's
content – the tearing of Müller's photo was the only prescribed image
that actually appeared – the spectator worked all the harder to find

7. Robert Wilson's production of *Hamletmachine* at New York University, 1986.

points of convergence. Who were these figures, one continually won-
dered, these identically dressed women who simultaneously scratched
their nails on a thin table, this hopscotching man in boxer shorts, this
man in jeans who kept dropping a book, and were they agents or
victims of the dramatic and historical processes, objects or subjects?

Wilson said: "You have these 18–19-year-old acting students
[the production was first done at New York University], they know
nothing about the context in which the play was written. . . And I
explained nothing about it, I said only: 'Speak these lines simply,
these slowly, these quickly,' and so on. They don't know what they're
saying, and that's exactly what you want."[32] Müller, for his part,
admired the openness and "sensuousness" of the staging, especially
Wilson's handling of text "like a body" – the way the choreography
was rehearsed for a week in silence, then "layered over" with words so
that "you still hear the silence that lies underneath" [15/41, 43]. One
could view the project as a delayed consummation of his principle of
theatrical "resistance," which he first described in 1975:

> When I write a play and I'm in doubt about which stage
> direction I should write for it, whether someone ought to walk
> on his hands or stand on his head or on all fours, then I know
> . . . that something's not right with the text. As long as the text
> is right, that's not interesting for me; it's a matter for the
> theater or the director. . . I believe fundamentally that
> literature is there to pose resistance to the theater.
>
> [14/17–18]

Perhaps the profoundest aspect of the production, however,
was the way it clarified and underscored Müller's true position on
authorly disappearance, and the relationship between that disappearance and his brand of literary "resistance."[33] Although Wilson disregarded the text when composing his stage pictures, he also left
Hamletmachine thoroughly intact, to the last line and stage direction.
(These latter were spoken by actors or, in the case of section three,
which was filmed, rolled across a screen like news flashes.) The text,
in other words, was simultaneously obliterated and preserved as a
monument – like the images in it of Stalin, Mao, Lenin, Marx, and like
Hamlet, the Hamlet Actor and his drama. Absolute text, sheltered and

preserved by the theater of images and its preference for absolute textlessness: the arrangement was based on the most venerable political gambit in art, the jester's gambit, maximum integrity at the price of zero authority.

7 Müller as Genet: *The Mission*

If Müller mentally transformed Artaud into something of a degraded Vergil who guided him through the purgatory of his own extreme theatrical ambitions, this was not, as discussed, a journey to which he dedicated his entire soul. Another part of him knew he would continue making practicable theater even as he stuffed the text of *Hamletmachine* with quotes from mad and otherwise incapacitated artists, and even as he watched impassively while the Cologne Schauspiel abandoned the work in frustration. This more earthbound Müller, who conceived wry rather than lethally serious theatrical ceremonies, who saw the theater's intrinsic sham, fakery, and pretense as ideal tools, sublimely diabolical traps for spectators, required other allies and guides. Among the most important of these others was Jean Genet – the only alter ego who ever provided him with a practical and affirmative channel (or a perfect alibi) for the unmaskable strain of insincerity in his avant-gardist work.

Müller always spoke of Genet, as of Kleist, with conspicuous warmth, and this was not merely due to his elective affinity with social outcasts. Müller was not a professional thief, a homosexual, a prostitute, or a convict, but he nevertheless felt that he and Genet made art for similar reasons, candidly declaring their "pleasure in catastrophes" [14/57] and building what might be called a negative aesthetics based as much on their repulsions as their attractions. Embracing the raw seductive power of evil for rhetorical effect (as opposed to Artaud's cathartic effect) was axiomatic for both. In an unhealthy world, "art may be a sickness . . . but it is the sickness with which we live," said Müller in 1980, with Genet in mind: "We have to live with this sickness and the paradox that we're parasites in the world as we exploit it" [14/57].

Sartre wrote that Genet was a "dreamer" who wanted to "contaminate" others with his dream, "make them fall into it" so that it acted on them "like a virus,"[1] and this was precisely Müller's attitude toward theater in the late 1970s and 1980s – that its only chance was to work by stealth, at least in the West. Asked by a 1983 interviewer, for instance, to explain his suggestion that the first part of *Verkommenes Ufer Medeamaterial Landschaft mit Argonauten* (*Despoiled Shore Medeamaterial Landscape with Argonauts* [7/91–101]) be performed during a peep-show (peep-shows did not exist in the GDR), Müller answered that it had to do with overcoming the "touristic" and "voyeuristic" attitude of West Germans, "the view from secure affluence down at the misery of the world," that had ensured "a superficial reception of my recent plays" [14/134]. Another aspect of this stealth-strategy was the deliberate violation of taboos; the man who blithely called Hitler and Stalin geniuses, and authored two plays (*Germania Death in Berlin* and *Germania 3*) in which Hitler appeared as an object of kitschy fantasy, was bound to be attracted by the proudly abject Frenchman who used Hitler as an object of sexual fantasy (in *Pompes funèbres* [*Funeral Rites*] and elsewhere) and breathed deep of the resulting hypocritical indignation among those who had flattered themselves that they were his partisans.

Both Müller and Genet thought symbols were stronger when built on facts, as in these uses of Hitler, yet neither felt any responsibility to historical facts per se. Indeed, what is most interesting about their connection is that both were so thoroughly committed to the idea of multiple or split selves, cultivating parts of themselves as Other or Others, that they never felt bound to maintain consistent viewpoints or smooth over their texts' jagged formal, tonal, or stylistic edges. And oddly enough, this ostensible naturalness, this readiness to accept the contradictions of self, is the immediate source of the air of calculation, of non-spontaneity, that surrounds their writing. For different reasons, insincerity became a dramatic strategy for both, a means of communicating their linked themes of betrayal and death. An art of deliberate insincerity makes betrayal a figure for life, with the effect of conflating life and death.

"Thanks for your / Betrayal which gives me back my eyes," says Müller's Medea to a disgustingly mercantile Jason in *Medeamaterial* ("I gave you two sons for one brother") [7/94–5]. "What you don't betray today will kill you tomorrow" [7/66], says Debuisson in *The Mission*, a bourgeois revolutionary who has just appeared as a powerless actor in a "theater of revolution." Betrayal and death are equally inevitable in a "prehistorical" world in which the rule of private property leaves the human being morally stillborn. The self cannot help but betray the Other, but in Müller and Genet where the Other *is* the self, betrayal also has a peculiar double edge: it becomes a circular game of dramatic masks, designed not to affect but rather "infect" spectators with its insincerity and with seductive images of moral opportunism. The goal? Müller in 1983: "Genet formulated it very precisely and correctly: the only thing an artwork can do is awaken yearning for another world-condition. And this yearning is revolutionary" [14/133]. I will come back to this point.

Genet was of more practical use to Müller than Artaud or the surrealists because of his formidable array of easily appropriable theatrical strategies based on disguises. Genet's role-exchanges, his insistence on truth-through-falseness (e.g. young boys as maids, revolutionary Arabs blowing on cartoon flames), his interpenetrating time-frames with the dead walking among the living, his pariah characters who have no normal or "default" existences beneath their acting rituals and repertoires of fantasy, all injected a host of fresh ideas into Müller's *Lehrstück* meditations. Each of his later plays (i.e. those from 1971 on) seem to me imbued with a consciousness of Genet's achievements – consider only the cross-gender playacting in *Gundling's Life . . .* and *Hamletmachine* – with the most flagrant examples being *The Mission* and *Quartet*. The latter play (including Müller's 1994 production of it, practically a homage to Genet) is the focus of chapter 10; but the former is really the more interesting case of Genet-*Kopien*, since it appropriates the structure of one particular Genet work.

Andrzej Wirth once called *The Mission* "an impossible collage at which only Heiner Müller could succeed," noting its explicit use of Brecht, Büchner, Kafka, Beckett, Marcuse, Reich, Artaud, and Genet, as well as earlier Müller texts.[2] Its complexity notwithstanding, though – and these are only some of its references – the foundation of the collage is, up to a point, a relatively straightforward imitation of *Les Nègres* (*The Blacks*). Subtitled *Erinnerung an eine Revolution* (*Memory of a Revolution*), Müller's play, like Genet's, is about theater as a distraction from, or substitute for, revolution, and hence it is about the betrayal of revolution as theater. And its main action involves the reenactment – the recollection through imperfect memory – of certain insurrectional events as a morbid *clownerie* (Genet's subtitle) for a gallery understood to consist of revolutionaries (blacks in Genet) wearing masks of oppressive authority – these parallels all becoming apparent not until the second scene.

The basic circumstance of *The Mission*, taken from Anna Seghers' story "The Light on the Gallows,"[3] involves three emissaries from the National Convention in revolutionary France sent to colonial Jamaica to foment a rebellion of slaves against the British Crown. Unlike the agitators in *The Measures Taken*, whom they clearly recall, Müller's characters neither succeed in their agitating nor, in failing, do they confront the old Party-minded question of *Einverständnis*, as in *Mauser*. Instead, their mission – the title "*Auftrag*," which also means task, assignment, and mandate, was a longstanding fetish for Müller, similar to "*Arbeit*" and "*Produktion*" – is annulled by the events of the 18th Brumaire, which left Napoleon in charge of the French government. The play bears approximately the same relation to the French Revolution and its aftermath as Genet's *The Screens* does to the Algerian War: it focuses on the mythic legacy of individual betrayals brought on by France's massive institutional betrayal. But the psychological landscape is recognizably Frantz Fanon's (whom Müller was also reading and paraphrasing around this time), with colonial domination seen as both a perversion and coercion to perversion, and with the French Revolution regarded as a paradigm, the more or less clearly perceived model, alas, for all subsequent revolutions.

The text opens with a letter, unassigned to a speaker, from one of the agitators to his former superior.

Galloudec to Antoine. I'm writing this letter on my deathbed. I'm writing in my name and in the name of Citizen Sasportas, who was hanged at Port Royal. I'm informing you that we must give you back the mission that the Convention assigned us through your person, since we couldn't fulfill it . . . From Debuisson you'll hear nothing more, he's well . . . traitors have a good time when peoples walk in blood.   [7/43]

The fate of all three emissaries – Galloudec, Sasportas, and Debuisson – is thus known from the outset, with the subsequent scene establishing that the letter was delivered by a sailor who had lain ill beside the dying Galloudec in a Cuban hospital. The bourgeois Antoine, in hiding and afraid of arrest and retribution, at first denies his identity to the sailor, thus betraying his dead colleagues once again, as Genia Schulz observes, in contrast to the commoner, who went to great risk and trouble to fulfill his mission of delivery.[4] Antoine is a veteran of the slaughter of monarchist peasants in the Vendée and soon is marked as a Danton-surrogate by quotations and paraphrases from Büchner. "Come to bed," says the woman he lives with at the end of the scene, for instance, the same line with which the troubled Danton exits to be comforted sexually by Julie in *Dantons Tod* (*Danton's Death*).

All this is a prelude to the main attraction of the *clownerie*, however. The shadow of Genet makes its appearance with an Angel of Despair, who speaks in the voice of the woman copulating with Antoine: "I am the knife with which the dead man forces open his coffin" [47]. From this point on the action is a flashback, a ritualistic memory narrated by a voice that may be dead – "We had arrived on Jamaica . . ." [47] – and lends the entire play the aura of a requiem or memorial service. (Recall that a catafalque is center-stage in *The Blacks*.) The three emissaries assume masks to perform their revolutionary drama (in the same way Genet's blacks assume masks to reenact the ritual murder of a white woman), with Debuisson doing double duty as a "whipping" director like Genet's character Archibald, correcting his colleagues when they become unruly: "You've acted twice out of character, Galloudec" [49]. Archibald: "Be careful, Village, don't start referring to your real life."[5] Also as in Genet, Müller's actors bicker over their roles, since Debuisson more or less plays himself, a physician and son of a colonial landowner returned home after supposedly being disgusted by the bloody revolution, whereas Galloudec plays his peasant-servant from Brittany and the black Sasportas plays his slave, ostensibly a refugee from the successful slave revolution in Haiti.

> GALLOUDEC: I know that you're playing the hardest role. It's written on your body.
> SASPORTAS: With the whips that will write a new alphabet on other bodies in our handwriting.   [49]

The most important alteration of Genet's basic circumstance is in the use of revolutionary "actors" from different social classes – not all blacks but rather one black and two ideological allies of his, one permanent (Galloudec), one all too temporary (Debuisson). The specter of black–black betrayal in *The Blacks*, communicated through an offstage trial and execution, is thus replaced with the far less subversive spectacle of republican–republican betrayal in *The Mission*, with the Fanonesque black rage of Sasportas lingering as a sort of unachievable utopian urge. Other unrealistic characters appear, such as Debuisson's father and mother and a mythically infuriated woman named First Love, all of whom enact with him a scenario called "the return of the prodigal son" and establish a separate category of observers akin to both Genet's Court (blacks in the white masks of Queen, Governor, Missionary, Judge, and Valet) and Peter Weiss' asylum director Coulmier and his family in *Marat/Sade*.

As their scenario changes to "the theater of revolution," however, as the characters called "SasportasRobespierre" and "GalloudecDanton" trade crude insults and play clownishly with each other's false heads in the manner of Brecht's *Badener Lehrstück*, it becomes clear that observers and observed are not so easily distinguishable. A prop-throne, for instance, is occupied successively by First Love, Debuisson, and Sasportas, who, newly crowned, speaks with vulgar violence about the evils of white violence: "we sentence you to death, Victor Debuisson. The snakes should eat your shit, the crocodiles your ass, the piranhas your balls" [56]. Like Archibald in *The Blacks* ("You're becoming a specter before their very eyes and you're going to haunt them"[6]) and Müller's unnamed rememberer in

The Mission ("THE REVOLUTION IS THE MASK OF DEATH DEATH IS THE MASK OF THE REVOLUTION" [51]), Sasportas speaks of death as revolution's sacred enabler. Müller's audience is charmed and entertained by clichéd images of inhumanly bloody leftist rebellion as Genet's white Court and white audience are charmed and entertained by demonstrations of stereotypical black viciousness, cravenness, and ineptitude.

At this point, having brought each of their plays to the brink of pornography – that is, with their audiences primed to see either Debuisson murdered or the white woman seduced and murdered – both authors employ the same surprise tactic, a peculiar climax in the form of a long monologue on a seemingly peripheral topic that broadens each work's geopolitical base and that temporarily replaces remembrance and rehearsal with immediacy. This climax in Genet is Felicity's extended paean to Dahomey – "To my rescue, Negroes, all of you! . . . Tribes covered with gold and mud, rise up from my body, emerge!"[7] – which calls the entire African continent to rebellion with an inspiring, uplifting rhetoric that seems, for the moment, more heartfelt than everything before. In Müller it is the "Man in the Elevator" section, a 2,200-word narrative also written in unprecedented tones (mostly anxiety) about a man who, summoned to meet "the boss," becomes trapped or lost in a surrealistic elevator in which "something is not right . . . with time" [58]. He convinces himself that his boss has committed suicide, and the elevator deposits him on a village street in Peru where he encounters ominous mechanical men who ignore him ("aren't I even worth a knife or the stranglehold of metal hands" [61]), a beckoning woman he avoids because a voice tells him she is "THE WIFE OF A MAN" [62], and other sights that reinforce the sense he has of lacking a definite task, or *Auftrag*.

Its abundance of real-world details notwithstanding, this vision is quasi-Beckettian, modern man bereft of a clear mission. The implication is that revolution will never be more than a means of filling time, a "war of landscapes" [67] or equipotent viewpoints, for people like the man in the elevator and Debuisson who have nothing material to gain by it. But as in *Anatomy of Titus* (which also contains echoes of *The Blacks*), Müller goes on to marry this vision to an explicit advocacy of the Third World that would have made Genet uncomfortable. Debuisson, explaining his belief that Napoleon's ascent to power means that "the world will be what it was, a home for masters and slaves" [62], describes a portentous dream in which Asia and Africa rise up as colored snakes on a run-down New York street. Like Brecht's plan to adapt *Waiting for Godot* by projecting films of Third World revolutionary movements behind the languishing Didi and Gogo, this dream attempts to superimpose a distinct political position, a policy statement, on a field of meticulously framed ambiguities and open questions. As Genet always knew and Müller apparently forgot at times, such positions and statements are the concern of enfranchised speakers, not of disenfranchised ones whose relations with the "loathsome" white public are *perforce* theatrical and hence conducted with filched language.

Much more could (and indeed should) be said about *The Mission* from other points of view – my comments do not begin to exhaust this dizzyingly polysemic text – but reading it through the lens of Genet seems to me especially important because of the light it sheds on Müller's self-image as a *Neger*.[8] *The Mission* is an important reminder that, for all his youthful isolation and poverty, Müller learned socialist principles from a blood parent, was comfortable from a young age with High German, and never suffered anything like the sort of segregation and degradation that made literary production unthinkable for the young Genet and continues to do so for multitudes of real untouchables and foundlings of all colors. (Genet: "what exactly is a black? First of all, what's his color?"[9])

The endings of *The Blacks* and *The Mission*, which both deal with the relationship between betrayal and beauty, could be used to illustrate this point. Genet allows his characters Virtue and Village to fall in love and find each other beautiful in the final scene, even though his play has treated beauty and love as treasons against perfect blackness, because that final gesture constitutes a consummate betrayal of ostensible first principles: consistency has value to him only in relation to an utterly unwholesome ideal. Müller, for his part, makes do with a string of mildly shocking images about the erasure of memory in the mind of the traitor, which convey an unmistakable note of weary resignation and pose no challenge whatever to the dominant sado-masochistic language he shares with Debuisson: "her beauty hit Debuisson like an axe . . . Then Betrayal threw herself on him like a sky, the happiness of her labia a dawn" [70].

The most penetrating critique of Müller's would-be blackness that I have encountered was written, aptly, by a black author: the prominent Australian Aboriginal writer Mudrooroo (born Colin Johnson) who, in 1991, accepted an invitation to participate in a university-sponsored workshop on *The Mission*, translated as *The Commission* on that occasion. The project was originally the brain-child of a Sydney-based German professor named Gerhard Fischer, who became convinced around the bicentennial celebrations of the European arrival on the Australian continent (1788–1988) that Müller's play could be made to speak strongly to Aboriginal interests. The "campaign of extermination waged against a race perceived as uncivilized," observed Fischer, began within a year of the French Revolution that forms the background to Müller's play set on another colonial island, Jamaica.[10] The project soon took on its own life, and out of the Sydney workshop grew an original play by Mudrooroo with (like *Marat/Sade*) a sprawling title: *The Aboriginal Protesters Confront the Declaration of the Australian Republic on 26 January 2001 with the Production of "The Commission" by Heiner Müller.*

Mudrooroo's play, which deserves to be studied in its own right, offers an eloquent commentary on the real ability of a work like *The Mission* (i.e. any text written by a white attempting to appropriate black rage) to "awaken yearning for another world-condition" among those in whose name it ostensibly pleads (to quote again Müller's own remarks on Genet, cited above). Seeing the text after close study as "a circular essay on defeat,"[11] Mudrooroo had doubts about its ability to awaken such yearning even among whites, but he did not pursue that matter in the play. Instead he set out to "highjack" and "Aboriginal-ise" *The Mission*, as he explains in an accompanying essay:

> as it is a European play the Jamaicans are not given a voice, are only a backdrop to these three characters. Picturesque slaves who only exist, or as Galloudec exclaims: ". . . and all for this lazy mass of black flesh that won't move except when kicked by the boot . . .". Familiar, isn't it? But then Müller is really not interested in the blacks of Jamaica. He is, as an East German,

interested in the stagnation of defeat; whereas I, as an Aborigine, a Nyoongah, am interested in combating the stagnation of defeat . . .[12]

Himself a master of interpenetrating time-frames and dream-like scenarios involving contemporary politics (a "Western Australian counterpart" to Müller, wrote Fischer[13]), Mudrooroo added another layer to the text, placing Aboriginal actors in the foreground. The action is set not during the 1988 bicentennial, as Fischer suggested, but rather thirteen years later on the fictional date when Australia declares itself fully independent from Britain. A group of Aborigines, feeling excluded from white-Australia's plans for the new republic, as they always were from decision-making in the Australian dominion, gather to rehearse Müller's play as part of a protest scheduled for the following day. Mudrooroo maintains a light banter among them, which lends the play a humor that *The Mission* lacks (but *The Blacks* possesses), and they share their opinions about Müller's lines as they move slowly and without conviction through their paces. Maryanne, for example, a Medical Service worker who plays the woman who sleeps with Antoine, says: "What I don't like about this play . . . is that women in it are treated like fuck bags. How would you like it, if I wrote a play with you starring that thing between your legs."[14]

As Fischer observes, most of them are middle-class professionals doing the play in their spare time, not illiterate and impoverished outcasts, the usual depiction of Aborigines even in Black Australian theater.[15] As a consequence, they are articulate and self-confident enough to express an increasing distaste for the project, for reasons that both an Aborigine and a white audience would respect. The text grows more and more foreign and irrelevant to them, the political arguments for sticking with it less and less persuasive. Clint, a black academic, for instance, makes an appeal that points up *The Mission*'s innocuous mainstream status by the early 1990s: "we got a lot of support from Germany for Landrights. So perhaps we should see this play as being a gift in return for that support, that is if we ever get it right."[16] Finally, the strongest motivation for continuing with the play is dismissed – the idea that the international coverage by

German television that they would receive is indispensable – and they vote not to perform, after already having presented the entire play in lackluster rehearsal, of course. "We got better things to do,"[17] says the director, inciting the group to direct political action as the Djangara (spirits) who have been onstage all along erupt with music and dance. The final note from this real Third World voice is one of defiant celebration.

8 Müller as Wagner: *Germania Death in Berlin*

In 1993, Müller directed a production of *Tristan und Isolde* (*Tristan and Isolde*) at the shrine on "the green hill," the Bayreuther Fest-spielhaus, that attracted a cult following and was later revived several times. In his autobiography he called Richard Wagner "a dramatist of genius." Nevertheless, as with Artaud, he generally downplayed his connections with the grandfather of the avant-garde who wrote "The Artwork of the Future." "Wagner interested me first of all more through Nietzsche's glasses, which of course also mirror Nietzsche, the conflict between two transposed perpetrators. I am more a utilizer than a connoisseur of music," he added in *War without Battle* [341]. Like so much else Müller said, these comments are both true and false – true in that Nietzsche's influence on him was indeed significant and music really was of secondary importance in his work, but false in that he knew perfectly well that Wagner's ghost exerted far more influence on him than his remarks implied, particularly on the group of texts known as his "German plays."

The veiled commitment of these plays to a utopian theatrical vision – all are collage-works, which he called "synthetic fragments" – makes them an ideal vehicle to begin speaking about Müller's ambition to be an epoch-making man of the theater. But, further, the obsession with German history and myth alone in them would mark them as Wagnerian: *Germania Death in Berlin* (1956/71), *The Battle* (1951/74), *Gundling's Life. . .* (1977), and *Germania 3* (1995). In fact, Müller's earliest significant recognition abroad was as a representative or pan-German artist in the tradition of Goethe and Wagner, precisely because the period when he assembled and published most of these texts, the 1970s, coincided with his first wave of fame in the West and his return to steady theater work in the GDR after twelve years of sporadic bans. No matter that the plays themselves are not celebrations but rather minefields of provocations concerning Germania (the personification of the German *Volk* as an armor-clad woman). The texts were, for years, less frequently read and produced than discussed, and Western journalists hungry for catch-phrases played frequently on the nickname "Müller-Deutschland" (see his first interview with the French scholar Sylvère Lotringer [19/33] and the 1989 television film *Müller-Deutschland* by Karl Heinz Götze).

Anger at Müller's derisiveness regarding things German – as well as anger at the presumptuousness of anyone, much less an East German, aspiring to pan-Germanness while Germany was separated – appears in many reviews of these plays. GDR radio condemned *Gundling's Life. . .* as "monstrous tastelessness," for instance, and Michael Schneider (as already mentioned) complained of Müller's "distorted, desperate hate-hymns to history."[1] Speaking in a 1994 lecture of the GDR's practice of replacing the word "German" with "GDR" in public titles as "a sort of defiant reaction to the West Germans' habit of regarding themselves as the only true Germans and designating themselves accordingly," Christa Wolf said, "I don't think we attached much importance to the adjective *German*."[2] Not so Heiner Müller, who chose rather to feed this seemingly quenched fire and to use the steady stream of interviewers who approached him at the time to fan the flames; as he told one of them, "fame consists in misunderstandings" [14/127]. Friedrich Dieckmann waxes lyrical about his interview persona with an explicit reference to Goethe:

> the hermetic dramatist appeared to a bewildered public as
> Germany-Germany's interview artist. He who brought the
> unsayable of reality before the people in images for mute
> discussion in the theater, turned from a respondent of
> unflappable pithiness to the preceptor of Germania, converting
> even the most incompetent interlocutor into his Eckermann.[3]

As with many of his other alter egos, it is important not to overstress Müller's affinities with Wagner, but a few conspicuous connections were drawn already in the early 1980s by some critics and more are salient today.[4] Wagner and Müller, for instance, were simi-

8.   The garden encounter of Tristan (Siegfried Jerusalem), Isolde (Waltraud Meier), King Mark (John Tomlinson), and Kurvenal (Falk Struckmann) in Act II of Wagner's *Tristan and Isolde,* directed by Heiner Müller, Bayreuther Festspielhaus, 1993. Erich Wonder's setting for this act featured hundreds of pieces of body-armor placed in grim rows.

larly egoistic and pugnacious personalities who, convinced of their genius, felt "called" to be artistic saviors of their communities – the main difference being that Müller assumed that "the German nation [was] dying" rather than awakening, his role being to "preserve the German experience" [19/86, 88]. Both artists also spoke of their art as "an affair of the *Volk*" (Müller's phrase [13/94, 98, 162]) yet lived to see their works become fetishized objects for a cultural elite (Müller's Bayreuth production of *Tristan and Isolde* being a prime example). Both traced the disastrous condition of their society and its *Kultur* to an "evil moment" in history – for Wagner, the end of classical Greece when tragedy supposedly split into its component arts, for Müller, the split in the German left after the Spartacus uprising in 1918. And both tried to heal those splits through myth, oblivious to the ways in which myth perpetuated much of what they abhorred.

If Kleist represented Müller's wounded but still proudly Prussian persona, Wagner was rather the focal point of a nervous ambivalence in him concerning the quintessentially German and how the quintessentially German applied to the world at large. With post-World War II hindsight, he was more alert than Wagner to literary-political issues such as the imperialistic implications of exalting a *Volkskunst* (people's art), or the "latent totalitarianism"[5] of the *Gesamtkunstwerk* ideal. But he was stuck with his German heritage and his penchant for viewing all heritage in terms of sweeping metaphors. Emblematic constructions such as "Wagner" and "Germany" were too convenient and provocative for him to bypass. As much as anything else, it was the field of hypersensitive emotions surrounding Wagner, Wagnerism, and Germany that drew Müller to them – the atmosphere of cultivated irrationality in which respectable patrons whistled Patrice Chéreau's *Götterdämmerung* (*Twilight of the Gods*) off the stage at Bayreuth and threw chairs at the Israel Philharmonic Orchestra when it tried to play the prelude to *Tristan and Isolde* in Tel Aviv.

One of the most interesting aspects of *Germania Death in Berlin*, the most explicitly Wagnerian of the synthetic fragments, is the nature of the provocations it caused. Clearly intended to elicit defensive chauvinistic reactions – consider only its title, Germania fused with death, suspended with death in eternal parallelism – it encountered mainly Cold War objections for nearly two decades. The GDR, true to its tradition of avoiding burdens of the German past that could not be ascribed to the Federal Republic, banned the play from stage and print until 1988. Its most egregious offense (Müller learned years later) was a "biassed" depiction of the workers' uprising of June 17, 1953, in which a communist is shown as a prisoner in a GDR jail [o/255]. When the play premiered in the Federal Republic in 1978, the prominent Frankfurt critic Georg Hensel harshly criticized that scene and others for being biassed the other way, saying that Müller had "dramatized the Party's views of June 17 straight down the line: SED legends for the GDR reader."[6] Only when it finally opened at the Berliner Ensemble in 1988, says Müller, was the work attacked (anonymously) for desecrating German honor [o/256].

Germania Death in Berlin was completed in 1971 and (although it had to wait six years for publication and seven for production) should therefore be placed beside *Macbeth* (1971) as one of the texts in which he first reached vigorously for Western forms and Western attention. *Germania Death in Berlin* enshrines an East–West tension in its very structure, alternating surreal, farcical, expressionistic and quoted scenes that flaunt their avant-gardism (and would thus have been opaque to most Eastern viewers in the 1970s) with scenes of everyday life in the GDR written predominantly in his 1950s style of Socialist Realism. This is why the play often figures in discussions of Müller's problematic subjectivity, his shifting or disappearing authorial position, and his so-called personal "crisis" of mid-career.[7] There is also much to be said about this alternation of styles, though, on the ordinary level of practical effect. The GDR scenes provide vital realistic ballast to the dizzying phantasmagoria of effects and abstractions around them, and they also add a tincture of humility to the magisterial attitude toward history that suffuses the play.

This most wide-ranging of the synthetic fragments touches, within its forty-one pages, on Arminius (a German national hero from the first century AD), the Nibelung myth, Frederick the Great, the revolutions of 1848 and 1918, Nazism and World War II, the splitting of the country in 1949, and the uprising of June 17, 1953. Disappearing-author theories notwithstanding, no satire or burlesque could possibly hide the comprehensive, even monumental, ambitions of such an overview. Müller said that his immersion in this historical material was a response to the pace of social change in his country during the 1960s and early 1970s.

> When you see that the tree won't bear apples anymore, that it's starting to rot, you look to the roots. The stagnation in the GDR in those years was absolute. In a case like that everything comes to the surface that lies beneath, hidden or buried. There was no movement anymore, nothing but braking maneuvers and fortification.   [o/256–7]

Like Wagner, in other words, whom Adorno once described as a "dissatisfied aesthete in . . . flight from banality,"[8] Müller was trying (among other goals) to drive away greyness and routine in a regimented, dully industrialized world, and ultimately arrived at a representation of historical stasis despite that far-flung quest for variety.

Müller's quest, moreover, led through a host of Wagnerian

obsessions, from Teutonic myth to death-as-salvation to mythic kitsch in the hallowed tradition of Brünnhilde dress-up dolls, Wotan pencil-sharpeners, and Rhine Maiden soft-porn (all of which have been on sale within blocks of the Bayreuther Festspielhaus). In one scene of *Germania*, ludicrously bloodthirsty Nibelung warriors upbraid corpses ("Malingerers. Slackers. Defeatists" [5/49]), drink beer out of skulls, and masturbate together before hacking each other to pieces, whereupon the pieces crawl together amid ear-splitting noise and form a "monster of scrap iron and human material" [51]. In another scene, a caricatured Hitler – a hybrid of Ubu, Arturo Ui, Chaplin's Great Dictator, and Joseph of the Holy Family – drinks gasoline and eats live soldiers while a clubfooted Goebbels gives birth to his child (understood to be West Germany), who turns out to be a thalidomide wolf.

What, if any, is the High Art purpose of this overwrought pulp-fiction aesthetic? A phrase of the filmmaker Hans-Jürgen Syberberg (an artist, equally obsessed with Wagnerian images of Germania, to whom Müller once dedicated an essay) comes to mind: "trivial sociology and psychology."[9] Syberberg says that this is the attraction and serious basis of the montages in his seven-hour *Hitler: A Film from Germany*, which link such disparate phenomena as Karl May, the reminiscences of Himmler's masseur, puppets of Hitler and his dog, Wagner's music, and the Christmas carol "Silent Night." Like Müller, Syberberg is interested not only in "the banality of evil" but also "the evil of banality." "The key to modern myths," Syberberg writes, "is in the banality (taken seriously) of kitsch success and the popularity of triviality – final traces of worlds gone under."[10] Müller, quoting the architect Hermann Henselmann, says similarly: "'Taste is the death of art' . . . As soon as you fear kitsch you stop yourself from moving and situate yourself in some niche" [15/145].

Müller's synthetic fragments were attempts to manufacture and exploit exactly what Syberberg meant by "modern myths." These plays present German history (which *is* history, for Müller) as a phantasmagoria of kitschy thrills in order to cast the public in the role of voyeur. This role is more typically associated with film than with theater, but Müller appropriated it for theater (like Genet) in order to pursue his old theme, the identity of perpetrator and victim. "The great criminals always make us voyeurs," writes a reviewer of *The Diary of Jack the Ripper*,[11] a recent "true crime" document written to collect some of the immense, television-age profits that have ineluctably accompanied sensationalistic journalism on cases from Lizzie Borden to Charles Manson and Jeffrey Dahmer. The cover of the German Rotbuch edition of *Germania Death in Berlin* reproduces a *New York Times* front page featuring adjacent articles on the condemned murderer Gary Gilmore and Japanese Emperor Hirohito.

Rather than criticize this prurient fascination with death, gore, and criminality, or lambast those who feed it, Müller feeds it himself, partly in order to laugh at a Teutonic cliché and partly in the hope that some onlookers will attack him as a pornographer and, in the process, become self-conscious about their voyeuristic feelings. (The strategy is reminiscent of the simultaneous duplication and satire of TV talk-show pandering in Oliver Stone's film *Natural Born Killers*.) The play's pantheon of sexily grotesque criminals is a lure, a blood-flavored sugar-coating for some tough dialectical thought about historical guilt and universal complicity, and that thought deserves close attention. Another interesting question behind it, though, is (to borrow a famous Brecht formulation): did the East German Müller truly have a grip on the commercial apparatus he was exploiting or did it in fact – as Adorno argued about Wagner – have a grip on him?[12]

The first of *Germania*'s six sets of paired scenes (plus one mimed Beckettian interlude titled "Night Play") begins with this laconic, ostensibly pedestrian exchange.

THE STREET I
Berlin 1918

MAN: So much for the war. It kept my arm.
WOMAN: You got out of it, man. Everything's as it was.
Children, there's bread, father's back.
MAN: When the bread belongs to us, and the factory.
Exit. Blackout. [37]

For Müller, this is neither banal nor an arbitrary starting point. As he made clear in many other texts, some of which also leap around in time (e.g. *Downfall of the Egoist Johann Fatzer*, *Hamletmachine*,

Volokolamsk Highway), the story of what Brecht called the "German *Misere*" [historical calamity] begins in 1918 for him, with the unique opportunity lost by the German Left at the end of World War I: the Spartacus rebellion, followed by the murders of Karl Liebknecht and Rosa Luxemburg, and the subsequent division of the Left into SPD (Social Democratic Party) and KPD (German Communist Party), which opened the way for the Nazis.[13]

This neo-primordial split or wound ("It kept my arm") – reiterated in the later splitting of Germany – is his theft of the Rhine-gold, his wound of Amfortas. Müller is loathe to betray or generate sentimentality toward any lost utopia, however, so he reduces the fateful national injury to a symbolic cipher in the manner of Brecht's most simplistic *Lehrstück*-parables. As the one-page scene continues, a loudspeaker announces a "GENERAL STRIKE," then "THE REVOLU-TION," a larger-than-life Baker (who has denied hungry children bread) closes his store, and a larger-than-life Sign-Distributor uses *Knit-telvers* (nursery-rhyme doggerel) and bribery to convince the children to march around with "DOWN WITH SPARTACUS" placards:

> What's being brewed there is no beer of yours
> To every man a dime, four times one's four
> Carry my sign the whole street through
> And say it's for Germany, if anyone asks you.   [37]

The loudspeaker declares "LAW AND ORDER. REESTABLISHED," and the Sign-Distributor cheats the children of their promised coins. "What does the dog get when he barks," he says, laughing along with the Baker like a caricature of the *Rhinegold* giant Fafner the moment before he murders his brother out of greed.

Absurdly abbreviated though it is, this scene establishes a theoretical platform for all that is to come. The fatal originating event, ground zero of the "explosion" of Müller's historical memory, is an inter-generational betrayal – a betrayal of bourgeois *capitalist* values. These German "children" will not learn the overt Brechtian *Lehre* about the Machiavellianism of capitalists (who will not even play by their own rules if they can get away with it) but rather a pre-conscious, Pavlovian lesson about not challenging authority. From now on, they will associate any such challenge with starvation and acute need; hence the resonance of *Nibelungentreue*, mindless loyalty to the tribe, as a metaphor. Müller shares with Nietzsche, Thomas Mann, the Frankfurt School and many others a view of Germany as a site of incompletely developed capitalism and, consequently, of stunted democracy. According to this theory, since Germany's late-blooming bourgeoisie was repeatedly cowed by brutally suppressed revolutions – especially that of 1848 in which Wagner participated – it developed obsessions with obedience and stability and became exceptionally amenable to totalitarian rule. (Wagner's celebration of Bismarck's *Reich* is thus a precedent for both Brecht's and Müller's opportunistic relationships to the GDR.)

Müller uses the play's scene pairings to build up the sense of a pathological syndrome based on these premises, with each first scene positing a historical thesis in crass, sardonic or absurd terms (presumably to avoid pathos) and each second scene demonstrating its "immediate" application in quasi-realistic GDR circumstances. "The Street 2," for instance, consists of a mélange of seemingly overheard comments on the founding day of the GDR in 1949, all of which bespeak German-on-German hostility, distrust and incipient violence. Quarreling prostitutes reminiscent of those in Reinhard Sorge's early Expressionist play *Der Bettler* (*The Beggar*, 1911), for instance, fantasize about exploiting rich customers, and a loudspeaker announces, "LONG LIVE THE GERMAN DEMOCRATIC REPUBLIC THE FIRST WORKERS-AND-FARMERS-STATE ON GERMAN SOIL":

> *Applause from the loudspeaker.*
> MAN: The Russian state.
> ANOTHER *strikes him down*: Mark the day.
> MAN *standing up, bloody*: You too.
> *Staggers away.*
> There are still trees with branches in Germany.
> We'll see each other again, Russian, when you hang.
> VOICES: Hold the troublemaker.   [38]

Similarly, the next pairing, "Brandenburg Concerto 1" and "2" – whose titles irreverently recall the patron-glorification practiced by baroque artists like Johann Sebastian Bach – suggests that the nascent German bourgeois identity was also handicapped by long-lived habits of feudal obeisance.[14] In the first scene, two clowns reverse the traditional point of the legendary tale of Frederick the Great and the Miller of Potsdam, who proved his burgherly stoutheartedness by refusing to move his noisy windmill away from Sanssouci Palace; the clowns mock the fable and add a new ending in which the Miller-clown eats the royal walking stick and marches militarily into a wall of flames. In the second scene, a GDR bricklayer, invited to a reception at Sanssouci as a "worker hero," wrestles with Frederick's vampirical ghost, demonstrating that the problem of emulating (internalizing) the demeanor of the "enlightened" Prussian despot continues and has spread beyond the would-be bourgeoisie to the ostensibly "triumphant" proletariat.

Indeed, as was described in *The Scab*, the GDR, in its eagerness to "build socialism," exploited the tradition of absolute loyalty to state power as fully as the Brandenburgs and the Nazis did. Again and again, the play's pairings imply, what ought to be the healing of the original wound (the new socialist state) turns out to be the tearing open of a fresh one (perceived theft of property and freedom in a populace perpetually cheated of its full measure of middle-class contentment). Betrayal and repression beget betrayal and repression in a more or less permanent state of smoldering *Bürgerkrieg*.

For Müller, this eternal civil war is not merely a German character flaw; it is driven by capitalism, a fundamentally deceitful and imperialistic system that places human beings – including those living under socialism, "encircled" by capitalism – under pressures they are constitutionally too weak to bear. He does imply that the Germans are particularly weak in this respect, but Germans are an aggravated case of a general human affliction to him.

The first scene of the third pairing, "Hommage à Stalin 1," makes this point by combining the old Marxist propaganda trope of cannibalism with a satirized myth. The Nibelung warriors already mentioned engage in a perpetual, self-deceiving battle (with "imaginary Huns") in which corpses count as wealth and foodstuff. Repeated references to entrapment in a "kettle" (a World War II nickname) place the scene at Stalingrad even though Julius Caesar, Napoleon, and soldiers from other eras also appear. One Nibelung suddenly demurs, complaining he has forgotten why they're fighting – "I don't want to die every night. I find it boring. It's no fun for me. I want to do something else" [50] – and the others mock him ("Are you a Hun, that you need reason to fight") before dismembering him and themselves in a squabble over money.

The obvious implication is that we are all, fundamentally, sado-masochistic Teutons trapped forever in the plutocratic war of all against all – a participatory spectacle that simultaneously horrifies and titillates us, snuffing out every spark of humanistic higher ambition that might arise in us. It is a mark of Müller's dramaturgical skill that he can repeat this platitudinous point, with minor variations, in nearly every pairing yet continue to command interest. The first scene in the fifth pairing, for instance, "The Brothers 1," is an unaltered quote from Tacitus describing a pre-battle colloquy in which Arminius tries to convince his brother, a soldier in the opposing Roman army, to switch allegiances out of national loyalty. The meeting ends in mutual fury, offering the underwhelming intelligence that the primordial *Bürgerkrieg* is also a *Bruderkampf* and hence especially nasty, but the fact that Müller can find support for his point even in the ancient text of Tacitus' *Annals* itself compels historical reflection.

Two features of the redundancy save it from tedium. First, like *Hamletmachine* and *The Mission* (both of which appeared later), it points to a durably fascinating paradox: a self-described heir to Brecht's dialectical theater has written yet another drama that, historically speaking, moves and points nowhere, that perpetually starts over, in fact, with its dozen different narratives. Second and more important, the redundancy itself is a compelling metaphor, recalling the stripped-down images of life as a cyclical purgatory in Camus, Ionesco, and especially Beckett. Adorno once referred to such metaphors as "the ritual of permanent catastrophe"[15] and traced them back to the "cycle" of Wagner's *Ring*:

> The eternity of Wagnerian music, like that of the poem of the *Ring*, is one which proclaims that nothing has happened; it is a state of immutability that refutes all history by confronting it with the silence of nature. The Rhine maidens who are playing with the gold at the start of the opera and receive it back at the

end are the final statement both of Wagner's wisdom and of his music. Nothing is changed; and it is the dynamics of the individual parts that reinstate the amorphous primal condition.[16]

As it happens (and I will take this connection up at greater length in the following chapter), *Germania Death in Berlin* is peppered with explicit allusions to Beckett – author, most famously, of "a play in which nothing happens, twice" (Vivian Mercier on *Waiting for Godot*[17]). The clowns in "Brandenburg Concerto 1" replay Hamm and Clov's game of centering the chair in *Endgame*. Hitler's guard offers a Clov-like report on events outside the bunker ("a dog walked by" [59]). And "Night Play" features a "man who may be a puppet" [74] who is suicidally frustrated by invisibly controlled props, as in *Act Without Words I*. Actually, though, Müller's "primal condition" in this play has much more in common with Wagner than with Beckett. The power and gravity of Müller's images, for one thing, depend on their being immersed in specific histories and constructs of nation (a specificity that impairs Beckett's plays in performance and that he abhorred). And for another, Müller's brand of morbidity is more Wagnerian than Beckettian, preferring the sanctification, even fetishization, of death itself (as in *Tristan and Isolde*, *Twilight of the Gods* and *Parsifal*) to any fixation on decrepitude or indomitability while dying ("I can't go on, I'll go on"). Müller in 1990: "When a civilization, a society, abolishes its death-cult – and it has been abolished in Europe – then it has used up its energies and begins to consume itself" [17/52].

Indeed, with "Hommage à Stalin 2" at the latest (second scene in the third pairing), it is clear that death is not merely a principal leitmotif but the focus of Müller's play, a sort of abstract protagonist pursuing its will through human pawns. Set in an East German pub on the day of Stalin's death in March, 1953, this is the longest scene in the play and one which ends the strict independence of the various narratives by introducing a plot that continues in subsequent scenes. Reacting to the death of Stalin, several patrons predict a new war – presumably East versus West – while another reminisces about the battle of Stalingrad and says the old war never ended. Deeply cynical

about the GDR's official Stalin myth (the benevolent despot who freed
Germany from Hitler), these patrons are nevertheless backhanded
admirers of what might be called the Western-cum-fascist Stalin myth
(the horrifically single-minded dealer of death). The French phrase
hommage à means both to pay respects and to pay tribute as a vassal.
("Myth" is used here not as a synonym for "lie" but in Roland
Barthes's sense, as a usage of speech circumscribing a concept among
a given group of people.)

Meanwhile, a young bricklayer – contemptuously referred to as
"Lohengrin" at one point – has fallen in love with a prostitute he has
mistaken for a virgin. In the final scene, "Death in Berlin 2," a
delirious dying worker named Hilse (also present in the pub) will
mistake her for Rosa Luxemburg, implying provocatively that she
represents the Party. Now the couple is approached by a mysterious,
vatic Skull-Seller who seems to have fallen out of an E.T.A. Hoffmann
tale in order to speak as death's mouthpiece: "Allow me to offer you a
small souvenir . . . A memento mori for the new home" [56]. He turns
out to be the most interesting character in the play, a sort of philosophical male Norn who reads the future and interprets the past in earth
rather than rope.

> I work on foundations. So to speak. We relocate graveyards
> without the public's knowledge. . . For me it's an occupation
> with some piquancy: I was a historian. Made an error in
> periodization, the thousand-year reich, you understand. Since
> history has banished me to the graveyards, to their theological
> aspect as it were, I'm immune to the ptomaine [*Leichengift*] of
> worldly promise. The golden age is behind us. Jesus is the
> afterbirth of the dead. Do you know Vergil.
> ALREADY A NEW RACE DESCENDS FROM THE RADIANT
>   HEAVENS,
> ENDS THE AGE OF IRON AND FREES THE LANDS FROM
>   TERROR.
> BEHOLD HOW EVERYTHING IN ITS PATH BREATHES OF
>   THE NEW CENTURY
> THAT ARRIVES ON WINGS BEARING GIFTS OF THE
>   EARTH. . .   [57]

The Skull-Seller is the face of Nazi history, which happens also to be the face of the GDR's vision of a new "foundation," of Vergil's ancient vision of a "new" or "golden race" of proto-Romans, and of Nietzsche's Zarathustra and Wagner's race of "free heroes" sprung from Siegfried. All these, Müller insinuates, are yearnings for death and stasis masquerading as utopian yearnings for life and progress, and all are driven by a basic human death-wish that, once again, lends universal relevancy to the extreme case of Germany. In Müller's dramatic world, death is not final, does not provide even the temporary rest and redemption of Valhalla. The dead have active appetites and desires, and the German *Volk*, having always viewed itself apocalyptically in relation to death (its own or other peoples') is more responsive to them than anyone else. That responsiveness is tantamount to devotion, which is why the Skull-Seller says that humanity (= Germania) was already lost when Christ arrived ("afterbirth of the dead"). By the same logic, all other redemption is also absurd, since all Valhallas are foredoomed to fall (surrounded by futile walls), as "the amorphous primal condition" ineluctably returns. The high-principled Lohengrins of this world are simply victims of "the ptomaine of worldly promise" – that is, oblivious fools.

That Müller thinks he is placing these thoughts about death in a critical context is obvious. The entire play is saturated with irony and sarcasm implying an underlying invitation to change the world. Lehmann writes, "What Adorno wrote about Wagner also applies to Müller: 'The changing of the world miscarries, but it has to do with changing the world.'"[18] The trouble is, in a structure like *Germania*'s that juxtaposes myth with a profusion of historical anecdotes and thereby mythologizes history, Müller's invitation reads as hopelessly weak. Sarcasm is a half-measure that provides a tone of critique while leaving the ancient truth-claims of myth firmly in place; myth is still used, as in the past, to identify primal tendencies in a particular *Volk* that are then shown to be tragically deterministic – and this is equally true of the mythic kitsch.

In "The Workers' Monument," for instance, second scene in the fourth pairing, set at a construction site on the day of the 1953 workers' strike, Hilse refuses to walk off the job with his colleagues and ends up being stoned "in rock rhythm" by three skinhead "youths" [67]. It is a chillingly realistic episode that, in the context of a play written wholly in one style, such as Müller's *The Scab* or *The Construction Site* (or Edward Bond's *Saved*, probably a deliberate allusion), might have prompted trenchant thoughts and discussions about alternative paths for the characters and the society. Surrounded as it is, though, by "The Holy Family" (the scene with Hitler and Goebbels), "The Brothers 1" (the Tacitus quote) and all the other emblematizing passages, it comes across flatly as yet another reconfirmation of the death-wish thesis, which is now dubiously enhanced by trivial socialist myths such as the plucky, self-sacrificing worker (recalling the proud prostitute who takes the day off in "The Street 2") and rock-and-roll as a sinister soundtrack for murder (recalling the apocalyptic use of a Pink Floyd song in *Gundling's Life. . .*). "Quick into the grave, grandpa," warns the Second Youth, "or there'll be no more room. Your / Comrades are already waiting in line at the cemetery" [66].

The play's structure casts the spell of the mythic over every scene, transforming all situations, no matter how commonplace or parochial, into symbols and archetypes grounded in nature. Müller seems to believe that such sweeping mythification will itself encourage a sort of deconstructive viewing, causing people to examine the artifices behind the myths. It is another example of his reaching toward Brechtian goals through the emotional channels that Brecht avoided – seduction by supposedly timeless truths intended to prevent similar seductions in the future. But, as Barthes once observed, because "myth is depoliticized speech," myth and left-wing politics do not mix very well:

> *Left-wing myth is inessential* . . . incidental . . . Statistically, myth is on the right. There, it is essential; well-fed, sleek, expansive, garrulous, it invents itself ceaselessly. It takes hold of everything, all aspects of the law, of morality, of aesthetics, of diplomacy, of household equipment, of Literature, of entertainment.[19]

Müller is so eager to be left-wing, he renders all his material "inessential" in this sense. His very strategy of overload deprives his satirized, superimposed, and attenuated myths of the power to seduce as Wagner's myths could. Interestingly, as if sensing this problem himself, he ultimately settles for *depictions* of seductions in blatantly ironic contexts in his final two GDR scenes.

Both of these scenes end with characters caught in the act of surrendering, as it were, to one or more myths. In "The Brothers 2," which takes place on June 17, 1953 – the scene Müller says the censor objected to most strongly – a communist political prisoner is locked in a cell with violent career criminals, one of whom is his Nazi brother. All except the communist hope to be freed momentarily by the workers' rebellion, and when the newcomer gloats over the sound of Soviet tanks arriving, the others descend on him murderously – the perpetrators and victims of that mythical day eternally and irrevocably blurred. The communist's last line ("Who am I" [74]) – implying that his sort of martyrdom begins with questioned individuality – is a quote from Walter Hasenclever's Expressionist passion play *Die Menschen* (*Humanity*, 1918), thus associating him explicitly with Christ.

In the final scene, "Death in Berlin 2," the nameless "Lohengrin"-bricklayer, recently disabused about the innocence of his now pregnant girlfriend, visits Hilse in a cancer ward. Christ-like, Hilse takes the younger man's "sin" of blindness (to the whore-like nature of the Party?) upon himself. Named after the weaver in Gerhart Hauptmann's 1893 *Die Weber* (*The Weavers*) who is killed by a stray bullet during a counter-revolutionary offensive, Hilse similarly dies of a chance cause (cancer) rather than from direct revolutionary activity (his standing up to the skinheads in "The Workers' Monument"). He expires grasping at inessential myth after inessential myth to lend his death meaning. To the Young Bricklayer: "We're a party, my cancer and I" [76]. To the girl: "The water didn't hold you, Rosa [Luxemburg] / And even if they make us all into soap / No soap'll wash your blood off them" [78]. His final speech is a panegyric to the invincible proletariat and the eternal feminine, delivered by a dying worker to a prostitute.

Much has been written about the form of *Germania Death in Berlin*, the synthetic fragment. This is generally celebrated as one of very few viable models for drama in a postmodern age when progressive and advanced artists supposedly distrust the rational and unitarian presumptions behind most drama. The form has been described, rightly, as an intensification of Brecht's pastiche structure (which Benjamin once likened to filmic montage – an interruptive technique in which pictures are "read" like verbal language).[20] Multiple and disjunctive actions range freely over different times and places and generate dissonance rather than harmony with their profusion of ideas, effects, and themes. In a 1975 open letter to the editor Martin Linzer, Müller explained his intentions this way:

> No dramatic literature is as rich in fragments as the German. That has to do with the fragmentary character of our (theater) history, with the tearing apart, again and again, of the connections between literature-theater-public (society) that results from that. . . the fragmenting of a process stresses its process character, prevents the disappearance of the production in the product, marketing, makes representation into a field of experiment in which the public can coproduce. I don't believe a story that "holds water" (the plot in a classical sense) captures reality anymore.   [4/125]

Part of this text amounts to yet another round of debate with Brecht over the *Lehrstück* – the issue of process and product, to be taken up in a moment. The gist, though, is a description of the synthetic fragment form as the basis of a new type of theater with a national foundation and universal ambitions. Müller suggests that what is contemporary (fragmentary, postmodern) is what is German – a suggestion strongly reminiscent of a remark Thomas Mann made about Wagner in the heyday of modernism: "Wagner's art is the most sensational self-portrayal and self-critique of the German nature that it is possible to conceive; it is calculated to make Germany interesting to a foreigner even of the meanest intelligence."[21] One needn't exaggerate Müller's nationalism – which is both self-evident and self-evidently equivocal – in order to see that it is the synthetic fragment's most telling political backdrop. (Indeed when he returned to the form at the end of his life, in *Germania 3*, it was to serve similar themes.[22]) This is a form that packages and markets the ills of Germany as avant-garde kitsch and employs Brechtian techniques to camouflage an inverted Wagnerian ideal: it is an anti-*Gesamtkunstwerk* that yearns for utopian wholeness by default in the process of ostentatiously foregoing it.

The best illustration is the use Müller makes of fragments and the fragmentary. (I will stay with *Germania Death in Berlin* since it has been my main example, but the point holds equally for *The Battle*, *Gundling's Life. . .*, and *Germania 3*.) Scission is the play's main recurrent figure, lacing itself through the action with the insistence of a musical leitmotif. By the time the Nazi pounces on his communist brother in "The Brothers 2," Müller has flooded the spectator's consciousness with numerous other deeply metaphorical splits, from the Spartacus uprising to the clowns' accidental breaching of a lion (traditional symbol of the fighting proletariat) in "Brandenburg Concerto 1" to Arminius' family troubles. Even the characters are often literally fragmentary, from the one-armed man at the opening to the other-worldly soldiers in "Hommage à Stalin 1" whose "bodies are no longer intact" to the Beckettian puppet-man who dismembers himself in "Night Play" to the cancer-eaten Hilse who complains, "I'm not half myself." The irony with which all these constituent "bits" are presented makes clear that they are meant to call the principle of unitary monumentality into question. At the same time, though, the theme or leitmotif of "fragment" (especially as couched here in clichés of Germanic brutality) lends compositional unity to the epic material, and also allows many sections of the play to appeal anti-intellectually like a freak show.

Müller once said that his technique was based on an aesthetic of "inundation" that leads to free choice among ideas:

> I always have the need when I write to pack the people up with so much that they don't know what to carry first, and I think that's also the only possibility. The question is how you achieve that in the theater. . . Today you have to bring as many points together at the same time as possible, so that people are forced to choose. I.e. perhaps they can't choose at all anymore, but have to decide quickly what they're going to carry.
>
> (1975) [14/20]

These remarks hark back to the dream of a "democratic Bayreuth" that he articulated as early as a 1970 text entitled "Six Points on Opera": "In the democratic the culinary is quashed; the parasitic moment is eliminated. . . So that the whole is more than its parts every part must be first of all a whole" [4/118].[23] It is difficult to see, however, how any artist as enamored as Müller is of military aggressiveness, sado-masochistic imagery, morbidity for morbidity's sake, and sheer volume, can argue that his spectators really have much to choose from. If Wagner's tasteful Teutonism sought to control people, to focus and guide their "bewildered, wandering, piecemeal minds"[24] through narcotizing, partriarchally directed hypnotism (as he more or less claimed), Müller's tasteless brand sought to accomplish the same goal through browbeating excess. Nothing in his deluges of superimposed and imbricated fragments ever overwhelms or disorients to the point where the spectator forgets the author's intense drive to lay bare the connections between everything and everything else. He is always clearly authoritative and possessed by a will to total synthesis as strong as his will to fragmentation, which is why comparison with the *Gesamtkunstwerk* ideal is unavoidable.

In the one substantial essay that has appeared on this subject, Schulz and Lehmann write that Wagner and Müller stand generally for "the polarity of wholeness and fragment":[25] "the one synthesizes the quotes, assembles the fragments into a great whole, the other isolates the component parts in precisely this 'montage' so separately that every attempt to arrive at a unity of sense stifles itself."[26] Their theory is that the synthetic fragments deliberately provoke a nostalgia or desire for [*Hang zum*] the organic wholeness of the *Gesamtkunstwerk* in readers and spectators in order to disappoint it. It's as if Wagnerism were a Romantic disease and Müller's plays, in effect, administered a homeopathic cure for it by promulgating and then suppressing its symptoms – Müller as a new-age historical doctor in spite of himself.

Equally likely, I suggest, is the possibility that he does not quite manage this, and that the plays consequently become examples of what they purport to criticize: commodity fetishes. Nicola Chiaromonte once made a pertinent observation about Erwin Piscator, originator of many of the stage effects generally considered Brechtian today: "Setting out from an extreme preoccupation with ideological content, Piscator arrived at the most extreme and self-defeating of formalisms," foretelling not "the advent of Socialism" but "the advent of the mass media."[27] Chiaromonte explains:

> in the political theater it is the theater of stagecraft, the theater-as-spectacle, that asserts itself, finding in the aim of political edification support for the aestheticism that characterizes it. Why aestheticism? Because, by its nature, this theater transforms into a more or less phantasmagorical scenic image the incitement to action it intends to produce, so that the formal element naturally gains the upper hand. . . "The director and the author both have a single purpose: the success of the work," [Piscator] proclaimed. He did not realize that, in making such pronouncements, he was giving dogmatic form to the law that rules artistic production in the mass society.[28]

Müller's theater of ostensibly political fragments, too, "has no ideological intentions; it is addressed not to the mind but to the nerves."[29]

In fact, one needn't accept Chiaromonte's thesis to argue this point; it can be made purely on the ground that Müller sets for himself. Marx once used the word "phantasmagoria" as a synonym for commodity fetishism, and Adorno reserved some of his harshest words for Wagner's "phantasmagorical style" whose "miracles have become as impenetrable as the daily reality of a reified society."[30] "The phantasmagoria tends towards dream not merely as the deluded wish-fulfilment of would-be buyers," writes Adorno, "but chiefly to conceal the labour that has gone into making it."[31] Müller claims (in the letter to Linzer) that the synthetic fragment "prevents the disappearance of the production in the product" [4/125]. One has only to see a few productions, however, to become convinced that his kaleidoscopic cascades of incidents, ideas, and effects (and *Gundling's Life. . .* adds photographic projections to the mix) – which are as compatible with his era's most advanced technical theater "miracles" as Wagner's music-dramas were with his – do not differ fundamentally from this sort of phantasmagoria.

In 1990, at the Frankfurt Experimenta festival, I had a rare chance to see, within days of each other, two different productions of *Germania Death in Berlin* that shed clarifying light on these issues. One was

Eastern, one Western, both had been mounted shortly before the fall of the Wall, and both were marked by a fidelity to text unusual among Müller's directors in the 1980s and 1990s. This fidelity – obviously a stiffening influence in both cases – was easier to understand with Fritz Marquardt's 1989 Berliner Ensemble staging, which was the GDR premiere, than it was with Frank-Patrick Steckel's 1988 staging from the Schauspielhaus Bochum, the seventh major West German production in ten years. For good or ill, though, the two directors' desire to serve Müller, give physical life to the images he originally imagined, made the projects easier to compare and more useful in discussing authorial intent than others might have been.

Marquardt's production, which opened ten months before the *Wende* (turning-point – the events leading to the fall of the Wall) and was not warmly received then by GDR audiences, was conceived very much in and for the East German context. Replete with "in jokes" that some natives found dated – such as the comically instantaneous arrest of pedestrians who start to sing the West German anthem (in "The Street 2"), or the arrogant loitering of a covey of superfluous *maître d*'s (in "Brandenburg Concerto 2") – it eschewed flashy spectacle for the most part in favor of low-tech, intentionally maladroit effects in the Ensemble's hallowed tradition of demonstrative humility. A simple trapeze bar, for instance, was used to lift the clowns in "Brandenburg Concerto 1" and then drop them flailing onto the lion below, two actors in a simple animal-suit who ran out in opposite directions.

The production did make frequent use of the stage's large motorized turntable, offering differing views of a central cutaway wall, and a brief clip of Fritz Lang's film *Die Nibelungen* (*The Nibelungs*) was seen at one point, but no attempt was made to accentuate what might be called the text's filmic conceits – that is, its scenic cross-blends, impossible stage activities, and numerous images inviting technical exertions that would stretch the theater's limits. These conceits, which are common to all the synthetic fragments, have already been described as Müller's first explicit play for Western attention. According to the critic Andreas Keller, they were also originally his contribution to a general movement in the 1970s intended to combat calcification in the GDR theater deriving from museum-

9.   Clown 1 (Hermann Beyer) and Clown 2 (Axel Werner) play at being Frederick the Great and the Miller of Potsdam in *Germania Death in Berlin*, directed by Fritz Marquardt, Berliner Ensemble, East Berlin, 1989.

ification of Brecht and a moribund Stanislavsky tradition.[32] Understandably uninterested in pursuing a 1970s agenda in 1989, Marquardt treated *Germania*'s technical novelties as moot, stressing instead the choppy disconnectedness of its structure and treating its inflammatory subject-matter as a set of pressing social questions submitted for sober consideration in the manner of Brecht's *Furcht und Elend des Dritten Reiches* (*Fear and Misery in the Third Reich*, 1935–38) – another collage work about terror that seemed dated by the time it was performed (in 1945).

There was no surprise or mystery about the absence of explicit kitsch-appeal in a pre-*Wende* GDR production, particularly one from the Berliner Ensemble, which had yet to overcome its museum-like stuffiness at this time. What was surprising was how easily Müller's ostensibly dystopian, postmodern valuing of fragments and fragmentariness could be rendered indistinguishable from the Brechtian modern one from which it supposedly departed. (Müller: "Brecht's

10. "The Holy Family": Hitler (Angelika Waller) waits for Goebbels (Simone Frost) to give birth to their child, a thalidomide wolf, in Fritz Marquardt's production of *Germania Death in Berlin*, Berliner Ensemble, 1989.

poetic entry was based on the idea of the world as a round thing . . . my globe consists of fighting segments that come together, at best, in the clinch" [4/8]).

In Marquardt's hands, Müller became, like the Brecht of *Fear and Misery*, the teller of a "rounded" series of thematically linked stories which, despite their disorienting leaps in time, mytho-historical references and otherwise enhanced disconnectedness, held interest like a singular story. Marquardt: "I discovered that [the play] is 'written through like an express train,' no collage but rather a synthetic fragment in which several plays are run together into a huge comprehensive concept that is a ruin."[33] According to Benjamin's famous essay, the mark of a "storyteller" is the offering of wisdom or "counsel," defined as "something useful . . . a moral . . . some practical advice . . . a proverb or maxim" growing out of the author's worldly experience.[34] Marquardt used Müller in just this way, with his recorded voice, for instance, as the sole action in "Nachtstück." "Hommage à Stalin 2" was a collection of visual quotes from Müller's recent, critically acclaimed Deutsches Theater production of *The Scab*. These gestures virtually ensured that, "fighting segments" notwithstanding, spectators would look to *Germania* as a fount of authorial wisdom, if not of a grand historical synthesis in the spirit of Wagner. No matter if one came away feeling that the fount had run dry; in Müller's devalued universe being thought of as a Wagnerian pretender could suffice as heroism.

The Bochum production, by contrast, was a slick, expensive cabaret that exploited every kitschy opportunity in the text and invented new ones. Its high production values generated a cynical, market-savvy, devil-may-care atmosphere whose sheer profligacy of means – the blood-red lighting effects against a giant cyclorama and brick wall are especially memorable – would have been astonishing in their own right had the director not ruined them with literalism and redundancy. "The Street 1" featured a Baker in a hugely fat dough-costume and a top-hatted Sign Distributor on stilts with jumbo buttons spelling out "S.P.D." – both figures recalling familiar advertisements. Frederick the Great in "Brandenburg Concerto 2" was a dwarf in a fierce mask whose freakish tininess was exaggerated by a giant empire chair. The soldiers in "Hommage à Stalin 1" wore dayglo Nazi uniforms and the Nibelungs elaborate Wagnerian regalia tricked up with green lamps that cast their faces in eerie light – every costume a sartorial one-liner. The moment these overstocked characters appeared their satirical dialogue was superfluous.

Like so many other German productions, East and West, this one was obviously driven by feelings of competitiveness with its predecessors; consciously or not, Steckel was playing the technical can-you-top-this? contest that has long been the bane of his culture's subsidized theater. That *Germania Death in Berlin* struck him as an ideal vehicle for his pyrotechnical exhibitionism, however, reflects back on the author whose images inspired the magnification and the parade of clichés. It may have been puerile of Steckel to use Death (dressed as a traditional skeleton with scythe) as a silent chorus lurking behind scenes and emerging whenever the theme of violence grew prominent, but that idea originated in the text. It may have been theatrically obtuse to impose an ironic diminutiveness on every last aggrandizing symbol of Germania – from the miniature Frederick to the costuming of Hitler in a fright wig and bug-eyes to the feeding of the Nibelungs with beer bottles lowered from the flies – but super-abundance of irony, too, was originally Müller's strategy.

That Steckel failed to give the play any chance to work on a subtle level is regrettable, but his phantasmagoric overkill and kitschily attractive violence (e.g. the dayglo Nazis, lovely tableaux of disembodied limbs, a vicious orgy at the end of "The Holy Family"), even his misguided effort to force theater to accommodate the visual emphasis and realistic effects of film, belong to a long tradition of Teutonic excess that Müller perpetuated as much for homage as critique. Müller's distaste for textual fidelity notwithstanding, his texts make obvious *his* penchant for phantasmagoria and hence invite an essentially apolitical immersion in phantasmagoria that vitiates the synthetic fragment as a progressive political instrument. To use stage technology to make already cartoonish exaggerations of Hitler, Goebbels, Frederick and the Nibelungs yet more ridiculous is to render them politically innocuous – which was precisely what Adorno meant by belittling Wagner's political landscape as a "musical fairyland."[35]

If Marquardt's production demonstrated that simply avoiding commodity fetishism is no way to give Müller's drama political teeth, Steckel's showed that indulging in it (by far the more common attitude in Germany) is no more effective. Such indulgence becomes simply a means of denying that the real nationalism behind the fetishized images remains dangerous and still holds any significant power over people. More, it is a mark of ambivalence on the part of both dramatist and director concerning the basic aesthetic value of the violently Teutonic. "Our aim is the irony of diabolical enlightenment," wrote Syberberg about "the risk of portraying the beauty of evil."[36] In Müller's case, the risk is that "enlightenment" too easily fails, is perhaps destined for failure, leaving behind mere diabolism.

9 Müller as Beckett: *Description of a Picture*

"Of our national epos he remembered only the calamities,
which did not prevent him from winning a minor scholarship
in the subject." Testimony of Mr Peaberry, market gardener in
the Deeping Fens and lifelong friend.

(Beckett, *Rough for Theater II*[1])

Samuel Beckett is the shadow figure whose importance to his own
work Müller most misjudged and whose centrality to twentieth-
century theater he most underestimated, at least publicly. Müller
was never hostile to Beckett, as was Georg Lukács, the quasi-official
tastemaker for many years in socialist countries. Lukács dismissed
Beckett as an extension of Kafka ("substituting his *angst*-ridden
vision of the world for objective reality") and Joyce ("attenuation of
reality . . . carried *ad absurdum* where the stream of consciousness is
that of an abnormal subject or of an idiot").[2] In fact, Müller was
generally critical of Brecht's notorious plan to adapt *Waiting for
Godot* as a socialist allegory (despite my comparison with *The
Mission* in chapter 7) [14/16, 49]. Still, his works, particularly the
later ones, are replete with altered Beckett quotations construable as
critiques of the originals, and his respectful comments about Beckett
over the years often included caveats. "Beckett is certainly a great
author, but *Godot* is simply too long for what he wants to say," he
said in 1985.[3] To me in 1993 he said: "The *Fatzer* material by Brecht
is much better than all the plays of Beckett."[4] To place these
remarks beside others such as this comment to Holger Teschke in
1994 – "You remember the scene from *Godot* in which Pozzo enters
with Lucky on the rope; that's the entirety of Brecht in a nutshell"[5] –

is to wonder whether Müller held any consistent attitude at all on the subject.

It seems clear that Müller admired Beckett. When one of Müller's accusers at the hearing on *The Resettler* in 1961 contemptuously called him "a Beckett of the East," he claimed that the epithet "helped me through a few minutes" [0/173]. Müller's predisposition to Beckett's sort of graveyard humor and severe concentration of means was apparently of concern to some officials as early as 1958, when he was warned by the editors of *Neue Deutsche Literatur* "against making a fetish of economy in language."[6] At some point, though – it is unclear when and perhaps it was the case all along – his admiration became mixed with envy; consider his description of *Waiting for Godot* as "the *Pillenknick* of recent drama" [9/262] in the 1985 text "The Wound Woyzeck," for instance (a *Pillenknick* is a decline in birthrate due to use of the pill). Believing he had "begun where Brecht left off" [14/129], Müller was irritated at the difficulty for himself or any younger dramatist to continue where Beckett left off – his attitude stemming no doubt as much from a desire to see this drama continue as from a desire to occupy the position of "last writer" himself. (Why else all his amassed images of apocalypse?) History is making him "the last German writer," he said to Lotringer in 1988 [19/88].

Müller tended to distinguish his sensibility from Beckett's by pointing out his greater immersion in history and politics. "If one really watched a play by Beckett intensively, one couldn't help but draw the conclusion that the next day one has to join the Communist Party," he said in 1976, two decades after he neglected to renew his Party card [14/49]. And in 1988: "Beckett's texts come out of the experience of a history-less world. For his characters there was no history and there won't be any. And I, for biographical or geographical reasons, have always been interested in history, or had to be interested in it. That's where I see the big difference" [15/131]. There is a truth in these remarks, of course, but it is a truth that amounts to another of Müller's deflecting screens. He wished to discourage others from looking more deeply into why a relationship existed between him and Beckett at all (by way of the latter's work, that is).

Much more important, I believe, is that, unlike Brecht, Beckett left no body of technique or theory upon which one might spend a career building, and unlike Genet, Kleist, and others, he was not easily imitated or inhabited vampirically – and Müller was frustrated by that. For years (in sympathy with Lukács despite the contempt he expressed for him [see 18/15, 25]), Müller tried to "write Beckett off" by inserting him schematically into his collages in ways that tacitly reduced him to categorical rubrics – "historical standstill" and "theater of the dead" being two of his minimizing descriptive phrases.[7]

In the mimed scene in *Germania Death in Berlin* entitled "Night Play" briefly discussed earlier, for instance, the main target is Beckett's *Act without Words I*, in which a silent figure simply called "the man" is teased by various enticing objects mysteriously controlled from the wings and flies until he finally stops pursuing them and lies still. In Müller, "a man" who is "larger than life, maybe a puppet" [5/74], and who is dressed in placards and has no mouth, is similarly teased by a bicycle and other props controlled from offstage. In frustration, he systematically tears off his limbs (an allusion to Brecht's *Badener Lehrstück*), after which "Beckett-goads" (from *Act without Words II*) pluck out his eyes and lice crawl out of the empty sockets, spreading over his face (an allusion to Artaud's *Spurt of Blood*). The scene's horror and willful strangeness notwithstanding, its last lines – "He screams. The mouth comes into being with the scream" [75] – are blatantly polemical. They imply that the mouth, newly born of Artaudian cruelty, will allow the character to complain, albeit inarticulately, a first Brechtian step toward overcoming Beckettian inertia and demanding his rights as a possible human.

Silent figures in *Medeaplay* and *Description of a Picture* are similarly depicted as entrapped by capricious and malevolent god-like forces working partly invisible theatrical machinery, as in the *Acts without Words*. And again polemically, the woman in *Medeaplay* demonstrates a capacity for rebellion in the end (read: revolutionary action) that wins her the alliance of the god-like forces: "The woman removes her face, tears apart her child, and throws the parts in the man's direction. From the flies, rubble, limbs, entrails fall on the man" [3/17]. Yet another example is the final scene of *Hamlet-machine*, in which defiant Ophelia sits center-stage in a wheelchair, like Hamm in *Endgame*, her body mummified in gauze rather than covered lightly with a handkerchief symbolizing a theatrical curtain ("Old Stancher! (*Pause.*) You . . . remain."[8]) – the implication being that Beckettian stasis amounts to an entombment, a phase of retirement from true drama to be endured "FEROCIOUSLY" like the father's armor until humanity is redeemed from the capitalist "ice age."

Interestingly enough, from the synthetic fragments on, schematic uses of Beckett such as these existed side by side with other references devoid of polemic and conceptions perhaps not consciously quoted but so close to Beckett that they might as well be quotations. The Skull-Seller in *Germania Death in Berlin* who speaks of "the ptomaine of worldly promise" [5/57], for instance, expresses precisely the same thought as Hamm in his story of the madman who looked at a field of rising corn and saw only ashes: "He alone had been spared."[9] Merteuil and Valmont's references in *Quartet* to the fact that they are performing (e.g. "Wouldn't we have full houses, Valmont, with the statues of our decayed desires" [7/73]) are made in the same blackly sardonic (and un-Brechtian) spirit as Didi and Gogo's and Hamm and Clov's. And Beckett's general melancholic attitude toward "the impossible heap" of humanist culture comes unavoidably to mind in the final pages of *Gundling's Life . . .*, when Müller's Lessing Actor speaks of feeling "burned by [his] more and more vehement yearning for silence" [7/35]. In the end, this character is left burrowing around in sand as "waiters fill the stage with busts of poets and thinkers" [36], recalling that other "burned" figure Winnie in *Happy Days*, who quotes snatches of the Bible, Shakespeare, Dante, *The Rubáiyát of Omar Khayyám* and more while sinking into the earth and reflecting, "One loses one's classics."[10]

There was also a sense in Müller's later directing projects that he had come round to a less qualified acceptance of Beckett toward the end of his life. In the multi-text evening *Mauser* at the Deutsches Theater in 1991, for instance, the action of the title work began with an obvious echo of the physical circumstances of *Rough for Theater II*: two men in heavy dark coats seated at two small tables set symmetrically at either side of the stage reading their lines tonelessly and mechanically (as a single boot sat inexplicably on another table – a satire of the single hat in Beckett's *Ohio Impromptu*?). The merciless words they spoke about Müller's condemned character A deepened the memory of Beckett's inquisitor-functionaries A and B who, with callous jocularity, discuss the possible condemnation of a man on the basis of notes and files they have collected. (There are indeed Beckett works, such as this one and *Catastrophe*, in which history is not absent but rather reduced to "a nuisance, like mosquitos in summer" [19/106], as Müller said admiringly about Pina Bausch.) Another example is the third act of Müller's 1993 Bayreuth production of *Tristan and Isolde*, in which Tristan awaited Isolde and death in a rubble-strewn gray space containing a single dilapidated armchair – the obvious allusion to *Endgame* strongly reinforcing the seriocomic impression left by the other two acts that this romantic hero's death-wish amounted to a histrionic conceit.

The net impression, however, is that Beckett was an object of profound ambivalence for Müller at most times, a cultural-historical presence to which he could not give due credit without seeming to diminish himself but whose necessity and significance he nevertheless fully understood. The following comments to Teschke in 1994 he left in the broadest terms, for instance: "theater must find its minimum once again, its zero point, from which outward steps can be taken again . . . The main point is to leave out . . . Reduction and concentration."[11] And this description of the plight of theater and the world from the following year he formulated as a gloss on Büchner's *Leonce und Lena* (*Leonce and Lena*):

> There's no more utopia, there's no more sense, there's no more
> meaning, nothing but this vacuum, this empty space. One
> doesn't know where to move in this empty space, how one
> should move, which direction makes sense. Therefore one
> plays. Out of that, play comes into being.[12]

A list of other occasions on which Müller conspicuously did *not* mention Beckett, before and after the fall of the Wall, could go on and on. "What's comical is that I write at all and don't simply do nothing," he said in 1982, reluctantly giving his assent when the interlocutor pointed out the Beckett association [14/115].

Speculation aside, the most telling document concerning Müller's relationship to Beckett, and the main reason this ambivalent connection is of principal significance in his art, is the 1984 text *Description of a Picture*. This work, very clearly influenced by the collaboration with Robert Wilson that began at that time, has been rightly seen by some critics as the acme of his formal innovation, and he himself identified it as "an endpoint or zero point" in his career [14/184].[13] Consisting of seven pages of dense prose broken only by commas and an occasional colon, and containing no stage directions or character indications, it describes a dreamlike "landscape between steppe and savanna, the sky Prussian blue" [8/7] – a nearly still, Wilsonesque picture that becomes the site and occasion of a theater event based primarily on the "movement" of the imagination.

Clouds, a tree, and a house are described in turn, followed by a woman in threadbare clothes "who dominates the right half of the picture," who may have returned from the dead, and who is "amputated by the picture's border" [8]. A man who may or may not be her murderer comes next, holding a bird in a death grip, the murder having possibly occurred during violent sex on a chair that is now broken. About two-thirds through, the narrator, without having resolved any of the myriad uncertainties about content, turns to hypotheses about the picture's meaning and about the future. Reference is made to a possible uprising of the dead and a "resurrection of the flesh" [12] driven by a mysterious historical wind that recalls Benjamin's famous storm of progress (the one that pushes the Angel of History in the ninth "Thesis on the Philosophy of History"[14]). In the end, the narrator announces a search for "the possibly redemptive error" [13] in the picture – a visual distraction of the killer, say, or laughter by the woman before the violent act. And then, unlike Beckett's Mouth in *Not I*, it resolves itself into an "I," or rather several of them:

> the MURDER is an exchange of sexes, FOREIGN IN ONE'S OWN BODY, the knife is the wound, the neck the axe, the fallible surveillance belongs to the plan, on which device is the lens attached that sucks the color out of the view, in which eye socket is the retina stretched, who OR WHAT asks about the picture, LIVING IN THE MIRROR, is the man with the dance step I, my grave his face, I the woman with the wound on the neck,

right and left in hands the divided bird, blood on the mouth, I
the bird, which shows the murderer the way into the night with
the writing of its beak, I the frozen storm.   [14]

The all-important idea that *Description of a Picture* is a specifically theatrical work, not merely a text for reading, might be explained
beginning with the closing phrase, "I the frozen storm," which makes
clear that the speaker *is* the picture, the picture a representation of the
speaker divided into multiple animate and inanimate identities (man,
woman, bird, storm). And since the picture is indeterminate, the
reader/spectator must mentally "construct" it in the course of listening; the largely mental theatrical action consists of the collision
between that construction process and the speaker's creative journey
(culminating in acceptance of the unifying "I"). Another collision is
also presumed, with a *mise-en-scène* that contrasts with rather than
duplicates the described images; "*Description of a Picture* can be read
as an overpainting of *Alcestis* which quotes the No play *Kumasaka*,
the 11th book of *The Odyssey*, Hitchcock's *The Birds*, and Shakespeare's *The Tempest* . . . The action is arbitrary" [14], writes Müller
in a postscript.

Staging is a matter for directors, however, and one reason this
seldom-produced text is particularly compelling is that, as with
Beckett's late stories, reading or listening to it feels in itself like a
dramatic experience. Because the mental construction of the timeless
picture necessarily occurs in time, the mind cannot help repeatedly
stopping to ponder what it has been told ("the sky Prussian blue"?),
momentarily regarding incomplete interim pictures as complete, like
theatrical scenes, despite the continual addition of new information.
Hence, willingly or not, the reader/listener/onlooker tends to be
pulled into the process of fragmentation that (in a final irony) binds
the narrative together ("who OR WHAT asks about the picture") – the
knife becoming the wound, the neck the axe, and the victim the
perpetrator precisely because the "surveillance" of the author/
speaker-cum-reader/spectator was "fallible." As Beckett once said,
"The key word in my plays is 'perhaps.'"[15] For Müller, too, maintaining indeterminacy is paramount: "a picture is always begun, and
then comes another that dissolves the old one or places it in question.

No picture ever materializes that you can really take home with you"
[15/92].

In a lucid 1987 essay, Hans-Thies Lehmann speaks of *Description of a Picture* as the culmination of Müller's later playwriting. The
"post-dramatic aesthetic" that the work consummates, Lehmann
says, dates back at least to *Cement* (1972), a play into which Müller
inserted nondramatic prose passages "that did not, however, break
apart the dramatic continuum."[16] In *Hamletmachine* and *The
Mission*, this "continuum" was broken apart since dialogue was
interrupted by long prose passages that stood independently –
"although at a pinch these could still be understood as monologues
overflowing their banks."[17] In both those works, *Anatomy of Titus*,
and *Quartet*, Müller also broadened his questioning of the "fixability"
of dramatis personae begun in the *Lehrstück* experiments; he introduced a "theater of voices" in which characters were no longer
"centering identities" but rather "carriers of discourses."[18] In
Description of a Picture, by contrast, the "last concessions to drama
(monologue, address, action) have disappeared," leaving behind "a
conflictive–dramatic encounter between a view and a picture, in
which the one brings the other to speech."[19] Lehmann:

> Müller's dissolving of dramatis personae results not merely
> from the historically shrinking significance of the single human
> subject. It has to do much more, for him, with the
> reconaissance of regions in which time, logic, space do not
> function, in which the subject does not experience itself as
> centered but rather as a contradictory imaginary *landscape*.[20]

This is a fine, illuminating discussion. The only point I would
add to it is that every one of the innovations attributed to *Description
of a Picture* was anticipated either in Beckett's late texts (which
Müller knew well) or in the uses they were put to by theater practitioners in the 1970s and 1980s. *Play* (1963), *Not I* (1972), and *That
Time* (1974–75), for instance, are long, monologic, possibly post-death
descriptions of physical and mental events which must be constructed
in time as pictures within spectators' minds during reading or performance; and these works all present fragmentary bodies (a mouth, a
head) as metaphors for damaged wholes, as Müller does with the

woman "amputated by the picture's border" and other figures (recall, for instance, the discussion of fragmentariness in chapter 8). Each of those Beckett plays, *A Piece of Monologue* (1979), *Rockaby* (1980), and *Ohio Impromptu* (1981) also presents a sculpted tableau on which spectators are meant to meditate as a flow of words with an ambiguous relationship to the tableau emanates from the stage, not necessarily from actors' mouths – Müller's preferred circumstance for productions of *Description of a Picture*.

Even more than Müller's other difficult works, this one depends as thoroughly as Beckett's on the ability of spectators to listen closely. Beckett was furthermore convinced of the dramatic value of onstage figures listening closely, their listening (in the media and late plays) usually being their means of access to ghostly presences. From *Play* and *Eh Joe* (1965) to *Ghost Trio* (1975) and *Ohio Impromptu*, Beckett was as obsessed as Müller was with otherworldly visitations – in the form of memories, dead loved ones, distorted reflections of self, and more – and with the relation of language to such visitations. (In the article just discussed, Lehmann speaks of Müller's specters largely in terms of Shakespeare, and in a later article devoted to the subject of ghosts in Müller he also makes no mention of Beckett.[21]) Lastly, to Beckett's consternation while he lived, a seemingly unending string of directors and would-be adaptors insisted on seeing his nondramatic writing (e.g. the novellas and stories such as *Imagination Dead Imagine*, *Ill Seen Ill Said* and *The Lost Ones*) as drama – a new sort of drama in which storytelling subjects become fused with mysteriously ambiguous scenes or landscapes, implicating listener-spectators in those processes of creative fusion.[22] All of Beckett's nondramatic works have been at some point adapted for the stage.

No disparagement of Müller or diminution of his achievement in *Description of a Picture* is intended in pointing out these similarities. Indeed, the grasping of directors at Beckett's nondramatic prose ought to be seen as evidence of a void in the theater of the 1980s, a void that Müller's text also might have filled (notwithstanding his claim that his later texts were written as ageless and indestructible "messages in a bottle"[23]). These observations are offered by way of description, since the history of Müller's *Kopien* is of enduring interest, even if he did invite more suspicious speculation by trying to deflect attention from Beckett as one of his shadowboxing partners. It is interesting in itself that the culmination of his far-flung quest for new theatrical forms – his thirty-year effort to peel away the layers of vestigial patriarchalism from Brecht's history-centered structures and to reach a purified, "democratic" core – was essentially achieved by applying Robert Wilson's pictorial aesthetic to the basic circumstances of Beckett's late drama.

In all likelihood, Müller understood that the power and magnitude of Beckett's work came from the authenticity of the renunciation it records, and his hesitations and ambivalence regarding Beckett grew out of uncertainty about how to react to it. Müller's life was hardly deficient in renunciation, but his sort of withdrawal (e.g. from faith in the future of socialism in the GDR) was never as thoroughgoing or as serious as Beckett's, and he could not simply "act" the part of the very private Beckett in his head, as he occasionally could the parts of Brecht, Kleist, Genet, Shakespeare, and others. Kafka – whose shadow is also visible in *Description of a Picture* and in many other Müller works[24] – might have been an acceptable substitute, since his works are a similar fount of entrapping landscapes and foredoomed subjects possessed of hopelessly vague "missions," if he had turned his attention more to drama and less to novels and stories.

Beckett, however, was the figure who pushed drama furthest toward the strategies of reduction and diminution that this virtuoso copyist (always attracted to extremes[25]) had need of in his later career. I will have more to say about this in the following chapter. Perhaps the greatest problem for Müller was that, in the end, Beckett's plays invariably celebrated the unaccommodated humans from whom they stripped everything away. The author of *Mauser*, who wrote, "Not before the revolution has triumphed absolutely / In the city of Witebsk as in other cities / Will we know what that is, a human being" [6/63], seems to have set himself the challenge of building on Beckett without being seduced by his humanism. *Description of a Picture* was – among its many other qualities, fortunately – the closest he came to that dubious goal.

10 Müller as Proteus: *Quartet*

KING: How fares our cousin Hamlet?

HAMLET: Excellent: Faith – of the chameleon's dish. I eat the air, promise-cramm'd. You cannot feed capons so.

KING: I have nothing with this answer, Hamlet.

(III.ii.96–100)

The protean character has been associated with theater, and with anti-theatrical prejudice, since antiquity. The chameleon, the changeling, the figure who wriggles out of all attempts to define his true nature and pinpoint his core, who insists that his essence *is* his masks if he offers any self-justification, has never inspired trust. Nor did it in me when I began research for this book. Even with other great protean figures in mind, the idea that expertise in eluding singular style, originality, or identity could be the defining characteristic of a writer of lasting importance ran contrary to every familiar concept of artistic achievement, including most of those rooted in the avant-garde. Ultimately, it was not textual investigations but rather the cumulative experience of productions – as it happens, numerous productions of one play – that convinced me of Müller's significance. The texts certainly revealed how deep his investment was in each of his various masks, but only the nine versions of *Quartet* I saw between 1985 and 1996 led me to understand the enduring value of his masks per se, the general importance of his aesthetic of malleability for the theater.

For this reason, this final chapter changes modes, concentrating not on a chosen alter ego but rather microscopically on a single play – the microscopic offering, in this case, a window on the expanse of Müller's vision. The availability of many productions of *Quartet* is due to its being a repertory favorite in Germany; it is staged frequently in France, the United States, and elsewhere as well – its serviceability and popularity due partly to its small cast and Müller's obvious effort to be pornographic in the manner of Marquis de Sade.[1] The extent to which this play has been different things to different people is at the center of this discussion. The productions were extraordinarily, even bewilderingly, various, yet as I grew more familiar with the text, I recognized that each was letter-faithful in its own way. And *Quartet* became, for me, a symbol and pinnacle of adaptability in Müller's quintessentially adaptable later oeuvre.

Quartet is the only one of his plays wholly grounded in aristocratic conventions. As its title implies, it is a chamber piece, recalling both the stage tradition of the *Kammerspiel* – small, intimate plays with fine-tuned atmospheres that touch obliquely on social issues – and the musical tradition of the quartet – an intimate form for four instruments, with roots in amateur medieval court entertainments, that blossomed in the eighteenth century. Müller's figural conception employs fictional eighteenth-century personages as "instruments" or "parts": two characters, Marquise de Merteuil and Vicomte de Valmont, play four – themselves and two innocents whom they plot to seduce, Volange (Merteuil's virginal niece) and the Presidente de Tourvel (a loyal wife). Notwithstanding the doubled roles and other devices to do with the work's operation as theater, the basic situation is taken from Choderlos de Laclos's 1782 novel *Les Liaisons Dangereuses*, which was written as a series of lurid letters exchanged by Merteuil and Valmont and was banned as obscene in France in its own and subsequent eras.

The novel has obvious temperamental affinities with Müller: the snide, icily urbane wit of the correspondents, their blithe assumption that morality is nothing but a game of appearances, tender feelings nothing but weaknesses to be exploited. "Love may be only a means of domination over people, of social achievement,"[2] writes Heinrich Mann in the introductory essay to his German translation of Laclos, an essay Müller once said had as much influence on him as the book itself [0/316]. Müller supposedly had the plan of adaptation in mind since the 1950s but could not finish the text until ideal circumstances occurred in 1980; that is, his third marriage having collapsed, he found himself working on the top floor of an Italian villa beneath which his estranged wife was sleeping with her new lover [0/317]. Apparently, what most appealed to Müller about *Les Liaisons Dangereuses* was its presentation of sexual relations so thoroughly drained of sentimentality that the narrative's very absence of warmth and tenderness becomes a source of titillation.

On the other hand, Laclos's baroque profligacy of words was not to Müller's laconic taste. *Quartet* was written, by contrast, in a hyper-concentrated, freeze-dried prose that doesn't so much dissolve as explode in the fluid of production. Nor was Laclos's causticity about the general idleness and hypocritical façade of the prerevolutionary French aristocracy a sufficiently conspicuous political platform for the dramatist, who adjusted it by immersing his play in Sadean salaciousness – Sade's greater political conspicuousness being that he was not only a fallen aristocrat but one famous for writing about pathological sexual behavior that appears normal in a pathological era.[3]

And this is the essence of *Quartet's* uniqueness in Müller's oeuvre. Cross prurience and graphic sexual description are vital to many of his works (*The Mission*, *Medeamaterial* and *Weiberkomödie* (*Womencomedy* [4/67–116]) come immediately to mind), but *Quartet* is the only text that uses sexual paradigms as its principal metaphorical medium. Like dozens of other Müller characters, Merteuil and Valmont are would-be Nietzschean *Übermenschen* held back from truly transcending morality by one or more inherited metanarratives (historical narratives embedded in the text that exert ideological influence on the immediate narrative). The metanarrative that mostly hinders them, though, is neither class heritage (as with Debuisson), nor family heritage (as with the Hamlet Actor), nor Enlightenment delusions of grandeur (as with Frederick the Great in *Gundling's Life. . .*), but rather the eternal Battle of the Sexes, a political conflict outside the arena of state power in which Müller usually preferred to work.

Quartet's single setting is enigmatically specified: "Timespace: salon before the French revolution / Bunker after the Third World War" [7/71] – a nod to Wagner and the tradition of fantastical stage transformation sprung from him (GURNEMANZ: "here time

176

becomes space" – *Parsifal*, Act I), as well as a nod to Brecht's *Fatzer* (CHORUS: "Just as ghosts came out of the past before / They'll come out of the future now"), as well as an indication traceable to Heinrich Mann that the aristocratic endgame about to be played has been played before and will be again (MANN: "A salon in the mid 18th century is a corrupt republic of the 15th, in mentality and predominant drives").[4] As will be seen, this stage direction has invited a variety of interpretations, the majority of which (to Müller's dismay, he told me) downplay the work's historico-political connections, focusing instead on stage effects or psychology.

Like many of Müller's later texts, *Quartet* is written mostly in long monologues – monologue functioning (as already mentioned) from *Hamletmachine* on as his preferred dramatic figure for frozenness, for a broadly conceived condition of political and psychological impasse in which true dialogue is no longer possible. The play's action consists of an elaborate masquerade-game whose rules and object are unclear, appear to change at five crucial points, and remain obscure in the end.[5] These five points, or beat shifts, are Müller's means of maintaining interest in what might otherwise quickly seem like a tedious playacting ritual derivative of Genet.

Merteuil begins speaking as if to a physically present partner –

MERTEUIL: Valmont. I believed your passion for me dead. Whence this sudden flare-up again. And with such youthful force. Too late, to be sure. You won't ignite my heart anymore.

[71]

– but the stage direction "Enter Valmont" a page later (Shift I) indicates that she was alone. In retrospect, her speech reads like a private rehearsal for a romantic rebuff, now fantasy, now anticipatory of some actual circumstance for which she wishes to be especially sharp. What is more odd is that, having confessed she is open to the physical advances of the imaginary Valmont even though she feels no emotion for him, she ends with an abrupt retraction ("That was well-played, wasn't it. . ." [72]) – the subtle implication being that she wishes to protect herself from even the appearance (before whom?) of emotional vulnerability.

In the next section, Valmont and Merteuil engage in vicious verbal sparring in their own persons, each accusing the other of finally stooping too low (Merteuil: "Tourvel is an insult. I didn't grant you your freedom so that you could climb onto this cow" [73]), the dialogue growing increasingly clever and savage, until Valmont waxes philosophical and breaks it off before exiting.

> VALMONT: I'm bored with the bestiality of our conversation. Every word rips a wound open, every smile bares a fang. We should let tigers play our parts. Won't you have another bite, another slash with a paw. The stage art of beasts.
> MERTEUIL: You're falling apart, Valmont. You're becoming sensitive. Virtue is an infectious disease.   [77]

At this point, without any transition or warning, Merteuil begins to speak as if she were Valmont (Shift 2), imploring Madame Tourvel, who is not there, not "to die partly unused" [80]. Reentering, Valmont just as quickly takes up the part of Tourvel, resisting Merteuil-as-Valmont's advances – that is, either he has been listening offstage, or the two are engaged in a ritualistic disguising in which both are rigorously rehearsed, or both.

In performance, this role exchange, if played as written, is an extraordinary *coup de théâtre*, partly because of the uncertainty about its basis. A woman, alone onstage, suddenly speaks in the person of a man, as if she had summarily swallowed him, demonstrating complete knowledge of how to play his part, which includes a subtle, skillful seduction speech. Her masterly sophistry ("Can it be less than a mortal sin not to do what we have been granted to think" [79] – a Sade argument that twists a church tenet of Tertullian's[6]) appears to have no effect on Valmont/Tourvel, until he suddenly tears open his shirt and faces her, announcing: "I am a woman, Valmont. Can you look at a woman and not be a man" [84]. "I can, Lady," says Merteuil, rebuffing him simultaneously as a make-believe man and actual woman.

The next transition (Shift 3) strengthens the suggestion from Merteuil's opening monologue that the game's stakes are inexplicably higher for her.

VALMONT: I believe I could get used to being a woman,
Marquise.
MERTEUIL: I wish I could.
> *Pause.*
VALMONT: Now what? Shall we go on playing?
MERTEUIL: Are we playing? Go on to what?   [84]

It seems she has been taking everything more seriously all along, and as Valmont launches into another scenario in which he plays himself and Merteuil plays the innocent niece, there is a sense that, though she plays along, he has transgressed some invisible line or failed some unspoken test of hers.

A graver political struggle over images of femaleness and maleness that has lain behind all the previous, jocund sexual skirmishing now moves closer to the fore, as Valmont delivers a male seduction speech as a male, perhaps implying greater responsibility or culpability on his part. It's as if the promulgation of a paradigm of female victimhood in an acted scenario set in another time and place (Valmont *playing* Valmont) constituted a greater violation of Merteuil than the similar promulgation made earlier when he sparred with her in the dramatic present (Valmont *being* Valmont). His earlier behavior might have been partly spontaneous and construable as harsh love-play, but now it is wholly calculated and there is an exhausted, even redundant quality to his domineering monologues at the niece's expense.

> On your knees, sinner. I know the dreams that pass through
> your sleep. Repent and I'll transform your punishment into
> grace. Have no fear for your innocence. God's house has many
> apartments. All you need do is open those astonishing lips and
> the dove of the Lord will fly and the holy spirit pour out. See,
> it's trembling with readiness. What is life without the daily
> death.   [86]

These speeches play on her convent upbringing by twisting quotations from the Bible, again in the style of Sade, but otherwise differ little in substance from the Tourvel seduction. Merteuil, as if bored, ends the scenario with a clipped summation: "The extermination of the niece" [87].

Her subsequent abrupt instigation of one final masquerade (Shift 4) – "And now we'll have the President's wife [Tourvel] die from her futile blunder" [88], requiring the earlier guises of Merteuil-as-Valmont and Valmont-as-Tourvel – reads in retrospect like a decision to go through with a preplanned murder of Valmont. She offers him "a last glass of wine" [89], and he then perorates heroically like a shamed heroine from sentimental tragedy seeking to regain her honor through suicide: "I'll push a needle into my crotch before I kill myself to be sure nothing is growing in me that you planted, Valmont" [89]. The play's final lines are deeply ambiguous, an anti-climactic figural orgasm in which Valmont switches to his own voice (Shift 5):

> VALMONT: . . . You don't need to tell me, Marquise, that the wine was poisoned. I wish I could watch you dying as I watch myself now. By the way, I still like myself. That even masturbates with the worms. I hope my acting didn't bore you. That would indeed be unforgivable.
> MERTEUIL: Death of a whore. Now we're alone
> Cancer my lover.   [90]

But is Valmont's death a murder or a suicide? Who has ultimately trumped whom? And, especially in light of the new information about cancer in the last line, which paradigms of maleness and femaleness, which images of power, may be said to dominate in the end? These questions are urgently posed and then left deliberately open, as if the masquerade's real content had to do with what Jean Baudrillard once called "the precession of simulacra" – life as a perpetual stalemate or Pyrrhic victory for all sides in which "power is no longer present except to conceal that there is none."[7]

One of the first effects of putting *Quartet* into performance is to stipulate a specific visual field against which all these open questions must be asked. Since general uncertainty about who is acting for whom is crucial to the basic conception of the work, *mise-en-scène* becomes an especially active agent of meaning, directors, designers, and actors facing a tremendous burden of supplying style without seeming to impose it, providing contexts for thematic questions without answering them.

In the 1985 American premiere directed by Gerald Thomas, for instance, designer Daniela Thomas transformed an already claustrophobic space at Theater for the New City in New York into a blackened crypt whose low archways were supported by thick pillars topped with griffins. The room had a dirt floor and was filled with fog as the audience entered, light coming only from one wing and two recessed openings in the ceiling. A dungeon? A deserted courtyard or monastery cloister at night? Eighteenth-century costumes and thick makeup featuring preternaturally red lips on two middle-aged actors completed the impression of a Sadean chamber specially outfitted for dangerous, perverse rituals. George Bartenieff played Valmont, a grotesque Valentino in a waistcoat, black cloak, combed gray wig and caked whiteface, his attitude permanently bemused. Amply endowed Crystal Field played Merteuil in a plunging black gown with a train that became soiled as it trailed in the dirt, her insinuating, gravelly voice conveying an air of forced coarseness.

The playacting in this production appeared solely driven by the characters' internal desires. True to their American heritage (even though both had long experience in the avant-garde), Bartenieff and Field had clearly sought psychological bases for all their line readings, and the director and designer's juxtapositions of elegance and sordidness was evidence of a somewhat single-minded indulgence in filth. The confessional tone of Field's soliloquies implied that the masquerades were primarily her idea and that, like Genet's maids and thieves, she saw herself as an outcast or "other" who had enjoined Valmont's participation in a compensatory ritual. The scene that sticks particularly in memory is the Volange seduction, in which Field groveled pathetically at Bartenieff's feet long enough to leave muddy knee-imprints on her gown. Admirable as it was as a first encounter with a theatrical idiom extremely foreign to everyone involved, the production lacked scale, an enduring sense that the characters represented historical, political, or sexual forces larger than themselves, and no subtleties in the design could compensate for this.

Lest one attribute too much to generalizations about American acting, however, let me add quickly that the earliest West German

Quartet I saw had many of the same problems. Carlo Tommasi's setting for Michael Haneke's 1987 production at Theater am Turm in Frankfurt was a rectangular platform with diverse and colorful costumes and props lying higgledy-piggledy in and around baskets, crates, and bizarrely hanging mirrors and furniture pieces, the audience seated along the two long sides in opposing bleachers. The scene brought to mind, by turns, a ransacked historical museum, a disorderly costume shop, and a rifled backstage storage area. During some moments, when the actors shifted beats abruptly to gesture like Thornton Wilder's Stage Manager for a spotlight or other technical effect, the stage represented a stage.

Performers Rüdiger Hacker and Elke Lang were both young and attractive enough so that aging was not a primary issue, and both alternated between formal and everyday demeanor in a forced attempt to avoid the appearance of singular personality. I might mention that part of the humor of this play, irretrievably lost in English translation, lies in the incongruousness of formal modes of address (*Sie*, not *du* – as Laclos and Sade use *vous*, not *tu*) being vehicles for unabashedly pornographic discourse, an incongruousness some directors and actors have turned to great advantage. These actors resembled aristocrats in isolated moments when their proprietary attitudes toward all the theatrical accoutrements implied that they saw themselves as lord and lady of this vague thespian realm, but most of their physical activity indicated meaner natures: silly costume changes, aggressive beer-drinking out of cans, playing of phonograph records, and bursts of slapping, whipping, and other low-key violence. None of the costume changes was especially pointed toward specific textual meanings; Hacker progressed, for instance, from a courtier's doublet and armor helmet to a woman's bathing suit with white overknee stockings to a leopard-skin robe with fur stole.

This production lacked scale largely because, despite their self-conscious attempts to pluralize themselves, the actors' recurring moments of abrupt aggression and snideness acted as everpresent reminders that two authentic, and hence privileged, characters underlay the array of "played" characters all the time. This Merteuil and Valmont toyed with Wilderesque metatheatrics, diverted themselves with various forms of hamming (Hacker, for instance, delivered one speech to a skull), but all that was durably real to them, and hence to us, was their sexually driven, mutually obsessive grasping and releasing, wounding and soothing, of each other. The avant-gardism, in other words, stood on glaringly conventional ground, one result of which was to drain the action of propulsive energy long before the end. With a third of the play still to go – after "Can you look at a woman and not be a man" [84] – Lang-Merteuil smacked her own face and fell to the floor in apparently real despair over losing Hacker-Valmont's love, her single remaining purpose the technical completion of a murder no longer invested with any interesting causal questions.

For a time, these two productions convinced me that nothing could be expected from conventional acting techniques in *Quartet*, that only the rarest of bizarre, perhaps even pathological, talents could ever exploit the work's multifarious facets to keep it from seeming "closed" in the sense discussed in chapters 2 and 4. But Hans Peter Cloos' 1988 production at the Schlosspark Theater in what was then West Berlin and Müller's own 1991 version at the Deutsches Theater in former East Berlin (both of which I saw long after their premieres) changed my mind. Interestingly enough, neither production pleased the author, as he told me himself, even though both were very powerful and popular with spectators. Müller said in 1993 that he thought his version (conceived as part of his *Mauser* evening) was "*schrecklich,*" that the *Quartet* actors had taken control of it away from him: "It had nothing to do with Brecht," he said with a dismissive wave.[8] His distaste notwithstanding, though, *Quartet* indeed permits some extremely rich readings in which Brecht is only a distant shadow.

Cloos built his production around another shadow, Beckett's *Endgame*, which other directors have also seen in the play but have acknowledged only fleetingly. (In the opening of Haneke's production, for instance, the actors moved and spoke only after removing coverings from their heads.) Taking literally the collision of epochs in Müller's initial stage direction, Cloos and designers Jean Haas (set) and Agostino Cavalca (costumes) juxtaposed a modern room devastated by an obviously modern war with actors in severely fatigued, eighteenth-century formal French garb. This juxtaposition remained more or less neutral politically since, apart from the sounds of planes and bombs occasionally mixing with soft classical music, the action never used it actively. This neutrality is what Müller found hardest to forgive (again apparently forgetting his affection for the way history appeared merely "as a nuisance" in Bausch). Mostly, the performers Sabine Sinjen and Joachim Bliese maneuvered moodily amid jagged concrete walls, gaping floor holes, and mangled metal scaffolding, now and then making use of a lone doorway at back that recalled the entrance to Clov's kitchen.

This Merteuil and Valmont were clearly taking shelter from immediate, physical danger outside (Hamm: "Outside of here it's death"[9]), as were Tristan and Kurvenal in Act III of Müller's Bayreuth *Tristan and Isolde*. And in both these cases, the politically indeterminate danger and shelter-like environment served to broaden rather than narrow the performance's pool of associations; the possibility that the various dangers stemmed from the characters' imaginations only increased the potential for humor. Again recalling Beckett, Sinjen and Bliese's studiedly stiff movements implied habitual behaviors that had developed in response to a feeling of entrapment. It was as if their use of roleplaying as a pastime had made them lose track of real time (Nell: "Ah yesterday!"[10]), binding them permanently to this intensely bitter, antagonistic dynamic which had once been a game. The surrender to their poisonous reality read emblematically as both consciously self-destructive and part of a nervous effort to keep playing, a fear of being crushed by boredom should they let up on the dialogue. So it went in caustic equilibrium for an indeterminate time, they implied, until this day, which for some reason was different – lethally so for Valmont (Merteuil: "Are we playing? Go on to what?" [84]; Clov: "Grain upon grain, one by one, and one day, suddenly, there's a heap"[11]).

What exactly did Sinjen and Bliese do that the other actors mentioned did not do? How did these two become expansive screens for projection, receptive fields for interesting ambiguities? The question revisits the nest of issues surrounding great Beckett acting, which I have written about elsewhere. There is no question that design can thwart or enhance this type of acting, but it cannot bring it about. Nor is it usually the result of deep character study or critical research. The

11. Merteuil (Sabine Sinjen) and Valmont (Joachim Bliese) in *Quartet*, directed by Hans Peter Cloos, Schlosspark Theater, West Berlin, 1988. Setting by Jean Haas.

12.   Merteuil (Dagmar Manzel) and Valmont (Jörg Gudzuhn) in *Quartet*, directed by Heiner Müller as part of *Mauser*, Deutsches Theater, East Berlin, 1991.

effect stems most often from extraordinarily specific physical and vocal choices that, "for reasons unknown but time will tell"[12] (Lucky), catalyze inquiring thought among spectators. Describing this effect is easier than isolating its causes, but those who have seen it know it can be the difference between forgettable and unforgettable theater. Though Müller did not want to talk about it much, at least with me, this supposedly apolitical effect is relevant to his work.

The author thought the performing of Dagmar Manzel and Jörg Gudzuhn in his Deutsches Theater *Quartet* was retrograde, he said, because it "turned into an apolitical clown act." And it is true that the play, flanked by intermissions, was used as comic relief between other gloomy and more explicitly political scenes built around *Mauser* and *The Foundling*. For this spectator at least, though, the contrast of this middle section magnified and sharpened the political impact of the others; the ultimately dubious display of variety and progress in *Quartet* prepared the mind to apprehend the full horror of cyclical killing and arrested historical development in the other plays. Through the originality of their choices, these actors proved that, in the right hands, the play can read as a battle of paradigms about sex and power, even in a case where the performers see it as a story of individual deception and revenge.

Quartet was performed mostly on the apron in front of the *Mauser* set, a busy, ominous assemblage by Jannis Kounellis of black panels, overcoats and other relatively colorless objects with a very high, rounded white wall at back and a metallic, smokestack-like cylinder center-stage.[13] During *Mauser* – recall that this is perhaps the most brutal of Müller's brutal texts, about a "worker" driven to orgiastic killing by his "work," which is to kill "enemies of the revolution" – a heavy coal-cart was pushed around the cylinder on a circular railroad track while furniture hoisted from below gradually crowded the space. (See fig. 1.) After *Mauser*, what was most jarringly different about Gudzuhn and Manzel's performance in *Quartet* was their engagement with each other in a focused, conversational manner and their interest in presenting a sensible, linear sequence of actions connected to their lines. Gone were the *Lehrstück*-based choral effects of *Mauser*, involving repetition of lines and distribution of speeches among multiple actors. Gone was Müller's trademark "deluge"-aesthetic, the general superabundance of activities, images, sounds, and texts whose oblique relation to one another characterized the rest of the evening.

The clarity and intelligence of the actors' choices were apparent at once.[14] Manzel-Merteuil, in contemporary dress, began onstage performing for Gudzuhn-Valmont, who wore an eighteenth-century wig and ruffles and was seated coldly and stiffly in a box seat. She proceeded to slice up her blouse with scissors during her opening soliloquy, blindfolding herself with one of the strips – "When I close my eyes, you're beautiful, Valmont. Or hunchbacked, if I want. The privilege of the blind" [71] – whereupon he (like a typical distracted eighteenth-century theatergoer) left his seat. Discovering his absence a few lines later – "I'm completely cold Valmont" [72] – she did not frown, or pout, or register any other familiar expression of pique, but rather, without a wince, stabbed herself in the wrist with the scissors, squirting blood and drawing a shocked laugh from the audience. The point in the text described above as Shift 1 thus became an opportunity to establish several complementary ambiguities and interpenetrating strata of meaning: Merteuil as a woman scorned who may or may not be truly in love; Merteuil as an actress intent on being watched, whose stage may or may not be in theatrical purgatory with the action occurring after death; and Merteuil as a gloriously demented monster of Individualism, played with proud aggressiveness by an East German actress as one of her first roles after the fall of Communism.

This last, most theoretical stratum was vital and pronounced, as was a sequence in which Manzel and Gudzuhn duplicated the earlier (Beckettian) circumstance of the two functionaries in *Mauser* by facing each other from opposing downstage desks, thus drawing a parallel between embattled former lovers and duelling socialist bureaucrats. To make too much of such explicitly political connections, though, would seem like acquiescence to the puerile attitude that sees all artworks as politically irresponsible unless they have direct contact with concrete social realities. My point, lest it get lost in the magnificent complexity of this production, is that the work of these actors, the startling specificity of their portrayals of two epically egotistical, comically histrionic souls, in itself promoted them from individuals to avatars of Individualism. Even for Müller, the theater is not obligated to teach history, only to offer people different orientations toward it than they have previously known.

Heinrich Mann wrote about Laclos's Valmont:

> Beneath the words of a roué who strives against love, the revolt of the personality against society becomes audible, muffled, rumbling. This species will accomplish the revolution in which "equality" is little more than a phrase but "freedom" is taken with the fiercest seriousness: the liberation of the Individual.[15]

How, exactly, did one see "beneath the words" of Müller's roué in this way? How did mere behaviors become filters through which one discerned such broad historical lines of significance? The answer lay in the way Gudzuhn and Manzel – like the best players of Didi and Gogo, Lucky and Pozzo, Hamm and Clov – rendered their exchanges simultaneously sensible and bizarre, hence memorable as archetypal patterns.

Both actors portrayed experts at seduction and deception whose constant effort was to throw each other off guard with mercurial shifts. Manzel used a well-stocked arsenal of bone-hard glances, sweet-talk, cajolery, and imposture, Gudzuhn an equally astonishing repertoire of rubbery movements and rigorously pointed switches between clownish mugging and strategic earnestness, all of which made his unctuous smugness oddly attractive. They seemed driven as much by feelings of actorly competitiveness as feelings of love – as if each was always challenging the other to a vaudevillesque duel to the death, only to offer a truce a moment later. Their urge to match each other "point" for "point" – like star actors in Laclos's age – had the sensation of a mental catherine wheel.

This contest was fascinating partly because one could never tell how seriously either party felt about it. Gudzuhn, for instance, spoke some of his more pretentious lines in mock self-deprecation, writing his words in the air ("LOVE IS AS STRONG AS DEATH" [87]). Another example is the point of Shift 4, when most other productions make clear that Merteuil has lost all patience and will now prepare for murder: here, both Manzel and Gudzuhn, with inscrutable tenderness, drew lines across each other's necks with blood from a pail, the "last glass of wine" [89] having been onstage, presumably poisoned, from the beginning. The ending, too, in other words, was foreknown – including hints of the historical aristocratic "ending" at the guillotine. Again like Hamm and Clov, this Merteuil and Valmont had no useful past and only the grimmest future; they were always locked in infernal, comic competition and always aspiring to virtuosity in their insatiable quest to entertain themselves and each other while awaiting the inevitable.

Merteuil ended as Valmont began, cold and stiff in an eighteenth-century dress, watching Valmont die from a box seat. The purgatory, in other words, was cyclical, "progress" being limited to the advancing decay of the flesh (as in Beckett). And this cyclical effect was why none of the acting conventions released spectators from the cyclical horror of *Mauser*, as Müller apparently feared.[16] *Quartet* merely sent the busy, physically overloaded worlds of *Mauser* and *The Foundling* into suspension for an hour or so; the historical impasse of Individualism (for which the psychological acting was a figure) temporarily replaced the historical impasse of revolution (for which the disassembled subject of the *Lehrstück* was a figure). At the

end of the evening, all easy escapes, whether into histrionic aestheti-
cism, suicide, murder, or hackneyed ideologies east or west of the
Wall (a main theme of *The Foundling*), appeared equally illusory.

One of most "aestheticist" *Quartet* productions ever done,
Robert Wilson's 1988 version at the American Repertory Theatre in
Cambridge, Massachusetts, a production almost entirely purged of
outside reference, contained some of the most radical ideas about
Müller's paradigms of maleness and femaleness that I have seen.
Wilson was rightly criticized by some commentators for the literalism
of his direction. With the exception of a 20-minute silent mime used
as a prologue and a few other sequences, the strict separation of stage
activity and text that had characterized his 1986 *Hamletmachine* was
absent, replaced with more-or-less direct illustration of actions and
metaphors that weakened both text and illustrative images. Despite
this and other problems (well described by Mona Heinze in a 1988
article entitled "Une Liaison Ennuyeuse"[17]), this project represented
an admirable stretch for Wilson. Not only did he atypically engage
with line-by-line meanings in a dense literary text, he also boldly
experimented with choreographic communication of complex themes
in the foreign (to him) tradition of tanztheater. The engagement of
these risks in itself deserves credit, and the results were more interesting than the reviews reported.

The set was among Wilson's sparest. Its economy combined
the cool asepsis and asexuality of his general aesthetic as a neutral
backdrop for the lurid language. (The same was true of his 1986
production of *Description of a Picture*, done as a part of his *Alcestis*.)
The main features were a table with six angular chairs and a re-
tractable diagonal scrim separating the stage into veiled and unveiled
triangular areas. Light circles and colored washes marked out playing
spaces, augmented at times by only a few isolated objects: a small
black triangular bench, one of Wilson's impossibly tall and thin
sculptural chairs, and a large rolling disk bearing a figure that recalled
Leonardo da Vinci's anatomical drawing of man defining both a circle
and a square ("man as the measure of all things").

These items rarely served discernible meanings of Müller's: the
choice of desultory, slow-motion activities to be partly obscured by
the scrim, for instance, seemed arbitrary, and there was no apparent

connection between the manipulations of the disk and specific lines of text. The mimed activity that served textual meanings did not escape redundancy or cliché; Valmont, for instance, threatened Merteuil with a belt, then wrapped it around his own neck and slapped himself on her line, "Be a good dog, Valmont, and follow the trail as long as it's fresh" [74]. The production's lasting distinction lay in its casting, primarily the use of dancer-choreographer Lucinda Childs as Merteuil, who was able to achieve the tense sculptural quality Wilson wanted.

Employing a cast of five, Wilson said he "did not want to repeat what [he] had done in *Hamletmachine*,"[18] and hence did not try to blur Merteuil's and Valmont's identities as he had Hamlet's and Ophelia's. Instead, the cast divided neatly into firmly anchored central characters (Childs as Merteuil, Bill Moor as Valmont) and accompanying choral figures (two men and one woman) who performed mimes based on the dialogue spoken mostly by the other two. It was the contrasts in style among these performers that made the production memorable. Childs opened the prologue with an extraordinarily slow and rigid turn like a figure on a music box and established from those first moments a standard of precise physical movement (later also a rigor of speech) that the men never matched.

The one other woman (Jennifer Rohn) sometimes approached this standard, occasionally mirroring Childs' actions, but the men (Jeremy Geidt, Scott Rabinowitz, and Moor) were always awkward and clumsy by comparison – which, given the nature of the text, seemed an intentional gender distinction. Geidt's padding entrances with stooped posture and hands outstretched like paws (holding an invisible newspaper?), Moor's naturalistic line readings filled out with emotional colorations and nuances, the loose-fitting suits on all three – all this seemed dangerously inefficient against Childs' ramrod-straight posture, bolt-steady arms (also true of Rohn), emotionless voice, floor-length slit-skirt, and cocoon-like bodice. Why dangerous? Because the implication was that she and her kind were hard where their opponents were flabby, that they had rigorously trained for a war that found the men woefully unprepared – bewildered lambs awaiting slaughter at the whim of female *Übermenschen*. Misogynistic Nietzsche turned on his head; the line, "It's good to be a woman,

13. Merteuil (Lucinda Childs) and The Old Man (Jeremy Geidt) in *Quartet*, directed by Robert Wilson, American Repertory Theatre, Cambridge, Massachusetts, 1988.

Valmont, and not a conqueror" [90], spoken here by a man, was pure self-delusion.

At one point, Childs-Merteuil, apparently so bored with Moor-Valmont's mistaken assumption that he had interrupted a tryst of hers that she could no longer be bothered to play along ("Through which window did he climb out" [72]), suddenly broke off speaking and laughed contemptuously as Moor and Rabinowitz *in*accurately mirrored each other's movements on either side of the scrim. Male ineptitude was repeatedly pitted against female facility and haughtiness in this way, or else was simply highlighted on its own: barechested Rabinowitz wearing a gaudy gold chain fell ignominiously to the floor after spilling wine on himself, for instance, and the arms of the male figure on the disk failed to reach the circle's perimeter like those of Leonardo da Vinci's Renaissance paragon. It is, of course, also possible that the whole schism of genders I am describing was accidental, that Wilson wanted uniformity of rigor in movement, speech, and design but had to make do with an imperfect cast and crew. No matter, really. Fortuitous calamity or not, the schism was the only aspect of the production that lifted it above its reductive literalism.

Even for those who might find the reverse Nietzschean schema itself a bit crude, Wilson's staging offered still another avenue of access: a fundamental battle for dominance between spoken language (logos) and the language of modern dance (image, movement, body). This recalled central themes in *Hamletmachine* (see the discussion in chapter 6) and *Description of a Picture.* Contrary to reputation, Wilson at his best can indeed make magnificent accommodations to what even André Breton readily admitted was the priority of language in human communication, surreal art included. The essence of many of Wilson's strongest pieces is a poetry not merely of dreamlike moving images but of unlocatable yet precise connections between words and images. As Walter Benjamin wrote in his essay on surrealism, quoting Breton:

> "Quietly. I want to pass where no one yet has passed, quietly! –
> After you, dearest language." Language takes precedence.
>
> Not only before meaning. Also before the self. In the
> world's structure dream loosens individuality like a bad tooth.[19]

What does it mean to "loosen individuality," and what were the places in Wilson's *Quartet* where language, quiet on its perch above meaning and self, accomplished this loosening through the dream of the dramatic world? One such place was certainly the ending, when Childs, chillingly placid after her act of murder, dwelled alone in silence, indulging in her strange, spider-like movements, sometimes manipulating a shoe, for *five minutes*, ultimately gliding upstage toward a sharply delineated light-rectangle where she uttered her enigmatic last line ("Now we're alone / Cancer my lover") and struck an equally enigmatic diamond-shaped pose with hands clasped behind her. This moment was beyond mere dream, immune from ("loosened" from) restrictive interpretations based on the individual dreaming subject. (Adorno: "something that is supposed to be a mere dream always leaves reality untouched, whatever damage is done to its image."[20]) Rather, it was a "marvelously" disturbing sculptural construction in which a quintessentially amoral human was granted the status of an object and left to stand mute and elegant, like a theatrical corollary to one of those Richard Serra multi-ton metal-slabs precariously balanced in a public square. No amount of interrogation of such an object with the "bad tooth" of individual reason can change its predisposition to depersonalize by crushing.

"I think a good text has to be like a thing, like a solid rock or stone," said Müller in a comment quoted in the program for Wilson's production. Appreciation of the pure dramatic object apparently weighed equally on his mind in 1994 when – three years after the Deutsches Theater "catastrophe" (his word) – he directed a free-standing *Quartet* at the Berliner Ensemble that owed much to Wilson's. In the interview after the opening, already quoted several times in connection with Beckett, Müller spoke of the importance of "moving away from the feeble-minded idea that theater has to be of immediate topical interest."[21] "Theater must not be allowed to show everything," he said, because too much "one-to-one representation" invariably kills the object-like "mystery" in a text.[22] He was referring to a Walter Benjamin quote he had received as a premiere gift: "Truth is not the disclosure that annihilates the mystery but rather the revelation that does justice to it." Revealingly, the two most enduringly mysterious *Quartet*s I have come across – this Berliner Ensemble version of Müller's and Bernd Peschke's short-lived 1989 production at Theater im Palast – were also the most politically powerful I have seen.

The main impetus for Müller's 1994 *Quartet* was the availability of Marianne Hoppe, 84-year-old doyenne of the German-language theater and former wife of Gustav Gründgens, to play Merteuil. "Realism," he explained, "arises not through less but rather more form." The theater not being "formalistic enough," this casting was "an example of a difference that compels form":

> To come away from age- or gender-specific casting notions. The great eras of the theater were always those when, for example, women weren't allowed onstage. You can also turn that around today and allow only women onstage, which compels a translation from the outset. You can't represent one-to-one anymore and then it becomes much more interesting.[23]

"Realism" here meant, first of all, the way an aged face inevitably led the mind toward associations outside the play: what twilights of which *anciens régimes* did this woman witness, one had to wonder, and which post-catastrophic future might she still live to see? Secondly, with 35-year-old Martin Wuttke playing Valmont, "realism" meant an acute magnification of what many have called the play's main theme: the aging female's rage at the loss of beauty and male attention.

The fact that the actor of Merteuil was 84 years old strikingly changed the coloration of all lines touching on mortality and decrepitude. "Ah, the slavery of bodies. The agony to live and not be God" [72], she said seated in a chair as if woolgathering, crowned by a bizarre, white, tufted wig two-and-a-half feet high. The next moment, wig off, she was clear-eyed and vigorous: "What does the pleasure of my body have to do with me, I'm no stable maid. My brain is working normally" [72]. This casting also affected all lines touching on the passage of time, which was rendered palpable by the production's slow pace (as it is in Wilson's and Beckett's work). Wuttke's leisurely, exquisitely gauged, digging deliveries particularly accentuated Valmont's cruelty.

> VALMONT: No rain has fallen on you in a long time; when did you last look in the mirror, friend of my soul.   [75]

> VALMONT: . . . our sublime occupation is to kill time. That occupies the entire person: there's too much of it. Ah, someone who could make the clocks of the world stand still: eternity as a

permanent erection. Time is the hole in creation; all of humanity fits into it. For the masses the church has stuffed it with God; we know that it's black and bottomless. When the masses find that out, they'll stuff us in afterward.

MERTEUIL: The clocks of the world. Do you have difficulty, Valmont, bringing your better self to a stand-still.

VALMONT: With you, Marquise . . .   [75–6]

The script gives Merteuil more than her share of retorts to this sort of humiliation, however, and Hoppe soon acquired her own potency. The spectacle of an old woman relentlessly assaulting a young man's masculinity with all this actress's commanding dignity made one listen ever closer to her hyperventilated monologues (which, more-over, were not always remembered and delivered precisely as Müller had written them, to put it mildly).

Like Wilson, Müller distributed lines and character respon-sibilities among a cast of five and separated the play into numerous scenes that had little to do with the five action shifts. (He believed the play had become too much of a classic and wanted to disturb con-gealed views of it.[24]) The scenes were divided by fadeouts and the simultaneous rising and lowering of a scrim whose movement re-sembled an eye; behind this was a desolate metal box of a room whose back wall sometimes opened onto a nearly identical wall behind – a trap within a trap (set by Hans-Joachim Schlieker). To this environ-ment Müller added not only his "formalistic" casting but also an entirely new plane of intertextual reference, called the "Dienst-botenebene" or "domestic servant level" in rehearsal: two maids, planted at the center of the action in explicit homage to Genet.[25]

These maids (Margarita Broich and Ruth Glöss) first entered on the lines quoted above about "the masses," when, with a routine air, they walked up behind Wuttke and Hoppe and cut their throats in mime. The moment was unfrightening, schematic, and condes-cending – the "masses'" rash, undiscerning condemnation of self-indulgent aristocrats. Fortunately, subtler sequences followed, such as a strange game of blindman's buff in which the bloodstained maids played joylessly with the actor Thorsten Heidel as he echoed Wuttke's lines, and a nasty struggle between the women for the privilege of sitting on a swing from which they had just rudely ejected Heidel (by then recognizable as a Valmont-surrogate).

These sequences gradually succeeded in delineating a time-collapsed universe in which revolution was always occurring and being betrayed, the underclass (represented by the maids) always in such a rush to enjoy its vulgar emulation of the overclass that it could never even share the fleeting pleasure of idealism (the subject of Valmont and Merteuil's cynicism). The pinnacle of dubious honor and position fell to Broich who apparently, as the younger and prettier of the two servants, earned the chance to be murdered by Valmont-Wuttke in lieu of Volange. A passage in Sartre describes the thrust of this device:

> When we see Solange and Claire [Genet's maids] in the presence
> of Madame, they do not seem real. Fake submission, fake
> tenderness, fake respect, fake gratitude. Their entire behavior is
> a lie. We are led to believe that this falsifying comes from their
> false relationships with their mistress. When they resume their
> joint solitude, they put on their true faces again. But when they
> are alone, they play . . . their truth is always elsewhere. . . for
> the truth of the domestic in solitude is to play at being
> master.[26]

I do not know whether Müller thought of this production, premiered a year and a half before his death, as any sort of culmination. For me, the way he handled the shadow of Genet in it had an unmistakable flavor of consummation. Over the years, the author seemed pained by the frequent characterizations of *Quartet* as a "boulevard play," an essentially apolitical capitulation to commercial images of historical pessimism. In 1992 he said that he "detested" the work while writing it but would have felt like a "traitor" had he not completed the text.[27] My perception is that, ever since what Tennessee Williams once called "the catastrophe of success" befell him in the 1970s, Müller had to struggle to remain a plausible outcast – an outsider, or "negro," or "Puerto-Rican," as he variously put it.[28] His explicit evocation of Genet in this late project suffused with awareness of mortality thus seemed like a form of headstrong grasping – an attempt to graft himself onto a nature that could still qualify as dangerously revolutionary, recalling his youthful relationship with Mayakovsky. And here again, he stopped his grafting process midway in order to display it as confessional art.

Müller's directing strategy in this production closely paralleled one of his characteristic writing strategies: selecting a literary paradigm and then demonstrating how it could *not* function as originally intended, could not lead him out of his various thematic impasses. What made this instance especially poignant was the singling out of a particular shadow figure (Genet) of whom he had always spoken warmly as a would-be negative redeemer. Unlike those in Genet's *Les Bonnes* (*The Maids*), the maids in *Quartet* were not the originators of their ritual but rather half-conscious emulators, perhaps figments, who tried to acquire the glory of aristocratic crimes by association, that is, largely by helping the aristocrats with *their* ritual rehearsals. Played by women, they were not even ostentatiously *fake*. "What is the real action in this ritual of betrayal?" Genet wanted his spectators to ask throughout his play. By contrast, Müller's preferred question was: "Can there be any 'real action' in a world where the exploited feel honored to be complicit in the system that exploits them, and where all rituals therefore amount to self-betrayal?"

Like Genet, Müller knew that the reign of overlaid masks and fantasies, based on the elemental attraction of Evil and Nothingness, would not end during his lifetime; his response was to leave it with a dying grande dame of a queen whose theatrical power issued from an inexorable, unmaskable "realism." A marquee name in dramatic classics under seven German Chancellors from Adolf Hitler to Helmut Kohl, Hoppe stood cloaked in undefinable yet ironclad authority in the end, the lyrical strains of Schubert's "Die schöne Müllerin" just faded out.[29] Nonplussed, she smoked a cigarette over the motionless body of Valmont, as orderly rows of flames rose, oven-like, along the edges of the metal box that entrapped them both.

The Germans have a wonderful word for the force of this type of fortuitous conjunction of fiction and actual fact about a performer or a performance venue, a word whose absence in English impoverishes theater criticism in our language. The word is *gegenwärtig*, the adjectival form of the ordinary word for present time, *Gegenwart*. But this Müller–Hoppe collaboration was not the most *gegenwärtig* production of *Quartet* I have seen. That distinction belongs to a version that never received much attention, though it was the play's GDR premiere. Opened on April 1, 1989, in Theater im Palast, this production was the Berlin directing debut of Bernd Peschke, an unknown young Dresdener whom Müller had recommended, who was killed in an automobile accident shortly after the fall of the Wall. By 1990, his *Quartet* too was history; its leading woman (also the theater's artistic director) had departed for the West, the aristocratic ruling class to which she belonged removed from power by an angry populace.

The political background of Peschke's production was explained to me by him and Müller on the evening of the premiere: Vera Oelschlegel, head of the theater and former wife of the Communist Party leader of the district of Berlin, had suffered the contempt of theater-world colleagues for years for having gained her position through nepotism, not talent. Determined to prove her abilities, she had chosen the role of Merteuil as an ideal vehicle, and Peschke had done his best both to serve that goal and to provoke a scandal at the same time. The scandal did not materialize – "unfortunately," he said. By 1989, Müller was at least as privileged as Oelschlegel, and concerned officials in the Culture Ministry had learned not to hand his Western supporters any more occasions to cry "censorship." In any case, the author claimed, all that those officials understood about Peschke's would-be provocation was that a high-ranking functionary's ex-wife was running around in public in her underwear. There was much more to be scandalized about than that, though, had they eyes to see it.

Theater im Palast was located on an upper floor of Palast der Republik, an enormous, boxy government edifice intended primarily to house the Volkskammer, the GDR's highest elective body. Built on the site of a Prussian royal palace torn down after World War II (even though it was still structurally sound) as a symbol of triumph for the new order, it shared a large public square with the Stasi and Communist Party headquarters. The Palast was one of those cheaply modern architectural monstrosities whose bombastic vulgarity stood as advertisement of the hypocrisy of the Communist ruling class (whose propaganda glorified the humble worker). The theater, an area at the corner of a large hall usually demarcated with grey and black curtains, was on this occasion opened to the spurious grandeur of the building itself.

With curtains and stage removed, spectators faced a tacky green carpet and impersonal white marble floor, a tall pillar wrapped in mirrors, modish brass light fixtures, forbidding marble steps, and tiers of windows through which the entire length of Unter den Linden could be seen in the setting sun, from the Stasi building to the Brandenburg Gate to the *Siegesäule* and Tiergarten in the distant West, which most East Germans (including Peschke) still were not allowed to visit. Except for a few stage lights and four incongruous TV-monitors stacked one atop another on the stair-landing, the setting *was* the Palast – the "Theater of the Palast," replete with the most realistic German-historical backdrop imaginable, its key player on this occasion one of its actual privileged residents.

After a few minutes in which the TV-monitors switched from program to program as if controlled by an unseen channel-surfer, Oelschlegel entered in a black slip and slicked-back blond hair, dancing lazily and sexily to music on a portable radio. Apart from a brief appearance by the actor of Valmont, Manfred Ernst, coolly smoking in a black suit and grey hat, the entire first half hour was devoted to establishing this woman as a bored, pampered, narcissistic beauty upon whom middle age was fearfully encroaching. Dressed as if for a date, she rode an unseen, noisy escalator (understood as her mechanical toy, a frivolous trapping of power) to the terrace atop the stairs, hung over the railing and spat, read aloud the technical printing on the back of one monitor, and crawled back down the stairs growl-ing – all the while speaking Merteuil's opening monologue in a sing-songy voice implying overfamiliarity with its content.

Here and elsewhere, Müller's words were treated as a pretext, the shell of an old drama no longer interesting to either party – astonishing in a national premiere. *Quartet* – already something of a classic in the West and hence an object of automatic interest for many Easterners – became a mere occasion for a sexual cat-and-mouse game whose real action the players seemed to invent anew each time they played it, their line readings and gestural communication telling a precise story that was related to but separate from Müller's. Valmont's line, "I'm bored with the bestiality of our conversation" [77], for example, was delivered with icy irony; Ernst obviously wished the dynamic were more bestial, having just pushed Oelschlegel down and brutally kicked her. (She had scratched bloody furrows in his back earlier.)

The sense of many sequences was utterly private: for example, when Ernst drew on his own chest with lipstick and dropped his pants during Merteuil's first discussion of Tourvel and Volange, or when each actor rudely interrupted the other's monologues with heckles, laughs, shouts, and singing ("I want to be loved by you"). Sometimes the performance seemed to cease entirely, the actors speaking Müller's words in inaudible colloquy as if on a break, relocating at one point to the windows where they gazed out and sipped coffee. And this exclusivity was the sharpest and clearest provocation of all; like most other spectacles at the Palast, *Quartet* had the flavor of a private affair – a public event watched by others like voyeurs at a keyhole. Müller in 1990: "the state- and Party-apparatus. . . never knew what people it governed. The oligarchy knew it gradually less and lived shielded from reality within a fiction" [17/83].

Courageous as he was, though, Peschke was unfortunately not willing to risk complete non-contingence of text and action, as Wilson was in *Hamletmachine* and as Müller recommended in *Description of a Picture*. The performers' private "internal" story was compelling because of their weird insouciant intensity. The one point where the director tried to pull text and action together straightforwardly, imposing a dominant interpretive idea on Müller, was where his production descended into cliché. After Ernst exited on the line, "The virgin tomorrow evening at the opera" [78], Oelschlegel broke down weeping, continuing to weep uncontrollably throughout her long subsequent monologue as Valmont seducing Tourvel. The implication was that she could not bear the thought of her playmate having left to seduce someone else, her self-indulgent nursing of her jealousy far more important to her than the game of impersonating him. Because of her uninterest in the complex thought in her monologues, this prolonged concentration on a single emotion pitifully reduced her to a woman exacting petty revenge in the end.

Fortunately, though, the ending redeemed itself in other ways.

14. Valmont (Manfred Ernst) and Merteuil (Vera Oelschlegel) taking a performed "break" from their roles in *Quartet*, directed by Bernd Peschke, Theater im Palast, East Berlin, 1989.

15. Merteuil (Vera Oelschlegel) practicing ferocity in Bernd Peschke's production of *Quartet*, Theater im Palast, 1989.

Among the most indelible memories of the production is of a voluptuous male aria from Bizet's *Les Pêcheurs de perles* (*The Pearl Fishers*) rising from loudspeakers as the monitors flashed to life during Ernst's final speech. On the screens one saw what seemed to be a time-delayed video of the action onstage. Beginning about ten minutes earlier, the videotape created a rich moment of disorientation when it continued past the presumably "present moment" (the actors had stopped to watch it) to show Valmont keeling over and dying. Victim and victimizer could both indeed watch him "die in the plural" [88], as Merteuil had just said she wanted, plurality being multiple kitschified playbacks at different times rather than Müller's multiple mirror images. After Ernst finally did keel over in the flesh, Oelschlegel stood at the upper-level railing lip-synching along with the monumentally romantic male singer of Bizet like a gender-bent German Evita. And at that moment she truly had risen again to the role of general proxy to all planters of hidden cameras, invaders of privacy, and conceited rationalizers of suffering and death.

Variety is the lifeblood of theater, of course, but it is not a value in itself. And all these descriptions of *Quartet* in performance are not intended as any genial celebration of directorial imagination in our time. I have used them in this last chapter as a means of summarizing general conclusions about Müller's protean identity and his place in the late twentieth-century theater. As I began to suspect after seeing about half of these productions, there is a special quality in their variety, unlike anything one sees with other playwrights. Consider Shakespeare, for example. Leaving aside adaptation projects such as Müller's *Macbeth* and *Anatomy of Titus*, I have seen, for instance, as many *Hamlet*s and *As You Like It*s as *Quartet*s, all with directors, designers, and actors striving for and sometimes achieving historical uniqueness. Some had abstract settings, some atextual concrete ones, some no scenery at all, some cross-race or -gender casting, some used masks or incorporated *Verfremdungseffekte*. It would make no sense, however, to place these productions in different classes of theater art. Each was a story-centered experience, identifiably tragic or comic, in which actors held one role each and were responsible for making those individuals as vivid as possible and the director was responsible for clarifying why a centuries-old text retained urgency in the present.

Quartet, by contrast, was the impetus for at least half a dozen different *kinds* of theater experience. Gerald Thomas and Michael Haneke directed essentially conventional evenings in which actors developed self-consistent characters and used the text to guide them on grounded psychological journeys. Hans Peter Cloos's actors, situated in an *Endgame* environment, used the same text to suggest, in the tradition of Beckett, that all such apparently consistent backgrounds were unreliable. Recalling another Beckettian tradition, Müller's Deutsches Theater actors intelligently transformed the play into a vehicle for their own clownish routines, providing a stark and significant cultural-political contrast between their individualism and the *Lehrstück*-based choral effects that dominated the rest of the evening. Robert Wilson directed a slow-moving tanztheater piece in which text was subordinated to image and movement, and two characterizations were distributed among five performers by way of a logic more sculptural or painterly than dramatic. Müller's Berliner Ensemble production was a marriage of Brecht and Genet that used the *verfremdet* acting of an 84-year-old woman and atextual maids ritually rehearsing crimes to force people to think historically about the emulation of aristocracies. And Bernd Peschke's production was primarily a deliberate political provocation designed for specific, unreproducible circumstances involving an actual political player.

This is an extraordinary range of approaches, and the list does not come close to exhausting the possibilities. I have yet to see any director do full justice, for instance, to Müller's 1983 remark that "*Quartet* is also a comedy . . . *Charley's Aunt* is in there as well" [14/139]. The point is, this range of possibilities is far wider than it could conceivably be with any other widely produced playwright – as long as we are speaking, again, of efforts to give particular plays theatrical life and not of adaptation. And this quality of malleability, or adaptability, applies equally to *Hamletmachine* and all the texts Müller published after it, which absorbed a number of chance events even during the writing process (as happened with some Gertrude Stein texts). Müller in 1991: "If I write, for instance, how Spartacus converses with Tiberius and the telephone rings and someone tells me a joke, then the joke can suddenly fit in. When the machine has started running, the different events suddenly become usable" [18/16].

Each of these Müller texts is an adamantine, occasionally impenetrable, formulation of interlocking mental impasses, a massively complex yet meticulously constructed collage of historical, political, social, and behavioral conundrums designed to serve numerous interpretive masters and seem perfectly compliant in every case. What is the true center, the authorially "privileged" attitude or meaning, in *Quartet*, in *The Mission*, in *Description of a Picture*, in *Despoiled Shore Medeamaterial Landscape with Argonauts*? The question is as nettling as the one about Müller's true identity, and just as unavoidable, and the apparent need for other people to complete the job of assigning significances for Müller has sent innumerable critics rushing to explain him through postmodern theory.

Postmodernism, however, regardless of whose version, is no more or less useful than any other totalizing explanation applied to him. It is constrictive, preventing his artistic whimsy and willful elusiveness from fulfilling themselves. (Müller in 1984: "The only Postmodernist I know of was August Stramm, a modernist who worked in a post office."[30]) Müller was not simply an abdicator of authority; he was a strong, clownish intellectual who enjoyed being seen as living proof of the Death of the Author, and who read postmodern theory himself in order to protect himself from it. One could say that he tried to act as his own deconstructionist critic by serving up puzzles of flagrantly contradictory meanings to begin with so that others wouldn't have to bother "embarrassing" him by cleverly searching them out. But that does not mean (as discussed in chapter 6) that he relinquished one iota of proprietorship over his words, *his* conundrums, in the collaborative maelstrom of the theater. For any commentator capable of thinking only in preconceived categories, he was indeed a bad accident waiting to happen.

Jonas Barish wrote of drama in general that it "cuts us off from direct access to the poet's self, which is a source of coherence, and replaces it with the competing selves of the various characters." Barish continued, "As the only available substitutes for the direct authorial presence, [the characters] afford at least a partial reassurance."[31] Müller would retort that his characters are scarcely more integral or determinate than the texts to which they belong, and that such reassurance is worthless in any case since, at least with him, the chase *is* the point, the difficulty of locating him as an author his most effective provocation to mental sharpness. And he might add, with Leo Bersani, that the special attraction of the theater in his era of embattled subjectivity lies in its being "a privileged arena for testing the viability of a fragmented *and* collectivized self. It can enact modes of escape from the ideology of a full and fully structured human character."[32]

I have never fully answered for myself why I needed to spend so much time and energy chasing Heiner Müller, pursuing the work and vision of a glacially infuriating writer who did not want to be so pursued, whose native theatrical context bore little comparison with my own, and whose general view of my country was woefully touristic in any case. What I have learned about my motivations has much to do with this Bersani quote, though. I come from a country in which "the ideology of a full and fully structured human character," as a function of capitalist Individualism, continues to help ensure that the serious theater is surrounded by a void of indifference. Müller came, by contrast, from a place in which myths and bromides about the "collectivized self" helped ensure that the theater (if only as a tension-release valve) was taken more seriously than film and television and where no one would think to question why an artist of major stature would want to work in it. Ours were worlds apart, yet I found his idiosyncratic ideas about arriving at Bersani's "privileged arena" strangely relevant to my own context. Despite his willed dilettantism in matters of detail, despite his exaggeration of his pariah status, and despite all the other aspects of his cultivated untrustworthiness, I am convinced more than ever that he saw much about theater and art internationally with unique clarity.

He saw, for instance, that overvaluation of originality, the bourgeois-era cult of the absolutely new, was a factor in the devaluation of history (in the West *and* East), and responded with a string of texts that refused to treat originality with proper capitalistic seriousness; partly because some of these texts also answer to Beckettian standards of precision and concision in language they will likely continue to puzzle, infuriate, and draw attention to this issue for a long while after their topical references become dated. He saw that the anxiety over technology and the relation of technology to self at the root of a moribund form called the *Lehrstück* pointed to an unmined lode of avant-gardist ideas and techniques suitable for the information age: "Preventing the subjugation of human beings through instrumentation is now the task of art," he said in 1991 [18/22]. And he saw the need, like Beckett and Wilson, for a theater that passes time, acting as a "brake" in the race of contemporary life and providing an opportunity for history-based "dialogue with the dead": "artworks need quiet in order to exercise their destructive power" [18/72].

For me, though, Müller's most disturbing insight was his more basic realization that in the late twentieth century – an age in which people on both sides of the now-invisible Wall are dangerously distracted by information inflation and media swarm, and the macro-conflict of capitalism and communism has moved underground, displaced by micro-conflicts around such matters as identity politics, multiculturalism, and terrorism – in such an era, the playwright of lasting importance cannot simply be an exquisitely feeling ego or "subject," like Strindberg, O'Neill, or Beckett. This playwright must rather be an engaged intellectual, someone capable of perceiving both the historical impasse in the theater (the end of bourgeois drama in a world not quite ready for the *Lehrstück*) and the historical impasse in subjective experience (the end of Individualism in a world not quite ready for Collectivism). Only such a writer would have the requisite indifference to reproaches of disingenuousness, evasion, charlatanism, and cynicism as he went about preparing literary bulwarks against the "ice age."

Notes

1 Müller as Müller

1 Eric Pace, "Heiner Müller, the Playwright and Social Critic, Dies at 66," *New York Times* (Jan. 3, 1996).

2 Stephen Kinzer, "Germany Can't Forget a Legendary Director," *New York Times* (Mar. 31, 1996).

3 Only two other book-length studies in English have been published: Arlene Akiko Teraoka, *The Silence of Entropy or Universal Discourse: The Postmodernist Poetics of Heiner Müller* (New York, Berne, Frankfurt-on-Main: Peter Lang, 1985), and the collection of essays from the 1994 Müller Symposium in Sydney edited by Gerhard Fischer, *Heiner Müller: ConTEXTS and HISTORY* (Tübingen: Stauffenburg Verlag, 1995).

4 Fried and Müller, *Erich Fried – Heiner Müller: Ein Gespräch* (Berlin: Alexander Verlag, 1989), 67.

5 Thomas Brasch, "Wiederbelebungsversuch," in Frank Hörnigk, Martin Linzer, Frank Raddatz, Wolfgang Storch, and Holger Teschke eds., *Ich Wer ist das Im Regen aus Vogelkot Im KALKFELL: für Heiner Müller: Arbeitsbuch* (Berlin: Theater der Zeit, 1996), 30. (Hereafter *KALKFELL*.)

6 In 1994 (a year after the news broke about Müller's Stasi contacts, and two years after the initial publication), a new expanded edition of *Krieg ohne Schlacht* was issued by Kiepenheuer and Witsch containing reproductions of the supposedly incriminating documents together with explanatory commentary. Pressed by the interviewer Thomas Assheuer for an answer to why he had said nothing about the contacts in the first edition, Müller said: "There is a human right to 'cowardice before the enemy'; I made use of it in that situation, that atmosphere back then. And that my image of the enemy was correct has certainly since been proven by the sensationalist press" [16/187]. No case of direct harm due to his Stasi association was ever proved.

7 Walter Benjamin, "Surrealism," in *Reflections*, ed. Peter Demetz, trans. Edmund Jephcott (New York: Schocken, 1978), 180.

8 *"Ich bin ein Neger": Diskussion mit Heiner Müller* (Darmstadt: Verlag der Georg Büchner Buchhandlung, 1986), 28.

9 Lecture by George Steiner at New York University, April 1991.

10 Heiner Müller, "Vampir," in Frank Hörnigk *et al.* eds., *KALKFELL*, 151.

11 Horst Drescher, "Der naive Erzgebirgler," in Frank Hörnigk *et al.* eds., *KALKFELL*, 122.

12 Michael Kluth, *Apokalypse mit Zigarre*, television film broadcast on German channel N3, June 14, 1995.

13 Interview with Jonathan Kalb, "Out-Takes: Fragments from an Interview with Heiner Müller," in Jonathan Kalb, *Free Admissions: Collected Theater Writings* (New York: Limelight Editions, 1993), 90.

14 Ibid., 91.

15 Thomas Mann, "Sufferings and Greatness of Richard Wagner," in *Essays of Three Decades*, trans. H.T. Lowe-Porter (New York: Alfred A. Knopf, 1965), 316.

16 Frank Schirrmacher in conversation with Heiner Müller, broadcast on German channel ZDF, Apr. 12, 1995.

17 Christa Wolf, "Einen Verlust Benennen," *Theater Heute* (Feb. 1996), 37.

18 Rosemarie Heise, "Begegnungen mit Heiner Müller," in Frank Hörnigk *et al.* eds., *KALKFELL*, 14.

19 Harold Bloom, *The Anxiety of Influence: A Theory of Poetry* (London, Oxford, New York: Oxford University Press, 1973), 5.

20 Ibid., 14, 15.

21 Ibid., 96.

22 Wolfgang Harich, "Der entlaufene Dingo, das vergessene Floss," *Sinn und Form* 25 (1973), no. 1, 215.

23 Müller wrote in *Krieg ohne Schlacht*: "There was a plagiarism trial with Dresen and Hamburger against my translation, which took place in Leipzig. [Gregor] Gysi [who would later be the last head of the GDR's Communist Party before the dissolution of the country] was our lawyer; Hamburger defended himself. He said it was historically proven that one could not make an independent translation of a Shakespeare play in two months. That was completely impossible. Gysi said: 'That's just evidence of the genius of my client.' He won the trial" [296].

In a letter to me (Dec. 1, 1996), Maik Hamburger explained that Müller had first seen and admired his and Dresen's *Hamlet* translation when it was performed in Greifswald in 1964. This text was then banned from publication and performance until 1973, Hamburger says, because its use of vernacular "subverted the sublimity of what was then taken to constitute a classical style" (Maik Hamburger, "'Are You a Party in this Business?' Consolidation and Subversion in East German Shakespeare Productions," *Shakespeare Survey* 48 [1995], 182). In 1976 or 1977, Müller himself recommended it for use at the Volksbühne, a major Berlin theater and hence a high-visibility

performance venue. Hamburger continues in his letter (and I quote him at
length because he has not had an opportunity to tell his story elsewhere):

> The Volksbühne made a contract with Henschelverlag [an East German
> publisher acting as Hamburger and Dresen's agent] for my *Hamlet*
> translation in 1977 and rehearsed this text for about 8 weeks without
> any exception. Three weeks before the opening of [Benno] Besson's
> production, Henschelverlag was informed they were doing a text by
> Matthias Langhoff and Heiner Müller instead. However, the actors had
> already memorized my text and as it turned out, the changes were
> minute. This was obvious at the run-through, when I first heard the
> alleged Langhoff/Müller version . . . As the Volksbühne proved obdurate,
> Henschelverlag, Dresen and I decided to apply for an *"einstweilige*
> *Verfügung"* [temporary injunction] to have the production stopped until
> we were correctly cited or the question of plagiarism had been decided at
> court. The hearing took place at a copyright court in Leipzig. Müller was
> defended by Gregor Gysi, but was not present himself. His description in
> *Krieg ohne Schlacht* is pure phantasy. Gysi did not talk about the
> question of plagiarism but only spoke of the unfortunate effects an
> injunction would have on the theatre, on the poor actors and on public
> opinion. Then the judge carried on a long telephone conversation with
> someone in authority – presumably in Berlin – and threw the case out of
> court . . . In fact Müller had continually altered the text at each stage of
> the proceedings. The version he submitted to Henschel was not the one
> acted, the version given to the court was a different one again and the
> one published by Rotbuch different again. However, I think you will find
> its debt to Hamburger/Dresen is evident even after all the
> metamorphoses.

The script of *Hamlet* included in Müller's volume *Shakespeare Factory 2*
is indeed quite similar at many points to the Hamburger–Dresen script
supplied to me by Hamburger (in a bound typescript from Henschelverlag).
Concerning his alleged "historical" argument in court, Hamburger added that
"I did not and could not have said that because my translation with Dresen
back in 1964 was itself done under extreme time pressure and completed in
about six weeks."

24 Jean-Paul Sartre, *Saint Genet: Actor & Martyr*, trans. Bernard Frechtman
   (New York: Pantheon, 1963), 426.
25 See Reiner Steinweg, *Das Lehrstück: Brechts Theorie einer Politisch-*
   Ästhetischen Erziehung, 2nd ed. (Stuttgart: J.B. Metzlersche
   Verlagsbuchhandlung, 1976), 144–5. In *The Brecht Memoir* (Evanston:
   Northwestern University Press, 1991), Eric Bentley quotes Brecht as saying,
   "Anyone can be creative, it's re-writing other people that's a challenge" [16].
26 Quoted by Erk Grimm, "The Backstage Performance: Heiner Müller and the

Young Poets from Prenzlauer Berg," in Gerhard Fischer ed., *Heiner Müller: ConTEXTS and HISTORY*, 80.

27 Hans-Thies Lehmann, "Heiner Müller's Spectres," in Gerhard Fischer ed., *Heiner Müller: ConTEXTS and HISTORY*, 88.

28 Ibid., 91.

29 Thomas Mann, *Reflections of a Nonpolitical Man*, trans. Walter D. Morris (New York: Frederick Ungar, 1983), 13.

30 I should mention that some usable English translations of Müller texts are available in various journals, notably those by Marc Silberman, Helen Fehervary, and Guntram Weber listed in the bibliography. Also, a competent volume translated by Marc von Henning entitled *Theatremachine* (London: Faber and Faber, 1995) exists in the United Kingdom but cannot be distributed in North America. Sylvère Lotringer's *Germania*, cited above, also contains usable material. The bulk of the texts published by Performing Arts Journal Publications, alas, need to be substantially reworked by a native speaker of English or, better, redone from scratch. For more on this subject, see my articles "Iconoclast Notes," *Village Voice* (Aug. 7, 1990), 90, and "On the Becoming Death of Poor H.M.," *Theater* (vol. xxvii, no. 1, 1996), 65–73.

2 Müller as Brecht

1 Tristan Tzara, *Seven Dada Manifestos and Lampisteries*, trans. Barbara Wright (London: John Calder, 1977), 8–9.

2 Peter Thomson, "Brecht's Lives," in Peter Thomson and Glendyr Sacks eds., *The Cambridge Companion to Brecht* (Cambridge: Cambridge University Press, 1994), 23, 27.

3 For other views on the relationship between Brecht and Müller, see: Helen Fehervary, "Enlightenment or Entanglement: History and Aesthetics in Bertolt Brecht and Heiner Müller," *New German Critique* 8 (Spring 1976); Theo Girshausen, "'Reject it, in order to possess it,': On Heiner Müller and Bertolt Brecht," *Modern Drama* (vol. xxiii, no. 4, Jan. 1981), 404–21; and Sue-Ellen Case, "From Bertolt Brecht to Heiner Müller," *Performing Arts Journal* 19 (vol. vii, no. 1, 1983), 94–102.

4 See, for example, Elizabeth Wright, *Postmodern Brecht: A Re-Presentation* (London and New York: Routledge, 1989), and Roswitha Mueller, "Learning for a New Society: the *Lehrstück*," in Thomson and Sacks eds., *The Cambridge Companion to Brecht*, 79–95 – the latter article an excellent summary of the ideas behind the *Lehrstück*, apart from this drawback. Her criticism of Esslin notwithstanding, Mueller points out herself that Brecht's stated goal of "discipline" "raises questions about the *Lehrstück* as a possible instrument of indoctrination," and that his corollary recommendation that parts of the texts be memorized before they are understood raises the "question [of] whether [the] leader/pupil distinction within the *Lehrstück*

implies authoritarian rule and the simple transmission of a number of revolutionary slogans" [88, 89].

5 Martin Esslin, *Brecht: The Man and His Work* (Garden City: Anchor, 1961), 43.

6 The best examples are the instances of Brecht offering *The Measures Taken* for performance as a *Schaustück* in Austria before his exile and in New York and London afterward. (See James K. Lyon, *Bertolt Brecht in America* [London: Methuen, 1980], 18, and John Willet, *Brecht in Context* [London and New York: Methuen, 1984], 30.) Martin Esslin characterizes Brecht's statement from 1956 that he has "repeatedly refused to permit performances of *The Measures Taken*" as "an example of typically Brechtian irony and delight in mystification" (*Brecht: The Man and His Work*, 157). Since *The Mother* was originally conceived as a *Lehrstück*, the disastrous 1935 Theater Union production of that play in New York is another example. For all Brecht's protests that his American collaborators betrayed his intentions, as Lee Baxandall reports in ample detail ("Brecht in America, 1935," *TDR* [Fall 1967]) there is no question that he was generally agreeable to the basic circumstance of thirty-six performances in a 1,100-seat house for a paying public and that the whole idea of using the play as a *Schaustück* was part of his general desire to broaden his fame in the United States. Brecht, of course, had a theory to explain this adjustment of purposes. In the absence of worldwide proletarian revolution, he said, *Lehrstücke* would have to settle for less, using dialectics to break down dominant ideologies, especially religious ones, among spectators in a process called "*Kleine Pädagogik*" ("little pedagogy"). Only after the radical revolutionary transformation of society would "*Grosse Pädagogik*" ("big pedagogy") be possible, whereby the plays would be performed by non-actors under the conditions described in this chapter. (See Reiner Steinweg, *Das Lehrstück: Brechts Theorie einer Politisch-Ästhetischen Erziehung*, 2nd ed. [Stuttgart: Metzlersche Verlagsbuchhandlung, 1976], 205–10.) This is all thoroughly understandable. The point, to reiterate, is not to embarrass Brecht or claim that his efforts to work outside conventional performance "apparatuses" were insincere, but rather to explain that he, not Martin Esslin or any other critic, bears the greatest responsibility for the misunderstanding of *Lehrstück* outside Germany.

7 Bertolt Brecht, *Gesammelte Werke 17: Schriften zum Theater 3* (20 vols., Frankfurt-on-Main: Suhrkamp, 1967), 1024–5.

8 Quoted from Roswitha Mueller, "Learning for a New Society: the *Lehrstück*," 85.

9 Reiner Steinweg, *Das Lehrstück*, 123.

10 Ibid., 119, 38. There is some dispute over whether Brecht also encouraged improvisation as a learning tool, as Lacis did with her children.

11 Francine Maier-Schaeffer discusses all three of these works in relation to the

Lehrstück in *Heiner Müller et le "Lehrstück"* (Berne *et al.*: Peter Lang, 1992).

12 Hans-Thies Lehmann, "Der Horatier," in Genia Schulz, *Heiner Müller* (Stuttgart: Metzler, 1980), 94.

13 Ibid., 95.

14 Martin Esslin, *Brecht: The Man and His Work*, 112.

15 Theodor Adorno, *Notes to Literature: Vol. 1*, ed. Rolf Tiedemann, trans. Shierry Weber Nicholsen (New York: Columbia University Press, 1991), 25.

16 Müller in 1987: "[*The Horatian*] really can't be played by adults. It's really a children's play, children playing politics . . . politics as children would practice them" (*Der Lohndrücker: Dokumentation 2*, protocol-book published by the Akademie der Künste der DDR [1987–88], 97). It is difficult to know how seriously he intended this remark, given the sharpness of his objections to proposed text changes by two groups of theater students involved with the work, one West German (in 1972), one East German (in 1988); see the published discussions in [6/73–81] and the protocol-book just cited, 96–8.

17 Steinweg, *Das Lehrstück*, 90.

18 Ibid., 188–90.

19 Bertolt Brecht, *Die Horatier und die Kuriatier*, in *Die Stücke von Bertolt Brecht in einem Band* (Frankfurt-on-Main: Suhrkamp, 1978), 421.

20 Wolfgang Schivelbusch discusses Müller in the context of a possible genre of "communist tragedy" in *Sozialistisches Drama nach Brecht* (Darmstadt and Neuwied: Luchterhand, 1974), as well as in "Optimistic Tragedies: The Plays of Heiner Müller," *New German Critique* 2 (Spring 1974), 104–13.

21 David Bathrick and Andreas Huyssen, "Producing Revolution: Heiner Müller's *Mauser* as Learning Play," *New German Critique* 8 (Spring 1976), 110–21.

22 Müller's repudiation of the parable is a central focus of the Theo Girshausen article referred to in note 3 above. Müller's explanation, in *War without Battle*, of why he didn't win a place as a *Meisterschüler* at the Berliner Ensemble in the 1950s also relates to this issue: "I was unable to write a story-plot and that's how I failed" [84].

23 Walter Benjamin, *Understanding Brecht* (London: NLB, 1973), 81. The German original may be found in Walter Benjamin, *Gesammelte Schriften* III (Frankfurt-on-Main: Suhrkamp, 1972), 440–9.

24 *"Ich bin ein Neger,"* 16.

25 Nicola Chiaromonte, *The Worm of Consciousness and Other Essays* (New York and London: Harcourt Brace Jovanovich, 1976), 138.

26 Interview with Müller in *Theater Heute*, "Das Vaterbild ist das Verhängnis" (Jan. 1984), 62.

27 The Müller text was published after a sixteen-year delay: Bertolt Brecht, *Der Untergang des Egoisten Johann Fatzer* (Frankfurt-on-Main: Suhrkamp, 1994). Those who have studied the *Fatzer* archive closely report that *Schaustück*

material greatly outweighs *Lehrstück* material in it. In his public comments, however, Müller was consistent in admiring *Fatzer* chiefly for its "experimental" *Lehrstück* aspects. (See Andrzej Wirth, "Brecht's *Fatzer*: Experiments in Discourse Making," *The Drama Review* 22:4 [Dec. 1978], 55–66.)

28 Richard Huelsenbeck, *Memoirs of a Dada Drummer*, ed. Hans J. Kleinschmidt, trans. Joachim Neugroschel (Berkeley, Los Angeles, London: University of California Press, 1991), 73.

29 *Der Lohndrücker: Dokumentation 2*, 12–22. Müller's "Note" to the play – which, as already mentioned, he disregarded – is quite specific: it calls for masks for the Romans, Albanians, sister and dogs, "no exits," as well as prop business such as the dropping of red cloths after each killing and the use of a puppet for the dead Horatian [6/54]. Interestingly enough, *The Horatians and the Curiatians* is the only *Lehrstück* for which Brecht wrote substantial performance instructions (see Bertolt Brecht, *Gesammelte Werke 17*, 1097–8), and *The Horatian* is the only one for which Müller did.

30 Elizabeth Wright, *Postmodern Brecht*. See Andrzej Wirth's article "Vom Dialog zum Diskurs," *Theater Heute* (Jan. 1980), 16–19, for a different, earlier discussion of the same topic.

31 For information on the Nazi *Thingspiel*, see: Günther Rühle, *Zeit und Theater III: Diktatur und Exil 1933–45* (Berlin: Propyläen, 1974), 33–41, 777–93, and Henning Eichberg, Michael Dultz, Glen Gadberry, and Günther Rühle, *Massenspiele: NS-Thingspiel, Arbeiterweihespiel und olympisches Zeremoniell* (Stuttgart and Bad Cannstatt: Friedrich Frommann, 1977). The latter book contains some material in English.

32 Bertolt Brecht, *Der Untergang des Egoisten Johann Fatzer*, 86.

3 Müller as Kleist

1 Lothar Trolle interviewed by Holger Teschke, "Eher kleistisch . . .," in Frank Hörnigk *et al.* eds., *KALKFELL*, 42.

2 Joachim Maass, *Kleist: A Biography*, trans. Ralph Manheim (New York: Farrar, Straus and Giroux, 1983), 130.

3 This would seem to be a main point of connection between Müller and Ernst Jünger as well.

4 Müller also saw his script of *Fatzer*, originally prepared as a "supplement" to Matthias Langhoff and Manfred Karge's 1978 Hamburg production of *The Prince of Homburg* [0/311], as relevant to the terrorism of the Baader/Meinhof group [14/53].

5 Wolfgang Emmerich, "Der Alp der Geschichte," in Paul Gerhard Klussmann and Heinrich Mohr eds., *Deutsche Misere einst und jetzt: Die deutsche Misere als Thema der Gegenwartsliteratur/Das Preussensyndrom in der Literatur der DDR* (Bonn: Bouvier Verlag Herbert Grundmann, 1982), 144,

123. For another discussion of similar issues in Müller, see Jost Hermand, "Fridericus Rex," in Ulrich Profitlich ed., *Dramatik der DDR* (Frankfurt-on-Main: Suhrkamp, 1987), 287–92.

6 J.H. Reid, "Homburg-Machine – Heiner Müller in the Shadow of Nuclear War," in W.G. Sebald ed., *A Radical Stage: Theatre in Germany in the 1970s and 1980s* (New York, Oxford, Munich: Berg, 1988, 1990), 145.

7 Heinrich von Kleist, *Prinz Friedrich von Homburg* (Stuttgart: Philipp Reclam Jun., 1968), 81.

8 J.H. Reid, "Homburg-Machine," 158.

9 Fried and Müller, *Erich Fried – Heiner Müller: Ein Gespräch*, 52.

10 J.H. Reid, "Homburg-Machine," 158.

11 Genia Schulz, *Heiner Müller*, 108.

12 Bertolt Brecht, *Die Massnahme*, in *Die Stücke von Bertolt Brecht in einem Band*, 265.

13 Wolfgang Schivelbusch, *Sozialistisches Drama nach Brecht*, 213.

14 Joachim Maass, *Kleist: A Biography*, 267.

15 Theodor W. Adorno, "On the Question: 'What Is German?'" *New German Critique* 36 (Fall 1985), 130.

16 Heinrich von Kleist, *Prinz Friedrich von Homburg*, 83.

17 Wolfgang Emmerich, "Der Alp der Geschichte," 154.

18 Interview with Jonathan Kalb, "Out-Takes," 84, and in numerous public forums. A related remark appears in Müller's acceptance speech upon receiving the Kleist Prize in 1990, printed in *Jenseits der Nation* [18/63]. Identifying the point with himself, Müller described "the feeling [when reading Kleist's letters], not without horror, of a terrible remoteness, a distance even to his own texts, his actual work, which is not addressed to people, not to a public, Goethe's reproach, not to a market."

4 Müller as Mayakovsky

1 For a fine account of this production, see Marc Silberman, "Heiner Müller's *Der Lohndrücker*, 1988," *Theater* (Fall 1988).

2 H.G. Huettich explains the "Fight Against Formalism" in *Theater in the Planned Society* (Chapel Hill: University of North Carolina Press, 1978), 26. Brecht's 1953 essay, "Cultural Policy and Academy of Arts," in *Brecht on Theater*, trans. John Willet (New York: Hill and Wang, 1964), 266–70, is an illuminating addendum.

3 The principles of Socialist Realism were originally formulated by Maxim Gorki and then codified by Andrey Zdhanov at the first All-Union Congress of Soviet Writers in 1934. Zdhanov's rules, which remained dominant during the entire period that Ulbricht and his circle were in exile in Russia, are quoted in H.G. Scott ed., *Problems of Soviet Literature* (New York: International Publ., 1935; Westport: Hyperion Press, 1981), 21.

4 For an account of the 1959 production, see Friedrich Luft, *Stimme der Kritik: Berliner Theater seit 1945* (Hanover: Friedrich Verlag, 1965), 289–91.

5 Interview with Peter Hacks, in Margaret Herzfeld-Sander, ed., *Essays on German Theater* (New York: Continuum, 1985), 304.

6 H.G. Huettich, *Theater in the Planned Society*, 31.

7 Ibid., 52. Rémy Charbon also writes about the milieu of the GDR at this time in "'Denn das Schöne bedeutet das mögliche Ende der Schrecken': Versuch über Heiner Müller und das Theater der DDR in der Epoche des Neuen ökonomischen Systems," *Wirkendes Wort* (May/June 1980), 149–77.

8 The precise nature of the collaboration between the Müllers will probably never be known. Interestingly enough, in 1959 (i.e. after the Party-friendly revision of *The Correction*), the East German Akademie der Künste selected them as co-recipients of the Heinrich Mann Prize for *The Scab* and *The Correction* [0/151, 154–5].

9 Emile Zola, *The Experimental Novel and Other Essays*, trans. Belle M. Sherman (New York: Cassell Publ. Co., 1893), 111.

10 See Peter Uwe Hohendahl and Patricia Herminghouse eds., *Literatur und Literaturtheorie in der DDR* (Frankfurt-on-Main: Suhrkamp, 1976), particularly the essays by Jost Herman and Jack Zipes.

11 See also Müller's 1987 interview with André Müller, in which he calls the revision a "mistake" [19/215].

12 The 1951 flight of Müller's father from the GDR involved a similar circumstance. A public building in Frankenberg collapsed due to substandard concrete work, that is, because of the bad faith of workers for whom he, as Bürgermeister, was ultimately responsible [0/69].

13 Müller's volume *Geschichten aus der Produktion 1* contains a partial transcript of the Schwarze Pumpe discussion as well as two contemporary commentaries: a terse and dispassionate *Zwischenbemerkung* (incidental remark) written by Müller after the Gorki Theater discussion and a breast-beating, "point for point" response by the director Hans Dieter Mäde to the "substantial advice" offered by Party officials. Müller says that the "open" form of *Correction 1* was a natural result of the "contradictions" of the contemporary GDR and adds that *Correction 2* is an "attempt to create a closed form" which, being "premature," may foster "political reaction." With strained earnestness, Mäde describes how the revised play turns nearly all the "ideological adjustments" into "real artistic deepenings" [1/59–66].

14 Müller tells the story of the Lenin text in *War without Battle* [103–4] and in *Zur Lage der Nation* [95–6], and the story of *Waldstück* in *War without Battle* [238–42]. The *Germania Death in Berlin* episode is related by Vladimir Koljasin, "Späte Saat – Heiner Müller und Russland," in Frank Hörnigk *et al.* eds., *KALKFELL*, 104. Müller refers to the *Germania Death in Berlin* episode but gives no details in *War without Battle* [302].

15 Vladimir Mayakovsky, "Left March," in *Selected Works in Three Volumes 1:*

Selected Verse, trans. Dorian Rottenberg (Moscow: Raduga, 1985), 77. Müller inserted this poem in his 1991 production of *Mauser* at the Deutsches Theater.

16 Vladimir Mayakovsky, "At the Top of My Voice," in *The Bedbug and Selected Poetry*, ed. Patricia Blake, trans. Max Hayward and George Reavey (Bloomington: Indiana University Press, 1975), 221, 223.

17 Quoted in Wiktor Woroszylski, *The Life of Mayakovsky*, trans. Boleslaw Taborski (New York: Orion Press, 1970), 83.

18 Interview with Klaus Völker, "Ein Stück Protoplasma: Heiner Müller über Majakowski," *Theater Heute* (Sept. 1983), 30.

19 Müller acknowledged Mayakovsky's technical influence on his writing on several occasions. See the 1957 text "Die Kröte auf dem Gasometer" [13/125], for instance, and the 1985 interview in which he said: "very important for me was Mayakovsky and the attempt – even in the translation into German – to bring the jargon of industry and the street into poetic writing" [14/147]. According to Holger Teschke (personal communication, Oct. 18, 1996), Müller knew no more than a few words of Russian; his third wife, Ginka Tscholakowa, who was fluent, provided rough translations from which he worked.

20 Vladimir Mayakovsky, *Selected Works in Three Volumes 1: Selected Verse*, 50.

21 Edward J. Brown, *Mayakovsky: A Poet in the Revolution* (Princeton: Princeton University Press, 1973), 370.

22 Victor Erofeyev, "Dying for the Party," *The Times Literary Supplement* (Jan. 7, 1994), 9. After the breakup of the Soviet Union, some of the public places named after Mayakovsky were changed back.

23 See, for example, the following articles on the 1990 "Experimenta 6" festival in Frankfurt, which was exclusively devoted to Müller: Gerhard Stadelmaier, "Mumienstücke," *Frankfurter Allgemeine Zeitung* (June 2, 1990); P.I. [Peter Iden?], "Dreifaches Debakel," *Frankfurter Rundschau* (May 21, 1990).

24 Fritz Mierau, "Majakowski Lesen," *Sinn und Form*, 30:3 (May/June 1978), 650–62.

25 There are several informative pieces on Inge Müller in Wolfgang Storch, ed., *Explosion of a Memory Heiner Müller DDR: Ein Arbeitsbuch* (Berlin: Hentrich, 1988), 197–205. See also Adolf Endler, "Fragt mich nicht wie: Zur Lyrik Inge Müllers," *Sinn und Form*, 31:1 (Jan./Feb. 1979), 152–61.

26 Letter to me January 27, 1994. My thanks to Wolfgang Storch for the idea of juxtaposing these poems (see his *Explosion of a Memory*, 114). Inge Müller's poetry, including this text, is collected in Inge Müller, *Wenn ich schon sterben muss* (Berlin and Weimar: Aufbau Verlag, 1985). Heiner Müller's poem first appeared in *Geschichten aus der Produktion 1* [83] without the lines "*Blut, geronnen / Zu Medaillenblech*"; I quote the text from Storch because Müller, also in the letter just cited, explained that the lines "were missing because I first found the manuscript after the printing."

27 Vladimir Mayakovsky, *The Bedbug and Selected Poetry*, 111.

28 Ibid., 83. Vladimir Mayakovsky, "War and the World," in *Selected Works in Three Volumes 2: Longer Poems*, trans. Dorian Rottenberg (Moscow: Raduga, 1986), 36–37.

29 Bertolt Brecht, *Poems: 1913–1956* (New York: Methuen, 1976), 405.

30 A 1930 clipping from a New York newspaper, with a headline belittling Mayakovsky's "Wounded Vanity," adorns the cover of *Kopien 2*, the Müller volume containing *Vladimir Mayakovsky: A Tragedy*. The woman named and depicted in the accompanying photo is his sometime lover and friend Lily Brik. It was actually another woman, Tatiana Yakovleva, who broke off with Mayakovsky and married a French Vicomte shortly before Mayakovsky's death.

31 See Adolf Endler, "Fragt mich nicht wie: Zur Lyrik Inge Müllers," 160. The other relevant poems by Inge Müller are "Das Gesicht" ("The Face"), a response to Mayakovsky's 1918 "Be Better to Horses," and "Nach Wolke in Hosen" ("After Cloud in Trousers"), in *Wenn ich schon sterben muss*, 26, 60.

32 Vladimir Mayakovsky, *Selected Works in Three Volumes 2: Longer Poems*, 39.

33 Paul Celan, *Last Poems*, trans. Katharine Washburn and Margret Guillemin (San Francisco: North Point Press, 1986), 14.

34 *The Scab* was submitted to and rejected by Peter Palitzsch at the Berliner Ensemble and Heiner Kipphardt at the Deutsches Theater in the 1950s, Müller says in *War without Battle*, both of whom later regretted their decisions. He also says that the Berliner Ensemble was actually in the forefront of the attack on *Resettler*, notwithstanding Helene Weigel's help on his self-critique [178–85].

35 Throughout his book about the *Resettler* affair, *Drama um eine Komödie* (Berlin: Christoph Links, 1996), Matthias Braun speaks as if Heiner and Inge Müller were definitely co-authors of the work, but he offers no evidence to support this. Marianne Streisand points out that the play's original title was taken from an Anna Seghers story published in a book that Heiner Müller reviewed in 1953 ("Heiner Müllers 'Die Umsiedlerin oder Das Leben auf dem Lande,'" *Weimarer Beiträge* 32 [1986] 8, 1,360).

36 Matthias Braun, *Drama um eine Komödie*, 9; Marianne Streisand, "Heiner Müllers 'Die Umsiedlerin oder Das Leben auf dem Lande,'" 1363–4.

37 This information is from Genia Schulz, *Heiner Müller*, 35–48. Schulz's chapter on *The Resettler* contains an interesting discussion connecting the work to the baroque *Trauerspiel*. See also Helen Fehervary's article, "Anna Seghers' 'Gothic' Realism and the Redemptive Moment in Heiner Müller's *Die Umsiedlerin*," in Gerhard Fischer ed., *Heiner Müller: ConTEXTS and HISTORY*, 21–39.

38 Matthias Braun, *Drama um eine Komödie*, 10–12.

39 Genia Schulz, "'Ein Bier und vor dir steht ein Kommunist, Flint'. Zur

Dialektik des Anfangs bei Heiner Müller," in Paul Gerhard Klussmann and
Heinrich Mohr eds., *Dialektik des Anfangs: Spiele des Lachens* (Bonn:
Bouvier Verlag Herbert Grundmann, 1986), 22.

40 As published by Rotbuch Verlag in 1975, *The Resettler* contains a single
surrealistic stage direction involving historical figures, implying that it, too
(like *Tractor*), could be considered an early harbinger of the fantasy worlds in
Germania Death in Berlin and the other "synthetic fragments" published in
the 1970s.

> *[The farmer] lets the books fall and exits. Flint picks up the books and
> walks with the bicycle, flag, sign and books. Enter Hitler with Eva Braun
> breasts, a gnawed carpet and a gasoline can, pursued by Frederick II of
> Prussia, his walking stick between his legs. Hitler leaps onto his back;
> Frederick II leaps onto Hitler's back. Repeated attempts by Flint to
> shake them off. At every attempt something different, or everything else,
> falls down: the bicycle, the flag, the sign, the books.   [3/25]*

Accounts of the 1961 performance make no mention of these actions,
however, and it is difficult to tell when the passage was added to the text.

5 Müller as Shakespeare

1 Harold Bloom, *The Anxiety of Influence*, 11.
2 This was also apparently a point of attraction for Robert Wilson, who said in a
1988 interview: "Heiner's plays are great because they're not written so that
one has to understand them. That's like Shakespeare." Interview with Frank
Hentschker *et al.*, "Be Stupid," in Wolfgang Storch ed., *Explosion of a
Memory*, 65. Many comments of Müller's concerning his eight-hour *Hamlet/
Machine* at the Deutsches Theater, directed amid the momentous events of
Fall 1989, also touch on this parallel. See Christoph Rüter's film about the
production, *The Time is Out of Joint* (1990).
3 No slight to Müller's powers of translation is intended here. Indeed,
notwithstanding the dispute over *Hamlet* mentioned in chapter 1, in German
Shakespeare circles his translations are considered to be (along with
Hamburger and Dresen's, B.K. Tragelehn's, and Eva Walch's) some of the most
important alternatives that were offered in the GDR to the Romantic classics
and to the officially sanctioned translations of Rudolf Schaller. For
discussions of these issues see: Thomas Sorge, "Unsere Shakespeares –
Nachdenken über einen Wegbegleiter," *Shakespeare Jahrbuch* (126/1990),
and Maik Hamburger, "Are You a Party in this Business?: Consolidation and
Subversion in East German Shakespeare Productions," 178.
4 Quoted in Benjamin Henrichs, "Die zum Lächeln nicht Zwingbaren," *Die
Zeit* (May 24, 1974), 19.
5 Wolfgang Harich, "Der Entlaufene Dingo, Das Vergessene Floss," 216;
Anselm Schlösser, "Die Welt hat keinen Ausgang als zum Schinder: Ein

Diskussionsbeitrag zu Heiner Müllers 'Macbeth'," *Theater der Zeit* (no. 8, 1972), 47.

6 Wolfgang Harich, "Der Entlaufene Dingo, Das Vergessene Floss," 216, 217.

7 Ibid., 210, 211.

8 Ibid., 214.

9 Ibid., 214, 217.

10 Martin Linzer, "Historische Exaktheit und Grausamkeit," *Theater der Zeit* (no. 7, 1972), 23; Friedrich Dieckmann, "Heiner Müller und die Legitimität," *Theater der Zeit* (no. 9, 1972), 46; Anselm Schlösser, "Die Welt hat keinen Ausgang als zum Schinder," 47.

11 Friedrich Dieckmann, "Heiner Müller und die Legitimität," 47.

12 Wolfgang Heise, "Notwendige Fragestellung," *Theater der Zeit* (no. 9, 1972), 46.

13 See the essays and interviews in Theo Girshausen ed., *Die Hamletmaschine: Heiner Müllers Endspiel* (Cologne: Prometh Verlag, 1978).

14 The Dec. 1982 issue of *Theater Heute* contains extensive photodocumentation of the production, including captions detailing the action depicted. For more details in English, see Eva and Günter Walch, "Shakespeare in the German Democratic Republic," *Shakespeare Quarterly* 35:3 (1984), 326–9.

15 Hans-Thies Lehmann, "Das Ende der Macht – auf dem Theater," *Theater Heute* (Dec. 1982), 16. Notwithstanding the rigor of Lehmann's analysis, no doubt justified in this case, Müller generally found it easier to achieve playfulness in his directing than in his writing. His meditations on fluid identity were never as carefree as, say, the young Sam Shepard's, but his productions, with their ample use of rock and roll, sometimes made him seem as though he wished they were.

16 Shortly before this production, Müller told Sue-Ellen Case that he had been reading *Kool Killer oder Der Aufstand der Zeichen* (Berlin: Merve, 1978), a collection of Baudrillard essays translated into German. The essay referring to "exchangeability" is "Unser Theater der Grausamkeit" ("Notre Théâtre de la Cruauté," 1977), but the rest of the book is also relevant. Sue-Ellen Case, "Developments in Post-Brechtian Political Theater: The Plays of Heiner Müller," unpublished doctoral dissertation at the University of California, Berkeley (1981), 71–2.

17 Quoted in *Theater Heute*, Dec. 1982, 21.

18 Hans-Thies Lehmann discusses this point in "Das Ende der Macht – auf dem Theater," 22–3.

19 Sue-Ellen Case, "Developments in Post-Brechtian Political Theater," ch. 2.

20 H.T. Price, "Construction in *Titus Andronicus*," in Alfred Harbage ed., *Shakespeare: The Tragedies: A Collection of Critical Essays* (Englewood Cliffs: Prentice-Hall, 1964), 26.

21 This production information is quoted from Norbert Otto Eke, *Heiner Müller:*

Apokalypse und Utopie (Paderborn: Ferdinand Schöningh, 1989), 304–5, 334–5.

22 Interview with Jonathan Kalb, "Out-Takes," 88.

6 Müller as Artaud

1 To mention only a few: Sue-Ellen Case's argument about Müller's "theater of terrorism" and the Theater of Cruelty was mentioned in chapter 5: see "Developments in Post-Brechtian Political Theater", ch. 2. Richard Herzinger writes that "Müller seizes on Artaud's concepts in order to link them with political content; he refers them to history": see his *Masken der Lebensrevolution: Vitalistische Zivilisations- und Humanismuskritik in Texten Heiner Müllers* (Munich: Wilhelm Fink, 1992), 75. For Klaus Teichmann, Artaud's "relevance" to Müller lies in the "confirmation" (*Beschwörung*) of a particular notion of human nature that places "equal emphasis" on subjectivity and resistance to "mediation by representation": see his *Der verwundete Körper: zu Texten Heiner Müllers* (Freiburg: Burg, 1989), 179. Frank Raddatz uses Artaud to describe the problematized "subject" in Müller's image of history: see his *Dämonen unterm Roten Stern: zu Geschichtsphilosophie und Asthetik Heiner Müllers* (Stuttgart: Metzler, 1991), 42. The most ambitious study of the Artaud–Müller connection to date is an article by Edward Scheer, "'Under the Sun of Torture' – A New Aesthetic of Cruelty: Artaud, Wilson and Müller," in Gerhard Fischer ed., *Heiner Müller: ConTEXTS and HISTORY*, 201-12.

2 "The GDR was lost when the people were allowed to watch television," said Müller in 1992 [16/165].

3 André Breton, *Manifestoes of Surrealism*, trans. Richard Seaver and Helen R. Lane (Ann Arbor: University of Michigan Press, 1972), 155.

4 Eugène Ionesco, *Notes & Counter Notes: Writings on the Theatre* (New York: Grove, 1964), 22.

5 Interview with Jonathan Kalb, "Out-Takes," 83.

6 Brecht's comments are from his journal entry for Dec. 11, 1940: *Arbeitsjournal 1938–1955: Vol. 1*, ed. Werner Hecht (Frankfurt-on-Main: Suhrkamp, 1973). Nietzsche's are from *The Birth of Tragedy*, trans. Francis Golffing (Garden City: Doubleday, 1956), 51.

7 Antonin Artaud, *The Theater and Its Double*, trans. Mary Caroline Richards (New York: Grove Press, 1958), 76.

8 Antonin Artaud, "Letter to André Gide, Feb. 10, 1935," *TDR* (June, 1972), 92–3.

9 Alfred Jarry, *The Ubu Plays*, ed. and trans. Simon Watson Taylor (New York: Grove Press, 1968), 106.

10 Friedrich Nietzsche, *The Birth of Tragedy*, 51–2.

11 Ibid., 29.

12 See, for example, Arlene Akiko Teraoka, *The Silence of Entropy or Universal Discourse*, ch. 3, and Elizabeth Wright, *Postmodern Brecht*, 132.

13 Müller also said, in connection with his advocacy of the Third World in the early 1980s: "European politics or history is based on a Father principle, a paternal principle. I see Asia as the rising of the maternal principle" [13/13].

14 Jacques Derrida, *Writing and Difference*, trans. Alan Bass (Chicago: University of Chicago Press, 1978), 234.

15 Antonin Artaud, *The Theater and Its Double*, 101. My acknowledgement to Norbert Otto Eke for his similar observations on these lines in *Heiner Müller: Apokalypse und Utopie*, 99.

16 Donald Kuspit, "Joseph Beuys: The Body of the Artist," *Artforum* (Summer 1991), 85. In *War without Battle*, Müller called Warhol "a car-body without a motor" [339].

17 Susan Sontag, "Artaud," in *Antonin Artaud: Selected Writings* (New York: Farrar, Straus and Giroux, 1976), xlvi.

18 Jacques Derrida, *Writing and Difference*, 235.

19 Friedrich Hölderlin, "Bruchstück 7," in *Sämtliche Werke*, vol. 2, part 1 (Stuttgart: Verlag W. Kohlhammer, 1951), 316.

20 Michael Schneider, "Heiner Müllers 'Endspiele,'" *Literatur Konkret* (Spring 1979), 32, 33.

21 Antonin Artaud, "Letter to Jacques Rivière, Jan. 29, 1924," in Susan Sontag ed., *Antonin Artaud: Selected Writings*, 34–5.

22 Compare Theodor Adorno's remark: "The splinter in your eye is the best magnifying glass" (*Minima Moralia*, trans. E.F.N. Jephcott [London and New York: Verso, 1974], 50) – itself probably an allusion to the Gospel of Matthew 7:3–5.

23 Michael Schneider, "Heiner Müllers 'Endspiele,'" 33.

24 Ibid.

25 Ibid.

26 Theo Girshausen ed., *Die Hamletmaschine: Heiner Müllers Endspiel*, 8.

27 Ibid., 68.

28 This information comes from Norbert Otto Eke, *Heiner Müller: Apokalypse und Utopie*, 104–5 n. 77.

29 Quoted in Ulrike Kahle, "Milk It or Move It," *Theater Heute* (December 1986), 4.

30 Interview with Frank Hentschker *et al.*, "Be Stupid," in Storch ed., *Explosion of a Memory*, 62.

31 Ibid., 63.

32 Ibid.

33 In a 1979 discussion of postmodernism in New York, Müller stated: "The great texts of the century work toward the liquidation of their autonomy . . . the disappearance of the author" [13/97]. Those who have rushed to quote this statement as an indication of his true and firm position on the matter,

however, would do well to consult this reference to it in his 1987 interview with Andre Müller: "I probably said that because the subject didn't interest me . . . The event was a means for me to get a free trip to New York" [19/203].

7 Müller as Genet

1 Jean-Paul Sartre, *Saint Genet: Actor & Martyr*, 369.
2 Andrzej Wirth, "Memory of a Revolution: Sado-Masochistic. Heiner Müller Produces his Text 'Der Auftrag' in East Berlin," trans. Olaf Reinhardt, in Gerhard Fischer ed., *The Mudrooroo/Müller Project: A Theatrical Casebook* (Kensington, Australia: New South Wales University Press, 1993), 62.
3 Anna Seghers, "Das Licht auf dem Galgen," in *Karabische Geschichten* (Berlin: Aufban Verlag, 1962).
4 Genia Schulz, *Heiner Müller*, 160.
5 Jean Genet, *The Blacks*, trans. Bernard Frechtman (New York: Grove, 1960), 43.
6 Ibid., 47.
7 Ibid., 81.
8 In *On the State of the Nation* (*Zur Lage der Nation*), Müller broadened to encompass his countrymen in general what had previously always been comments to this effect only about himself (see chapter 1, note 9). The GDR people, he said, were "treated for forty years like negroes [*Neger*], at any rate they felt that way, and like housepets" [17/92].
9 Jean Genet, *The Blacks*, 10.
10 Gerhard Fischer, "Genesis of a Theatre Project," in Fischer ed., *The Mudrooroo/Müller Project*, 3.
11 Mudrooroo, "The Aboriginalising of Heiner Müller," in Gerhard Fischer ed., *The Mudrooroo/Müller Project*, 21.
12 Ibid., 20.
13 Gerhard Fischer, "'Twoccing' *Der Auftrag* to Black Australia: Heiner Müller 'Aboriginalised' by Mudrooroo," in Fischer ed., *Heiner Müller: ConTEXTS and HISTORY*, 160.
14 Mudrooroo, *The Aboriginal Protesters Confront the Declaration of the Australian Republic on 26 January 2001 with the Production of "The Commission" by Heiner Müller*, in Gerhard Fischer ed., *The Mudrooroo/ Müller Project*, 86.
15 Gerhard Fischer, "'Twoccing' *Der Auftrag* to Black Australia," 145.
16 Mudrooroo, *The Aboriginal Protesters Confront . . .*, 88.
17 Ibid., 120.

8 Müller as Wagner

1 Genia Schulz, *Heiner Müller*, 139; Michael Schneider, "Heiner Müllers 'Endspiele,'" 32.

2 Christa Wolf, "Parting from Phantoms: The Business of Germany," trans. Jan van Heurck, *PMLA* (May, 1996), 401.

3 Friedrich Dieckmann, "Zeit-Wege," in Wolfgang Storch ed., *Explosion of a Memory*, 13.

4 In his article "Raum-Zeit" (*Text + Kritik* 73 [Jan. 1982], 80], for instance, Hans-Thies Lehmann observed that "in each case a political message is articulated by way of recourse to archaic and exotic fantasy-spaces, which make possible the representation of figures and conflicts that have historical significance according to a theory or philosophy but can't be pocketed."

5 Genia Schulz and Hans-Thies Lehmann, "Protoplasma des Gesamtkunstwerks: Heiner Müller und die Tradition der Moderne," in Gabriele Förg ed., *Unsere Wagner* (Frankfurt-on-Main: Fischer, 1984), 71.

6 Georg Hensel, "Schlacht-Szenen aus der DDR," *Frankfurter Allgemeine Zeitung* (April 22, 1978), 25.

7 See, as only a few of many possible examples: Michael Schneider, "Heiner Müllers 'Endspiele'"; Henning Rischbieter, "Nur heilloser Schrecken? 'Germania Tod in Berlin' an den Münchner Kammerspielen," *Theater Heute* (June 1978), 7–11; Andreas Keller, *Drama und Dramaturgie Heiner Müllers zwischen 1956 und 1988* (Frankfurt-on-Main: Peter Lang, 1992), 182.

8 Theodor Adorno, *In Search of Wagner*, trans. Rodney Livingstone (London and New York: Verso, 1981), 105.

9 Hans-Jürgen Syberberg, "Introduction" to *Hitler: A Film from Germany*, trans. Joachim Neugroschel (New York: Farrar Straus Giroux), 15.

10 Ibid., 9.

11 Thyrza Nichols Goodeve, "Drear Diary," *Artforum* (March 1994), 14.

12 See Bertolt Brecht, *Brecht on Theater*, trans. John Willet (New York: Hill and Wang, 1964), 34.

13 Müller also speaks candidly about this issue in numerous interviews. See, for example [14/182–94; 18/8–9].

14 The following comments of Müller's from *On the State of the Nation* elaborate on this view: "The Peasant Wars were a premature revolution; that's why the potential could be destroyed for centuries. Or, as Brecht put it, the German national character was pulverized back then. Then came the Thirty Years War and that destroyed the rest. Because these catastrophes are always a negative selection: whoever opens his mouth dies first, and all that remains are the cowed masses. Since this premature revolution the tendency toward delay has ruled in Germany; everything always comes too late in Germany. And the delay also means that the energies can be discharged only in catastrophe." [17/13]

15 Adorno, *In Search of Wagner*, 119.

16 Ibid., 40.

17 Vivian Mercier, *Beckett/Beckett* (New York: Oxford University Press, 1977), xii. The remark originally appeared in a review in the *Irish Times*.

18 Hans-Thies Lehmann, "Raum-Zeit," 81.

19 Roland Barthes, *Mythologies*, trans. Annette Lavers (New York: Noonday, 1972), 147–8.

20 See, for example, the discussion by Christian Klein in *Heiner Müller ou l'idiot de la république: le dialogisme à la scène* (Berne: Peter Lang, 1992), 103–11. Benjamin's comments are in "The Author as Producer," in *Reflections*, 234–5. Müller's churlish remark in *War without Battle* – "It's an error to read [*Gundling's Life* . . .] as a montage of parts. What's interesting are the fluent transitions between the disparate parts" [269] – is a defensive reaction to critics who had noticed the primacy of verbalism in his synthetic fragments. *Description of a Picture* notwithstanding, he was indeed much more of a verbalist than a visual artist.

21 Thomas Mann, "Sufferings and Greatness of Richard Wagner," 350.

22 *Germania 3: Gespenster am Toten Mann* (*Germania 3: Ghosts at the Dead Man*), his last published play, deals centrally with Hitler and Stalin – whose linked ideological obsessions and mass murders set the premises for the contemporary world, Müller thought – and also a potpourri of other figures from GDR politics, daily life in the Third Reich and the GDR, Nibelung myth, Croatia, tabloid newspapers, Kleist, Grillparzer, Kafka, Hölderlin, and (in one particularly scathing scene) the Berliner Ensemble after Brecht's death. "The Dead Man" is the nickname of a mountain near Verdun, the site of World War I's bloodiest trench warfare and Müller's preferred site of the play's premiere. In the fall of 1995, the mayor of Verdun revoked Müller's invitation to produce the play as part of the city's cultural commemoration of the battle's eightieth anniversary the following June. The mayor was angered by a published interview in which Müller criticized recently erected Verdun memorials as "monumental theatrical production": "One has the feeling they were erected in order to excuse having sent the soldiers to their deaths and to lend the war a meaning it doesn't have . . . They're an ersatz; the kitsch is a symptom of bad conscience" (quoted from Daniela Pogade, "Heiner Müller bleibt ausgeladen," *Berliner Zeitung* [Oct. 31, 1995], 29). According to the Berliner Ensemble dramaturg Holger Teschke, *Germania 3* – which, to my mind, lacks the unified tone of Müller's other synthetic fragments – is really a compilation of material from which he intended to construct seven different plays. His decision to publish the variegated scenes amounted to a hasty response in 1995 to the news that he was terminally ill. Teschke also says that the numeral "3" in the title was intended simply as mystification: "'Actually it ought to be *Germania 2*,' he said, 'but let's call it *Germania 3* and watch people search for deep meanings in it'" [interview in Berlin, June 21, 1996]. If all this is true, it is especially interesting that Müller published the text with the apparent confidence that its Germania-related themes sufficed to hold it together.

23 The phrase "democratic Bayreuth" is from Müller's interview with Holger Teschke, "Theater muss wieder seinen Nullpunkt finden," *Theater der Zeit* (May/June 1994), 7.

24 Richard Wagner, "Art and Revolution," *The Art-Work of the Future and Other Works*, trans. William Ashton Ellis (Lincoln and London: University of Nebraska Press, 1993), 52.

25 Schulz and Lehmann, "Protoplasma des Gesamtkunstwerks," 71.

26 Ibid., 64.

27 Nicola Chiaromonte, "The Political Theater," in *The Worm of Consciousness and Other Essays*, 137. Chiaromonte continues: "In speaking of Piscator, we should not forget the influence that directors like Vsevolod Meyerhold and Alexander Taïrov exercised on him – men who distinguish themselves by the attempt to translate the revolutionary idea into a language of scenic design derived from the aesthetics of the Russian artistic and literary avant-garde of their time" (135–6).

28 Ibid., 135–6, 137.

29 Ibid., 146–7.

30 Adorno, *In Search of Wagner*, 91.

31 Ibid.

32 Andreas Keller, *Drama und Dramaturgie Heiner Müllers zwischen 1956 und 1988*, 10.

33 Fritz Marquardt, "Ich spiel euch nicht den Helden: aus einem Gespräch mit Martin Linzer," in Frank Hörnigk *et al.* eds., *KALKFELL*, 22. At the performance of Marquardt's production I saw in 1990, a scene was inserted (read from scripts by two actors) in which Ernst Thälmann and Walter Ulbricht chatted as guards on patrol atop the Berlin Wall. It is a mark of the fluidity of the texts of the synthetic fragments in the author's mind that this scene, which Müller said was originally written for *Germania Tod in Berlin*, was later included in *Germania 3*.

34 Walter Benjamin, in "The Storyteller," *Illuminations*, trans. Harry Zohn (New York: Schocken, 1969), 86.

35 Adorno, *In Search of Wagner*, 86.

36 Syberberg, *Hitler: A Film from Germany*, 13–14.

9 Müller as Beckett

1 Samuel Beckett, *The Collected Shorter Plays* (New York: Grove, 1984), 80.

2 Georg Lukács, *The Meaning of Contemporary Realism*, trans. John and Necke Mander (London: Merlin, 1963), 26.

3 *"Ich bin ein Neger,"* 27.

4 Interview in Berlin, May 25, 1993.

5 Interview with Holger Teschke, "Theater muss wieder seinen Nullpunkt finden," 10–11.

6 H.G. Huettich, *Theater in the Planned Society*, 73.

7 The latter phrase is from my 1989 interview with him ("In Search of Heiner

Müller," in Jonathan Kalb, *Free Admissions: Collected Theater Writings*, 72),
the former phrase from the 1993 interview cited in note 4 above.

8 Samuel Beckett, *Endgame* (New York: Grove, 1958), 84.

9 Ibid., 44.

10 Samuel Beckett, *Happy Days* (New York: Grove, 1961), 57.

11 Interview with Holger Teschke, "Theater muss wieder seinen Nullpunkt
finden," 7.

12 Interview with Olivier Ortolani, "Georg Büchner: Die Verwiegerung des
Überblicks," in Frank Hörnigk *et al.* eds., *KALKFELL*, 72.

13 Robert Wilson says Müller wrote *Description of a Picture* in response to his
request for a prologue text to his already planned production of Euripides'
Alcestis. (Interview Frank Hentschker *et al.*, "Be Stupid," in Storch ed.
Explosion of a Memory, 62.) In his essay on *Description of a Picture*, Florian
Vassen quotes a less definitive comment on the subject by Müller: "The way
the piece was written has something to do with the fact that I worked with
Bob before" (Florian Vassen, "Images become Texts become Images: Heiner
Müller's *Bildbeschreibung*," in Gerhard Fischer ed., *Heiner Müller:
ConTEXTS and HISTORY*, 174).

14 Walter Benjamin, *Illuminations*, 257–8.

15 Interview with Tom Driver, "Beckett by the Madeleine," *Columbia
University Forum* 4, no. 3 (Summer 1961), 23.

16 Hans-Thies Lehmann, "Theater der Blicke: Zu Heiner Müllers
Bildbeschreibung," in Ulrich Profitlich ed., *Dramatik der DDR* (Frankfurt-on-
Main: Suhrkamp, 1987), 186.

17 Ibid., 186–7.

18 Ibid., 187.

19 Ibid., 189.

20 Ibid., 188–9. Compare this 1988 remark of Müller's in response to a question
about Robert Wilson and anthropocentrism: "The American magic word is
'space.' E.g. the Grand Canyon: that is a dimension of landscape in which one
no longer stands in the center as an observer. And that certainly applies also
to my own texts when they're produced. The conventional theater, especially
in Europe, is still always oriented toward the central perspective. But this
ordering principle doesn't grasp the texts, because they're no longer written
out of the central perspective" [15/147].

21 Hans-Thies Lehmann, "Heiner Müller's Spectres," in Gerhard Fischer ed.,
Heiner Müller: ConTEXTS and HISTORY, 87–96.

22 For documentation of stage adaptations of Beckett's nondramatic prose, see
Jonathan Kalb, *Beckett in Performance* (Cambridge: Cambridge University
Press, 1989), ch. 7. Given Beckett's notorious insistence that directors follow
his stage directions and that his works be kept in the genres for which they
were written, it is usually assumed that he and Müller held diametrically
opposed views on authorly authority. As I hope my discussion in chapter 6

made clear, the matter is not so straightforward. Müller told me himself in 1989 that he sympathized with Beckett's position but thought it unenforceable. Referring to Herbert König's recent version of his *Philoctetes* at the Schaubühne, he said: "Yes, it was a stupid production. Quite clear. No question about that. But there's only one possibility – you can forbid it, and you don't get away with that. Beckett tried it in the past, to forbid productions. I understand it quite well, but he didn't get away with it" (Interview with Jonathan Kalb, "In Search of Heiner Müller," 72).

23 *"Ich bin ein Neger"*, 16.

24 The German title of Müller's *The Construction Site* (1963/64), *Der Bau*, for example, is also the title of a Kafka story that plays on the word's secondary meanings of burrowing and digging a grave.

25 Müller in 1976: "For me Beckett is only important because he's an extreme" [14/47].

10 Müller as Proteus

1 One source says that *Quartet* had twenty-two foreign productions in 1993 and 1994 alone. Reinhard Tschapke, *Heiner Müller* (Berlin: Morgenbuch, 1996), 55.

2 Heinrich Mann, "Choderlos de Laclos," in Pierre Choderlos de Laclos, *Schlimme Liebschaften*, trans. Heinrich Mann (Berlin: Aufbau Taschenbuch Verlag, 1995), 403. "Love is a metaphor for false consciousness," said Müller similarly in *Jenseits der Nation* (*Beyond the Nation* [18/81]).

3 Müller writes in *War without Battle*: "Laclos always declared himself to be a moralist who described all these abysses in order to warn humanity about them. But that was merely the moralistic posture of an author intensely interested in the dark reaches of the soul. It was exactly the same with de Sade; his posture was also that of a moralist, of an Enlightener" [0/290].

4 Richard Wagner, *Parsifal* (Stuttgart: Reclam, 1950), 24; Bertolt Brecht, *Der Untergang des Egoisten Johann Fatzer*, 73; Heinrich Mann, "Choderlos de Laclos," 408. Asked by a 1982 interviewer to elucidate his opening stage direction, Müller answered as follows:

> The stage direction issues from the hope that the play will also be performed after a Third World War. Then we'll know how a bunker after the Third World War looks. It's simply an expression of historical optimism. I believe not only in a Third but also in a Fourth World War.
>
> [14/107]

5 Other critics have divided the play differently, making cases for four and five parts or "acts," but each of these readings recognizes the importance of the five shifts I mention. See Genia Schulz, "Abschied von Morgen: Zu den Frauengestalten im Werk Heiner Müllers," *Text + Kritik* 73 (Jan. 1982), 66; and Norbert Otto Eke, *Heiner Müller: Apokalypse und Utopie*, ch. 6.

6 Sade speaks in this spirit frequently, but the most direct link to *Quartet* is probably the argument of the brigand Coeur-de-fer to Justine, which contains many formulations Müller apparently borrowed or paraphrased (e.g. "the peristyles of first one and then the other of Nature's altars"; "one can offer to Venus in many a temple"). (Marquis de Sade, *Justine, Philosophy in the Bedroom & Other Writings*, trans. Richard Seaver and Austryn Wainhouse [New York: Grove, 1965], 485, 488.) Tertullian, condemning the pollution of mind that accompanies the witnessing of fictional sin in the theater, asks, "Why . . . is it right to look on what it is disgraceful to do?" ("On the Spectacles," in Bernard Dukore ed., *Dramatic Theory and Criticism: Greeks to Grotowski* [Fort Worth *et al.*: Holt, Rinehart and Winston, 1974], 90.)

7 Jean Baudrillard, *Simulations*, trans. Paul Foss, Paul Patton, and Philip Beitchman (New York: Semiotext(e), 1983), 46.

8 Interview in Berlin, May 25, 1993. All quoted comments by Müller about his Deutsches Theater production are from this conversation.

9 Samuel Beckett, *Endgame*, 9.

10 Ibid., 15.

11 Ibid., 1.

12 Samuel Beckett, *Waiting for Godot* (New York: Grove Press, 1954), 29.

13 The following remarks concerning Christoph Nel's 1980 production of *Mauser* in Cologne, from *War without Battle*, may illuminate why Müller believed the two plays belonged together: "Christoph Nel's dramaturg was Urs Troller; both came from good middle-class homes and were politically sinless. They thought, for that reason, that they could represent the whole thing only as a male–female relationship. That was the only violent relationship they knew from the sphere of their own experience and life. *Mauser* was thus played by a man and a woman, and with every shot the man slapped a cream pie between the woman's legs. It sounds pretty stupid but it wasn't silly. When I later wrote *Quartet* I knew that they had directed *Quartet* with the text of *Mauser*" [o/317].

14 Müller disliked this sort of personal choice by actors on principle. "That's where impurities come [into a production]; the private element effaces the contours. That's Wilson's problem with West German actors," he said in *War without Battle* [o/334].

15 Heinrich Mann, "Choderlos de Laclos," 406–7.

16 In a 1991 interview Müller offered the following remarks about this production:

> I'm working on the production of three texts of mine . . .: *Quartet* (after Laclos, 1782), *Mauser* (action around 1920), *The Foundling* (after 1968). The strange thing about these three texts is that the most historically distant, that is *Quartet*, is the closest to the public and the most historically recent, *The Foundling* . . . which plays primarily in the GDR

of 1968, is the most distant from the public. The production is a trip out of the past backwards into the present, because the past lies before us and the future, which was contained in the present, lies behind us.

[16/123]

17 Mona Heinze, "Une Liaison Ennuyeuse: Wilson's Production of Müller's *Quartet*," *Theater*, Fall 1988.

18 Interview with Frank Hentschker *et al.*, "Be Stupid," in Storch ed., *Explosion of a Memory*, 67.

19 Walter Benjamin, "Surrealism," in *Reflections*, 179.

20 Theodor Adorno, "Looking Back on Surrealism," in *Notes to Literature: Vol. 1*, 86–7. Another remark from this essay is relevant to Wilson's production:

> Surrealism's booty is images, to be sure, but not the invariant, ahistorical images of the unconscious subject to which the conventional view would like to neutralize them; rather, they are historical images in which the subject's innermost core becomes aware that it is something external, an imitation of something social and historical.   (89)

21 Interview with Holger Teschke, "Theater muss wieder seinen Nullpunkt finden," 8.

22 Ibid., 7, 9.

23 Ibid., 7.

24 Ibid., 9. Müller said he believed that the distaste most people around him expressed for the *Dienstbotenebene* demonstrated "a need for hierarchies; a text is viewed as sacrosanct or classic, and you're not allowed to mess it up or rough it up. But if a text can't take that, such messing and roughing up, then it can't be classic at all."

25 This information comes from an interview in Berlin with Holger Teschke, the production dramaturg, on June 21, 1996.

26 Jean-Paul Sartre, *Saint Genet: Actor & Martyr*, 618–19.

27 Here are Müller's remarks in context:

> *You once made a comment to the effect that one occasionally writes texts that one detests. But one would be a traitor if one didn't write them. Which of your texts do you detest today?*
> During the writing, for example, *Quartet*. A very evil, cynical play. One could also characterize it as religious. The union of religiosity and cynicism is, I believe, the essence of this play.
> *It surprises me that you name this play.* Quartet *is one of the few plays of yours that has only marginally to do with history.*
> If the concept of history has any meaning at all then it surely describes also the structure and destruction of human relationships. To that extent *Quartet* has a historical theme. *Quartet* is perhaps not a political but certainly a historical play.   [16/152]

28 In *Beyond the Nation*, Müller made a case for this outcast position being perhaps the only effective vantage-point for the artist at that time (1991): "One can't think anymore except from the position of minorities. Thinking is nowhere but on the margins, because movement is nowhere but on the margins" [18/54]. See also chapter 7, note 8.

29 Müller says he listened to this Schubert *Lied* on a small radio while writing *Quartet* [0/318].

30 Heiner Müller, "19 Answers by Heiner Müller," in *Hamletmachine and Other Texts for the Stage*, trans. Carl Weber (New York: PAJ Publ., 1984), 137. The following comments from *Beyond the Nation* are also pertinent: "The main theme of science fiction literature in the West is the disappearance of the subject. That is also the central theme of the French postmodern. Virilio, Baudrillard, or Lyotard try to establish ideologically that that's good. That's the attempt to arrive at the connection [*Anschluss*] with the machine, to run after the machine on foot. The endeavor of theory in the West is confined to standing on the side of the winners, the machines . . . The postmodernists are simply afraid of not belonging to the winners but rather to those who – in an intellectual sense – are sent to the concentration camp" [18/46–7].

31 Jonas Barish, *The Anti-Theatrical Prejudice* (Berkeley, *et al.*: University of California Press, 1981), 446–7.

32 Leo Bersani, *A Future for Astyanax: Character and Desire in Literature* (New York: Columbia Univ. Press, 1984), 258. Barish also quotes this passage himself as a contrasting view.

Bibliography

Primary

The following is a list of Müller texts in English translation. Potential users are referred to chapter 1, note 30 above. See pp. xviii–xix for Müller's works in German.

Müller, Heiner, *The Battle: Plays, Prose, Poems by Heiner Müller*, ed. and trans. Carl Weber (New York: PAJ Publ., 1989).
Cement, trans. Helen Fehervary, Sue-Ellen Case and Marc Silberman, *New German Critique* 16 (Winter 1979 Suppl.), 7–64.
Explosion of a Memory: Writings by Heiner Müller, ed. and trans. Carl Weber (New York: PAJ Publ., 1989).
Hamletmachine and Other Texts for the Stage, ed. and trans. Carl Weber (New York: PAJ Publ., 1984).
The Horatian, trans. Marc Silberman, Helen Fehervary and Guntram Weber, *The Minnesota Review* (Spring 1976), 40–50.
Mauser, trans. Helen Fehervary and Marc Silberman, *New German Critique* 8 (Spring 1976), 122–49.
Philoctetes, trans. Oscar Mandel in collab. with Maria Kelsen Feder, in Oscar Mandel, *Philoctetes and the Fall of Troy* (Lincoln and London: University of Nebraska Press, 1981), 215–50.
The Slaughter, trans. Marc Silberman, Helen Fehervary and Guntram Weber, *Theater* (Spring 1986), 23–9.
Theatremachine, trans. and ed. Marc von Henning (London: Faber and Faber, 1995).

Secondary

This list contains secondary sources mentioned in the notes and
selected others. Articles in books predominantly about Müller are not
listed separately. For more in-depth research, readers should consult the
indispensable bibliography by Ingo Schmidt and Florian Vassen, now in
two volumes: *Bibliographie Heiner Müller: 1948–1992* (Bielefeld:
Aisthesis, 1993); *Bibliographie Heiner Müller Band 2: 1993–1995*
(Bielefeld: Aisthesis, 1996).

Adorno, Theodor, *In Search of Wagner*, trans. Rodney Livingstone
(London and New York: Verso, 1981).
  Minima Moralia, trans. E.F.N. Jephcott (London and New York:
    Verso, 1974).
  Notes to Literature: Vol. 1, ed. Rolf Tiedemann, trans. Shierry Weber
    Nicholsen (New York: Columbia University Press, 1991).
  "On the Question: 'What Is German?'" *New German Critique* 36 (Fall
    1985), 121–31.
Allen, Pam, "Skeletons in the Closet that Smell of Stalin: Heiner
  Müller's *Wolokolamsker Chaussee*," *University of Dayton
  Review* 3 (1990), 21–7.
Arnold, Herbert, "On Myth and Marxism: The Case of Heiner Müller
  and Christa Wolf," *Colloquia Germanica* 21 (1988), 58–69.
Artaud, Antonin, *Antonin Artaud: Selected Writings*, ed. Susan Sontag
  (New York: Farrar, Straus and Giroux, 1976).
  "Letter to André Gide, Feb. 10, 1935," *TDR* (June, 1972), 92–3.
  The Theater and Its Double, trans. Mary Caroline Richards (New
    York: Grove Press, 1958).
Assheuer, Thomas, "Der böse Engel," *Frankfurter Rundschau* (Jan. 2,
  1996), 9.
Baranczak, Stanislaw, "Voltaire's Vomit," *The New Republic* (Apr. 23,
  1990), 36–9.
Barish, Jonas, *The Anti-Theatrical Prejudice* (Berkeley, *et al.*: University
  of California Press, 1981).
Barthes, Roland, *Mythologies*, trans. Annette Lavers (New York:
  Noonday, 1972).
Bathrick, David, "'The Theater of the White Revolution is Over': The

Third World in the Works of Peter Weiss and Heiner Müller," in Reinhold Grimm and Jost Hermand eds., *Blacks and German Culture* (Madison: Wisconsin University Press, 1986), 135–49.

Bathrick, David and Andreas Huyssen, "Producing Revolution: Heiner Müller's *Mauser* as Learning Play," *New German Critique* 8 (Spring 1976), 110–21.

Baudrillard, Jean, *Kool Killer oder Der Aufstand der Zeichen* (Berlin: Merve, 1978).

Simulations, trans. Paul Foss, Paul Patton and Philip Beitchman (New York: Semiotext(e), 1983).

Baxandall, Lee, "Brecht in America, 1935," *TDR* (Fall 1967), 69–87.

Becker, Peter von, "Gespenster am toten Mann: Heiner Müller oder Eine Variation über Vampire," *Theater Heute* (special number, 1996), 108–10.

Beckett, Samuel, *The Collected Shorter Plays* (New York: Grove, 1984).

Endgame (New York: Grove, 1958).

Happy Days (New York: Grove, 1961).

Waiting for Godot (New York: Grove, 1954).

Bendkowski, Halina, "Der theatralisch verlassene Mann," in Sonja Düring and Margret Hauch eds., *Heterosexuelle Verhältnisse: Beiträge zur Sexualforschung* 71 (Stuttgart: Ferdinand Enke, 1995), 14–26.

Benjamin, Walter, *Gesammelte Schriften* III (Frankfurt-on-Main: Suhrkamp, 1972).

"The Storyteller," in *Illuminations*, trans. Harry Zohn (New York: Schocken, 1969), 83–109.

"Surrealism," in *Reflections*, ed. Peter Demetz, trans. Edmund Jephcott (New York: Schocken, 1978), 177–92.

"The Work of Art in the Age of Mechanical Reproduction," in *Illuminations*, trans. Harry Zohn (New York: Schocken, 1969), 217–51.

Understanding Brecht (London: NLB, 1973).

Bentley, Eric, *The Brecht Memoir* (Evanston: Northwestern University Press, 1991).

Bersani, Leo, *A Future for Astyanax: Character and Desire in Literature* (New York: Columbia University Press, 1984).

Bibliography

Biermann, Wolf, "Die Müller-Maschine," *Der Spiegel* (Jan. 8, 1996),
154–61.
Birringer, Johannes, "Brecht and Medea: Heiner Müller's Synthetic
Fragments," *Gestus* 3 (1987), 67–79.
"*Medea* – Landscapes Beyond History," *New German Critique* 50
(1990), 85–112.
Bloom, Harold, *The Anxiety of Influence: A Theory of Poetry* (London,
Oxford, New York: Oxford University Press, 1973).
Braun, Matthias, *Drama um eine Komödie* (Berlin: Christoph Links,
1996).
Brecht, Bertolt, *Arbeitsjournal 1938–1955: Vol. 1*, ed. Werner Hecht
(Frankfurt-on-Main: Suhrkamp, 1973).
Brecht on Theater, trans. John Willet (New York: Hill and Wang,
1964).
Der Untergang des Egoisten Johann Fatzer (Frankfurt-on-Main:
Suhrkamp, 1994).
Die Stücke von Bertolt Brecht in einem Band (Frankfurt-on-Main:
Suhrkamp, 1978).
Gesammelte Werke 17: Schriften zum Theater 3 (20 vols., Frankfurt-
on-Main: Suhrkamp, 1967).
Poems: 1913–1956 (New York: Methuen, 1976).
Breton, André, *Manifestoes of Surrealism*, trans. Richard Seaver and
Helen R. Lane (Ann Arbor: University of Michigan Press, 1972).
Brown, Edward J., *Mayakovsky: A Poet in the Revolution* (Princeton:
Princeton University Press, 1973).
Calandra, Denis, *New German Dramatists* (New York: Grove Press,
1983).
Case, Sue-Ellen, "Developments in Post-Brechtian Political Theater:
The Plays of Heiner Müller," unpublished doctoral dissertation
at the University of California, Berkeley, 1981.
"From Bertolt Brecht to Heiner Müller," *Performing Arts Journal* 19
(vol. VII, no. 1, 1983), 94–102.
"Notes on Directing *Cement*: Conversation with Heiner Müller,"
New German Critique 16 (Winter 1979 Suppl.), 71–80.
Celan, Paul, *Last Poems*, trans. Katharine Washburn and Margret
Guillemin (San Francisco: North Point Press, 1986).
Charbon, Rémy, "'Denn das Schöne bedeutet das mögliche Ende der

Schrecken': Versuch über Heiner Müller und das Theater der
DDR in der Epoche des Neuen ökonomischen Systems,''
Wirkendes Wort (May/June 1980), 149–77.

Chiaromonte, Nicola, *The Worm of Consciousness and Other Essays*
(New York and London: Harcourt Brace Jovanovich, 1976).

Cohn, Ruby, *Modern Shakespeare Offshoots* (Princeton: Princeton
University Press, 1976).

"DDR-Dramatiker über Brecht,'' in Werner Hecht ed., *Brecht 71:
Brecht-Woche der DDR 9.-15. Februar 1973 Dokumentation*
(Berlin: Henschel, 1973), 197–230.

Der Lohndrücker: Dokumentation 2, protocol-book published by the
Akademie der Künste der DDR, 1987–8.

Derrida, Jacques, *Writing and Difference*, trans. Alan Bass (Chicago:
University of Chicago Press, 1978).

Dieckmann, Friedrich, "Das grosse Worttheater: *Mauser* und andere
Stücke von Heiner Müller am Deutschen Theater,'' *Neue Zeit*
(Sept. 17, 1991), 12.

"Heiner Müller und die Legitimität,'' *Theater der Zeit* (no. 9, 1972),
46–7.

"Wanderer über viele Bühnen,'' *Theater der Zeit* (Mar./Apr. 1996),
4–7.

Domdey, Horst, "'Ich lache über den Neger': Das Lachen des Siegers in
Heiner Müllers Stück *Der Auftrag*,'' in Paul Gerhard Klussmann
and Heinrich Mohr eds., *Die Schuld der Worte* (Bonn: Bouvier,
1987), 220–34.

Driver, Tom, "Beckett by the Madeleine,'' *Columbia University Forum*
4 (no. 3, Summer 1961).

Dudley, Joseph M., "Being and Non-Being: the Other and Heterotopia in
Hamletmachine,'' *Modern Drama* 35:4 (1992), 562–70.

Dukore, Bernard ed., *Dramatic Theory and Criticism: Greeks to
Grotowski* (Fort Worth, *et al.*: Holt, Rinehart and Winston,
1974).

Eckhardt, Thomas, *Der Herold der Toten: Geschichte und Politik bei
Heiner Müller* (Frankfurt-on-Main *et al.*: Peter Lang, 1992).

Eggers, Ingrid, "Heiner Müller's *Cement*'' and "An Interview with
Heiner Müller,'' *Theater* (Fall/Winter 1979), 80–4.

Eichberg, Henning, Michael Dultz, Glen Gadberry, and Günther Rühle,

Massenspiele: NS-Thingspiel, Arbeiterweihespiel und olympisches Zeremoniell (Stuttgart and Bad Cannstatt: Friedrich Frommann, 1977).

Eke, Norbert Otto, *Heiner Müller: Apokalypse und Utopie* (Paderborn: Ferdinand Schöningh, 1989).

Emmerich, Wolfgang, "Der Alp der Geschichte," in Paul Gerhard Klussmann and Heinrich Mohr eds., *Deutsche Misere einst und jetzt: Die deutsche Misere als Thema der Gegenwartsliteratur/ Das Preussensyndrom in der Literatur der DDR* (Bonn: Bouvier Verlag Herbert Grundmann, 1982), 115–58.

Endler, Adolf, "Fragt mich nicht wie: Zur Lyrik Inge Müllers," *Sinn und Form*, 31:1 (Jan./Feb. 1979), 152–61.

Erofeyev, Victor, "Dying for the Party," *The Times Literary Supplement* (Jan. 7, 1994).

Esslin, Martin, *Brecht: The Man and his Work* (Garden City: Anchor, 1961).

Fanon, Frantz, *The Wretched of the Earth*, trans. Constance Farrington (New York: Grove, 1966).

Fehervary, Helen, "*Cement* in Berkeley," in Reinhold Grimm and Jost Hermand eds., *Brecht-Jahrbuch 1980* (1981), 206–16.

"Enlightenment or Entanglement: History and Aesthetics in Bertolt Brecht and Heiner Müller," *New German Critique* 8 (Spring 1976), 80–109.

"Heiner Müller and *Cement*," *New German Critique* 16 (Winter 1979 Suppl.), 3–5.

"Heiner Müllers Brigadenstücke," in Reinhold Grimm and Jost Hermand, *Basis*, vol. 2 (1971), 103–40.

Fiebach, Joachim, *Inseln der Unordnung: Fünf Versuche zu Heiner Müllers Theatertexten* (Berlin: Henschel, 1990).

Fischborn, Gottfried, *Stückeschreiben: Claus Hammel, Heiner Müller, Armin Stolper* (Berlin: Adademie-Verlag, 1981).

Fischer, Gerhard ed., *Heiner Müller: ConTEXTS and HISTORY* (Tübingen: Stauffenburg Verlag, 1995).

The Mudrooroo/Müller Project: A Theatrical Casebook (Kensington, Australia: New South Wales University Press, 1993).

Fried, Erich and Heiner Müller, *Erich Fried – Heiner Müller: Ein Gespräch* (Berlin: Alexander Verlag, 1989).

Fuchs, Elinor, "The PAJ Casebook: *Alcestis,*" *Performing Arts Journal* 28 (10:1, 1986), 79–105.

Fuchs, Elinor and James Leverett, "Back to the Wall: Heiner Müller in Berlin," *Village Voice* (Dec. 18, 1984), 62–4, 67.

Genet, Jean, *The Blacks,* trans. Bernard Frechtman (New York: Grove, 1960).

Girshausen, Theo, "'Reject it, in order to possess it,': On Heiner Müller and Bertolt Brecht," *Modern Drama* (vol. xxiii, no. 4, Jan. 1981), 404–21.

Girshausen, Theo ed., *Die Hamletmaschine: Heiner Müllers Endspiel* (Cologne: Prometh Verlag, 1978).

Goodeve, Thyrza Nichols, "Drear Diary," *Artforum* (Mar. 1994), 14.

Hacker, Doja and Urs Jenny, "'Theater ist feudalistisch': Dramatiker Heiner Müller über das Berliner Ensemble, DDR-Nostalgie und Rechts-links-Verwirrungen," *Der Spiegel* 12 (1995), 224–6.

Hacks, Peter, interview in Margaret Herzfeld-Sander ed., *Essays on German Theater* (New York: Continuum, 1985), 304–10.

"Über Heiner Müllers 'Philoktet,'" *Theater Heute* (Oct. 1969), 27.

Hamburger, Maik, "Are You a Party in this Business?: Consolidation and Subversion in East German Shakespeare Productions," *Shakespeare Survey* 48 (1995), 171–84.

Harich, Wolfgang, "Der entlaufene Dingo, das vergessene Floss," *Sinn und Form* 25 (1973), no. 1, 189–218.

Harris, Max, "Müller's *Cement:* Fragments of Heroic Myth," *Modern Drama* 31:3 (Sept. 1988), 429–38.

Heinitz, Werner, "'Das Vaterbild ist das Verhängnis': Heiner Müller im Gespräch mit Werner Heinitz über Brecht und die Dramatik der Gegenwart," *Theater Heute* (Jan. 1984), 61–2.

Heinze, Mona, "Une Liaison Ennuyeuse: Wilson's Production of Müller's *Quartet,*" *Theater* (Fall 1988), 14–21.

Heise, Wolfgang, "Notwendige Fragestellung," *Theater der Zeit* (no. 9, 1972), 45–6.

Henrichs, Benjamin, "Die zum Lächeln nicht Zwingbaren," *Die Zeit* (May 24, 1974), 19.

Hensel, Georg, "Schlacht-Szenen aus der DDR," *Frankfurter Allgemeine Zeitung* (Apr. 22, 1978), 25.

Hermand, Jost, "Fridericus Rex," in Ulrich Profitlich ed., *Dramatik der DDR* (Frankfurt-on-Main: Suhrkamp, 1987), 287–92.

Herzinger, Richard, *Masken der Lebensrevolution: Vitalistische Zivilisations- und Humanismuskritik in Texten Heiner Müllers* (Munich: Wilhelm Fink, 1992).

Hohendahl, Peter Uwe and Patricia Herminghouse eds., *Literatur und Literaturtheorie in der DDR* (Frankfurt-on-Main: Suhrkamp, 1976).

Hölderlin, Friedrich, *Sämtliche Werke*, vol. 2, part 1 (Stuttgart: Verlag W. Kohlhammer, 1951).

Holmberg, "A Conversation with Robert Wilson and Heiner Müller," *Modern Drama*, 31:3 (Sept. 1988), 454–8.

Hörnigk, Frank ed., *Heiner Müller Material: Texte und Kommentare* (Göttingen: Steidl, 1989).

Hörnigk, Frank, Martin Linzer, Frank Raddatz, Wolfgang Storch, and Holger Teschke eds., *Ich Wer ist das Im Regen aus Vogelkot Im KALKFELL: für Heiner Müller: Arbeitsbuch* (Berlin: Theater der Zeit, 1996).

Huelsenbeck, Richard, *Memoirs of a Dada Drummer*, ed. Hans J. Kleinschmidt, trans. Joachim Neugroschel (Berkeley, Los Angeles, London: University of California Press, 1991).

Huettich, H.G., *Theater in the Planned Society* (Chapel Hill: University of North Carolina Press, 1978).

"Ich bin ein Neger": Diskussion mit Heiner Müller (Darmstadt: Verlag der Georg Büchner Buchhandlung, 1986).

I., P. [Iden, Peter], "Dreifaches Debakel: Misslungener Auftakt," *Frankfurter Rundschau* (May 21, 1990).

Iden, Peter, "'Kunst hat und braucht eine blutige Wurzel,'" *Frankfurter Rundschau* (Jan. 2, 1996), 9.

Ionesco, Eugène, *Notes & Counter Notes: Writings on the Theatre* (New York: Grove, 1964).

Jarry, Alfred, *The Ubu Plays*, ed. and trans. Simon Watson Taylor (New York: Grove Press, 1968).

Kahle, Ulrike, "Milk It or Move It," *Theater Heute* (Dec. 1986), 4.

Kalb, Jonathan, *Beckett in Performance* (Cambridge: Cambridge University Press, 1989).

"Iconoclast Notes," *Village Voice* (Aug. 7, 1990), 90.

"In Search of Heiner Müller" and "Out-Takes: Fragments from an Interview with Heiner Müller," in *Free Admissions: Collected Theater Writings* (New York: Limelight Editions, 1993).

"On the Becoming Death of Poor H.M.," *Theater* (vol. 27, no. 1, 1996), 65–73.

Kamath, Rekha, *Brechts Lehrstück-Modell als Bruch mit den bürgerlichen Theatertraditionen* (Frankfurt-on-Main, Berne: Peter Lang, 1983).

Keller, Andreas, *Drama und Dramaturgie Heiner Müllers zwischen 1956 und 1988* (Frankfurt-on-Main: Peter Lang, 1992).

Kinzer, Stephen "Germany Can't Forget a Legendary Director," *New York Times* (Mar. 31, 1996).

Klein, Christian, *Heiner Müller ou l'idiot de la république: le dialogisme à la scène* (Berne: Peter Lang, 1992).

Kleist, Heinrich von, *Prinz Friedrich von Homburg* (Stuttgart: Philipp Reclam Jun., 1968).

Klussmann, Paul Gerhard, "Deutschland-Denkmale: umgestürzt. Zu Heiner Müllers *Germania Tod in Berlin*," in Paul Gerhard Klussmann and Heinrich Mohr eds., *Deutsche Misere einst und jetzt: Die deutsche Misere als Thema der Gegenwartsliteratur/ Das Preussensyndrom in der Literatur der DDR* (Bonn: Bouvier Verlag Herbert Grundmann, 1982), 159–76.

Klussmann, Paul Gerhard and Heinrich Mohr eds., *Dialektik des Anfangs: Spiele des Lachens: Literaturpolitik in Bibliotheken: Über Texte von Heiner Müller, Franz Fühmann, Stefan Heym* (Bonn: Bouvier Verlag Herbert Grundmann, 1986).

Kruger, Loren, "Heterophony as Critique. Brecht, Müller and *Radio Fatzer*," *The Brecht Yearbook 17: The Other Brecht I* (1992), 235–50.

"'Stories from the Production Line': Modernism and Modernization in the GDR Production Play," *Theatre Journal* 4 (1994), 489–506.

Kuspit, Donald, "Joseph Beuys: The Body of the Artist," *Artforum* (Summer 1991), 80–6.

Lacis, Asja and Walter Benjamin, "Building a Children's Theater," *Performance* 5 (1973), 22–32.

Lehmann, Hans-Thies, "Das Ende der Macht – auf dem Theater,"
　　Theater Heute (Dec. 1982), 16–24.

"Dramatische Form und Revolution in Georg Büchners 'Dantons
　　Tod' und Heiner Müllers 'Der Auftrag,'" in Peter von Becker ed.,
　　Georg Büchner. Dantons Tod. Kritische Studienausgabe des
　　Originals mit Quellen, Aufsätzen und Materialien (Frankfurt-
　　on-Main: 1985, 2nd ed.), 106–21.

"Georg Büchner, Heiner Müller, Georges Bataille Revolution und
　　Masochismus," in Hubert Gersch, Thomas Michael Mayer, and
　　Bünter Oesterle eds., *Georg Büchner Jahrbuch* 3 (1983), 308–29.

"Mythos und Postmoderne – Botho Strauss, Heiner Müller," in Albrecht
　　Schöne ed., *Akten des VII. Internationalen Germanisten-*
　　Kongresses Göttingen 1985, vol. 10 (Tübingen: 1986), 249–55.

"Raum-Zeit," *Text + Kritik* 73 (Jan. 1982), 71–81.

"Theater der Blicke: Zu Heiner Müllers *Bildbeschreibung*," in Ulrich
　　Profitlich ed., *Dramatik der DDR* (Frankfurt-on-Main:
　　Suhrkamp, 1987), 186–202.

Linzer, Martin, "Historische Exaktheit und Grausamkeit," *Theater der*
　　Zeit (no. 7, 1972), 22–3.

"Wechselvoller Umgang mit einem Autor: Heiner Müller und
　　Theater der Zeit," *Theater der Zeit* (Mar./Apr. 1996), 12–15.

Lücke, Detlev and Stefan Reinecke, "Deutscher sein, heisst Indianer
　　sein: Gespräch mit Heiner Müller über den 8. Mai deutschen
　　Ewigkeitsanspruch und Brecht (Teil 1)," *Freitag* (May 5, 1995), 3;
　　"Eigentlich hat Hitler den Krieg gewonnen: Gespräch mit Heiner
　　Müller über Hitler und Stalin und den Humanismus als letzten
　　Mythos (Teil 2)," *Freitag* (May 12, 1995), 11.

Luft, Friedrich, *Stimme der Kritik: Berliner Theater seit 1945* (Hanover:
　　Friedrich Verlag, 1965).

Lukács, Georg, *The Meaning of Contemporary Realism*, trans. John and
　　Necke Mander (London: Merlin, 1963).

Lyon, James K., *Bertolt Brecht in America* (London: Methuen, 1980).

Maass, Joachim, *Kleist: A Biography*, trans. Ralph Manheim (New York:
　　Farrar, Straus and Giroux, 1983).

Maier-Schaeffer, Francine, *Heiner Müller et le "Lehrstück"* (Berne *et al.*:
　　Peter Lang, 1992).

Malkin, Jeanette R., "Mourning and the Body: Heiner Müller's Fathers and *The Foundling* Son," *Modern Drama*, 34:3 (Fall 1996), 490–506.

Mann, Heinrich, "Choderlos de Laclos," in Pierre Choderlos de Laclos, *Schlimme Liebschaften*, trans. Heinrich Mann (Berlin: Aufbau Taschenbuch Verlag, 1995), 403–16.

Mann, Thomas, *Reflections of a Nonpolitical Man*, trans. Walter D. Morris (New York: Frederick Ungar, 1983).

   "Sufferings and Greatness of Richard Wagner," in *Essays of Three Decades*, trans. H.T. Lowe-Porter (New York: Alfred A. Knopf, 1965).

Mayakovsky, Vladimir, *The Bedbug and Selected Poetry*, ed. Patricia Blake, trans. Max Hayward and George Reavey (Bloomington: Indiana University Press, 1975).

   Selected Works in Three Volumes 1: Selected Verse, trans. Dorian Rottenberg (Moscow: Raduga, 1985).

   Selected Works in Three Volumes 2: Longer Poems, trans. Dorian Rottenberg (Moscow: Raduga, 1986).

Mayer, Hans, "Rede über Heiner Müller," *Theater Heute* (special no., 1996), 129–49.

Mercier, Vivian, *Beckett/Beckett* (New York: Oxford University Press, 1977).

Merschmeier, Michael, "Heiner & 'Heiner,'" *Theater Heute* (Feb. 1993), 1.

Mierau, Fritz, "Majakowski Lesen," *Sinn und Form*, 30:3 (May/June 1978), 650–62.

Motoyama, Kate T., "*Mauser*: A Critique of *The Measures Taken*," *Texts and Performance Quarterly* 11:1 (1991), 46–55.

Müller, Inge, *Wenn ich schon sterben muss* (Berlin and Weimar: Aufbau Verlag, 1985).

Nietzsche, Friedrich, *The Birth of Tragedy*, trans. Francis Golffing (Garden City: Doubleday, 1956).

Pace, Eric, "Heiner Müller, the Playwright and Social Critic, Dies at 66," *New York Times* (Jan. 3, 1996).

Pogade, Daniela, "Heiner Müller bleibt ausgeladen," *Berliner Zeitung* (Oct. 31, 1995), 29.

Poulet, Jacques, "Viv(r)e la contradiction! Jacques Poulet s'entretient avec Heiner Müller," *France nouvelle* (Jan. 29, 1979), 43–50.

Price, H.T., "Construction in *Titus Andronicus*," in Alfred Harbage ed., *Shakespeare: The Tragedies: A Collection of Critical Essays* (Englewood Cliffs: Prentice-Hall, 1964), 24–7.

Profitlich, Ulrich ed., *Dramatik der DDR* (Frankfurt-on-Main: Suhrkamp, 1987).

Raddatz, Frank, *Dämonen unterm Roten Stern: zu Geschichtsphilosophie und Ästhetik Heiner Müllers* (Stuttgart: Metzler, 1991).

"Im Jensiets ist jetzt mehr los: Mein Gespräch mit Heiner," *Theater der Zeit* (Mar./Apr. 1996), 8–11.

"Das Schweigen des Müller: Frank Raddatz befragte Heiner Müller zu kulturellen und politischen Ereignissen," *Theater der Zeit* (Mar./Apr. 1995), 2–3.

Reid, J.H., "Homburg-Machine – Heiner Müller in the Shadow of Nuclear War," in W.G. Sebald ed., *A Radical Stage: Theatre in Germany in the 1970s and 1980s* (New York, Oxford, Munich: Berg, 1988, 1990).

Rischbieter, Henning, "Deutschland, Ein Wilsonmärchen," *Theater Heute* (Dec. 1986), 4–6.

"Nur heilloser Schrecken? 'Germania Tod in Berlin' an den Münchner Kammerspielen," *Theater Heute* (June 1978), 7–11.

Rouse, John, "Heiner Müller and the Politics of Memory," *Theatre Journal*, 45:1 (1993), 68–73.

Rühle, Günther, *Zeit und Theater III: Diktatur und Exil 1933–45* (Berlin: Propyläen, 1974).

Sade, Marquis de, *Justine, Philosophy in the Bedroom & Other Writings*, trans. Richard Seaver and Austryn Wainhouse (New York: Grove, 1965).

Sartre, Jean-Paul, *Saint Genet: Actor & Martyr*, trans. Bernard Frechtman (New York: Pantheon, 1963).

Schechter, Joel, "Heiner Müller and other East German Dramaturgs," *Yale/Theater* 8 (Spring 1977), 152–4.

Schivelbusch, Wolfgang, "Optimistic Tragedies: The Plays of Heiner Müller," *New German Critique* 2 (Spring 1974), 104–13.

Sozialistisches Drama nach Brecht (Darmstadt and Neuwied: Luchterhand, 1974).

Schlösser, Anselm, "Die Welt hat keinen Ausgang als zum Schinder: Ein Diskussionsbeitrag zu Heiner Müllers 'Macbeth' ", *Theater der Zeit* (no. 8, 1972), 46–7.

Schneider, Michael, "Heiner Müllers 'Endspiele,' " *Literatur Konkret* (Spring 1979), 32–7.

Schulz, Genia, "Abschied von Morgen: Zu den Frauengestalten im Werk Heiner Müllers," *Text + Kritik* 73 (Jan. 1982), 58–70.

" 'Bin gar kein oder nur ein Mund' Zu einem Aspekt des 'Weiblichen' in Texten Heiner Müllers," in Inge Stephan and Sigrid Weigel eds., *Weiblichkeit und Avantgarde* (Berlin and Hamburg: 1987), 147–64.

" 'Ein Bier und vor dir steht ein Kommunist, Flint'. Zur Dialektik des Anfangs bei Heiner Müller," in Paul Gerhard Klussmann and Heinrich Mohr, eds., *Dialektik des Anfangs: Spiele des Lachens* (Bonn: Bouvier Verlag Herbert Grundmann, 1986), 15–28.

"Gelächter aus toten Bäuchen: Dekonstruktion und Rekonstruktion des Erhabenen bei Heiner Müller," *Merkur* 9 (1989), 764–77.

Heiner Müller (Stuttgart: Metzler, 1980).

"Kein altes Blatt: Müllers Graben," *Merkur* 8 (1993), 729–36.

"Medea. Zu einem Motiv im Werk Heiner Müllers," in Renate Berger and Inge Stephan eds., *Weiblichkeit und Tod in der Literatur* (Cologne and Vienna: Böhlau, 1987), 241–64.

"Something is Rotten in this Age of Hope: Heiner Müllers Blick auf die (deutsche) Geschichte," *Merkur* 5 (1979), 468–80.

Schulz, Genia and Hans-Thies Lehmann, "Protoplasma des Gesamtkunstwerks: Heiner Müller und die Tradition der Moderne," in Gabriele Förg ed., *Unsere Wagner* (Frankfurt-on-Main: Fischer, 1984), 50–84.

Schumacher, Ernst, "Ein Deutscher ohne Widerruf," *Berliner Zeitung* (Jan. 2, 1996), 3.

Scott, H.G. ed., *Problems of Soviet Literature* (New York: International Publ., 1935; Westport: Hyperion Press, 1981).

Seghers, Anna, "Das Licht auf dem Galgen," in *Karabische Geschichten* (Berlin: Aufban Verlag, 1962).

Silberman, Marc, *Heiner Müller*, Forschungsberichte zur DDR-Literatur
  2 (Amsterdam: Rodopi, 1980).
  "Heiner Müller's *Der Lohndrücker*, 1988," *Theater* (Fall 1988),
  22–34.
Sorge, Thomas, "Unsere Shakespeares – Nachdenken über einen
  Wegbegleiter," *Shakespeare Jahrbuch* (126/1990).
Stadelmaier, Gerhard, "Mumienstücke: 'Experimenta' oder Wie Heiner
  Müller unters Drama kam," *Frankfurter Allgemeine Zeitung*
  (June 2, 1990), 25.
  "Orpheus an verkommenen Ufern," *Frankfurter Allgemeine Zeitung*
  (Jan. 2, 1996).
Steinweg, Reiner ed., *Auf Anregung Bertolt Brechts: Lehrstücke mit
  Schülern, Arbeitern, Theaterleuten* (Frankfurt-on-Main:
  Suhrkamp, 1978).
  Brechts Modell der Lehrstücke: Zeugnisse, Diskussion, Erfahrungen
  (Frankfurt-on-Main: Suhrkamp, 1976).
  *Das Lehrstück: Brechts Theorie einer Politisch-Ästhetischen
  Erziehung*, 2nd ed. (Stuttgart: J.B. Metzlersche
  Verlagsbuchhandlung, 1976).
Storch, Wolfgang ed., *Explosion of a Memory Heiner Müller DDR: Ein
  Arbeitsbuch* (Berlin: Hentrich, 1988).
Streisand, Marianne, "Heiner Müllers 'Die Umsiedlerin oder Das Leben
  auf dem Lande': Entstehung und Metamorphosen des Stückes,"
  Weimarer Beiträge 32 (1986) 8, 1358–84.
Swackhammer, John, "Composing Music for *Cement*," *New German
  Critique* 16 (Winter 1979 Suppl.), 76–80.
Syberberg, Hans-Jürgen, *Hitler: A Film from Germany*, trans. Joachim
  Neugroschel (New York: Farrar Straus Giroux, 1982).
Taubeneck, Steven, "Deconstructing the GDR: Heiner Müller and
  Postmodern Cultural Politics," *Pacific Coast Philology* 26:1–2
  (1992), 184–92.
Teichmann, Klaus, *Der verwundete Körper: zu Texten Heiner Müllers*
  (Freiburg: Burg, 1989).
Teraoka, Arlene Akiko, *The Silence of Entropy or Universal Discourse:
  The Postmodernist Poetics of Heiner Müller* (New York, Berne,
  Frankfurt-on-Main: Peter Lang, 1985).

Teschke, Holger, "Theater muss wieder seinen Nullpunkt finden: Heiner Müller im Gespräch mit Holger Teschke," *Theater der Zeit* (May/Jun. 1994), 6–11.

Theweleit, Klaus, "Artisten im Fernsehstudio, unbekümmert," *Die Zeit* (Aug. 25, 1995), 14–15.

Thomson, Peter and Glendyr Sacks eds., *The Cambridge Companion to Brecht* (Cambridge: Cambridge University Press, 1994).

Töteberg, Michael, "Vorgeschichte eines Autors," *Text + Kritik* 73 (Jan. 1982), 2–9.

Tschapke, Reinhard, *Heiner Müller* (Berlin: Morgenbuch, 1996).

Tzara, Tristan, *Seven Dada Manifestos and Lampisteries*, trans. Barbara Wright (London: John Calder, 1977).

"Untergang des Egoisten Fatzer von Bertolt Brecht," *Theaterarbeit in der DDR 15* (Berlin: Brecht-Zentrum der DDR, 1987).

Vassen, Florian, "Der Tod des Körpers in der Geschichte," *Text + Kritik* 73 (Jan. 1982), 45–57.

Völker, Klaus, interview with Heiner Müller, "Ein Stück Protoplasma: Heiner Müller über Majakowski," *Theater Heute* (Sept. 1983), 30.

Wagner, Richard, *Parsifal* (Stuttgart: Reclam, 1950).

   The Art-Work of the Future and Other Works, trans. William Ashton Ellis (Lincoln and London: University of Nebraska Press, 1993).

Walch, Eva and Günter Walch, "Shakespeare in the German Democratic Republic," *Shakespeare Quarterly* 35:3 (1984), 326–9.

Weber, Betty Nance, "*Mauser* in Austin, Texas," *New German Critique* 8 (Spring 1976), 150–6.

Weber, Carl, "Heiner Müller: The Despair and the Hope," *Performing Arts Journal* 12 (vol. IV:3, 1980), 135–40.

Widmann, Arno, "Witz, Pathos, Zynismus," *Die Zeit* (Jan. 12, 1996).

Wieghaus, Georg, *Heiner Müller* (Munich: C.H. Beck, 1981).

   Zwischen Auftrag und Verrat: Werk und Ästhetik Heiner Müllers (Frankfurt-on-Main, *et al.*: Peter Lang, 1984).

Wilke, Sabine, "The Role of Art in a Dialectic of Modernism and Postmodernism: The Theatre of Heiner Müller," *Paragraph* 3 (1991), 276–89.

Wille, Franz, "Das Rad der Geschichte Dreht Durch: Heiner Müller inszenierte Heiner Müller – *Mauser* und manches mehr am Deutschen Theater in Berlin," *Theater Heute* (Oct. 1991), 3–7.

Willet, John, *Brecht in Context* (London and New York: Methuen, 1984).

Wirsing, Sibylle, "Der Mann im Feuerofen und Hochsicherheitstrakt," *Der Tagesspiegel* (June 27, 1992).

Wirth, Andrzej, "Brecht's *Fatzer*: Experiments in Discourse Making," *The Drama Review* 22:4 (Dec. 1978), 55–66.

"Vom Dialog zum Diskurs," *Theater Heute* (Jan. 1980), 16–19.

Wittstock, Uwe, "Die schnellen Wirkungen sind nicht die Neuen: Ein Portrait des Dramatikers Heiner Müller," *Text + Kritik* 73 (1982), 10–19.

Wolf, Christa, "Einen Verlust Benennen," *Theater Heute* (Feb. 1996), 37.

"Parting from Phantoms: The Business of Germany," trans. Jan van Heurck, *PMLA* (May, 1996), 395–407.

Woroszylski, Wiktor, *The Life of Mayakovsky*, trans. Boleslaw Taborski (New York: Orion Press, 1970).

Wright, Elizabeth, *Postmodern Brecht: A Re-Presentation* (London and New York: Routledge, 1989).

Zhdanov, A.A., "Soviet Literature – The Richest in Ideas, The Most Advanced Literature," in H.G. Scott ed., *Problems of Soviet Literature: Reports and Speeches at the First Soviet Writers' Congress* (Westport: Hyperion Press, 1935), 13–24.

Zola, Emile, "Naturalism on the Stage," *The Experimental Novel and Other Essays*, trans. Belle M. Sherman (New York: Cassell Publ. Co., 1893), 109–57.

Zurbrugg, Nicholas, "Post-Modernism and the Multi-Media Sensibility: Heiner Müller's *Hamletmachine* and the Art of Robert Wilson," *Modern Drama* 31:3 (Sept. 1988), 439–53.

Films and television broadcasts

Barbier, Dominik, *Ich war Hamlet*, 1993 (broadcast on German channel WDR June 12, 1996).

Conrad, Gabriele, *Der Krach um die Komödie*, 1995.

Bibliography

Götze, Karl Heinz, *Müller-Deutschland: Ein Filmportrait von Karl Heinz Götze zum 60. Geburtstag von Heiner Müller*, broadcast on German channel NDR II, Jan. 6, 1989.

Kluth, Michael, *Apokalypse mit Zigarre: Der Dramatiker Heiner Müller*, television film broadcast on German channel N3, June 14, 1995.

Rüter, Christoph, *The Time Is Out of Joint*, 1990.

Schirrmacher, Frank, "Heiner Müller im Gespräch mit Frank Schirrmacher," broadcast on German channel ZDF, Apr. 12, 1995.

Index

Index